The Poetry of Life

Shelley and Literary Form

To understand the force Shelley has exerted in our literary and political culture, we must first dispel the image of him, promoted by the ruling class of nineteenth-century Britain, as the author of fragile and ineffectual lyrics. The starting point of Ronald Tetreault's analysis is the view of Yeats, who admired Shelley and described his work as 'the poetry of desire.' From this perspective, the crucial categories of Shelley's verbal universe are not skepticism and certainty or truth and beauty, but desire and anxiety, power and authority.

Shelley was more an artist than he was either a philosopher or a politician; while philosophical and political issues are often material from which he makes his poetry, there are formal and final causes in his work that define him more precisely as a poet. A tireless experimenter with poetic form, Shelley throughout his career sought a rhetorical vehicle adequate to his vision. The major published lyrics of Shelley's great Italian period are by no means art for art's sake; they are poems artfully designed to make things happen, lyrics that employ speech to dramatize an unfolding process in the poet's mind and to project that process outward toward an audience.

Shelley's eventual adoption of dramatic form was the practical artistic consequence of his mythopoeic mode, the strategy by which he solved the creative problem of poetic narcissism, and the instrument with which he made his poetry into a social discourse. It is through the drama's decentred form that Shelley finally legitimates his language of desire.

RONALD TETREAULT is associate professor of English at Dalhousie University.

RONALD TETREAULT

The Poetry of Life:
Shelley and Literary Form

University of Toronto Press
Toronto Buffalo London

© University of Toronto Press 1987
Toronto Buffalo London
Printed in Canada

ISBN 0-8020-5696-2

Canadian Cataloguing in Publication Data

Tetreault, Ronald, 1947-
The poetry of life
Includes bibliographical references.
ISBN 0-8020-5696-2
1. Shelley, Percy Bysshe, 1792-1822 – Criticism
and interpretation.   2. Shelley, Percy Bysshe,
1792-1822 – Technique.   I. Title.
PR5438.T48 1987   821'.7   C86-094565-0

This book has been published with the help of a grant from the Canadian
Federation for the Humanities, using funds provided by the Social Sciences
and Humanities Research Council of Canada.

For my wife
BETTE
with love and gratitude

Contents

Acknowledgments

A book whose gestation takes place over a long period naturally incurs many debts. Though not every influence upon its growth can be traced, its seeds were planted during my years in graduate study at Cornell University. It was there that Reeve Parker first taught me to appreciate the variety and complexity of Shelley. I owe special thanks to him, and to M.H. Abrams, who not only helped me find my bearings in the period but also introduced me to rhetorical criticism and thereby awakened a lifelong interest in literary theory. Other members of the Cornell faculty also deserve my thanks, especially Stephen M. Parrish and Donald Eddy of the English Department, who gave me help when I most needed it, and Max Black, Allen Wood, and Russell Dancy of the Philosophy Department, who helped me place literature in a larger intellectual context. To these, to my friends in the Classics Department, to my fellow students of those days, and to the others from whom I learned I shall always be grateful.

More recently, this particular project has benefited from the wisdom and support of numerous colleagues. Among these, Tilottama Rajan, now at the University of Wisconsin, and Leonard Findlay, of the University of Saskatchewan, deserve special thanks for reading the whole manuscript and offering advice vital to its improvement. I would also like to thank those who read parts of the manuscript at earlier stages of its development and were generous with their advice and encouragement. I am grateful in this regard to Milton Wilson of the University of Toronto, and to Stephen Gill of Lincoln College, Oxford, both of whom backed my work on Shelley from the beginning; to Stuart Curran of the University of Pennsylvania, Geoffrey Hartman of Yale University, and Jerome McGann of Cal Tech, who helped me focus my topic; and to Anne Mellor of UCLA, whose work on Romantic irony added a new dimension to my thinking. Among the members of my own department at Dalhousie University, I am grateful to Malcolm Ross for reading my work and setting a standard of achievement, to Alan Kennedy for sharing my interest in literary theory and helping me to sharpen my argument, and to James Gray for timely advice on publication. Finally, I would like to thank Bruce Barker-Benfield of the Bodleian Library, Oxford, for helping me to thread my way through the labyrinth of the Shelley manuscripts.

The only part of the present book to see previous publication is chapter 8, 'The Lyrical Drama,' which is a revised version of my article 'Shelley at the Opera,' which appeared in 1981 in *ELH*, 48, pp. 144–71. I am grateful to the editors of *ELH* for permission to reprint it. Some of the material in chapter 3 derives from my article 'Quest and Caution: Psychomachy in Shelley's *Alastor*,' which appeared in *English Studies in Canada*, 3 (1977), 289–306, while the parallels between Coleridge and Shelley in chapter 4 were noted in my article 'Shelley and Byron Encounter the Sublime,' *Revue des langues vivantes*, 41 (1975), 145–55; however, this material has been much reworked and now appears in quite a different context.

I would like to thank the Social Sciences and Humanities Research Council of Canada (SSHRC) for their generous support of my research, especially for providing me with a Leave Fellowship that was crucial to the writing of this book. I would also like to thank the Canadian Federation for the Humanities for a grant in aid of publication no less crucial to its appearance in print. Finally, special thanks are due to my wife, Bette, who not only guided me through the intricacies of word-processing and did yeoman service in typing and proof-reading, but without whose love and faith in me I could not have accomplished my purpose.

THE POETRY OF LIFE

'How can it be said that ethics belongs merely to philosophy, when the greatest part of poetry relates to the art of living?'

Friedrich Schlegel, *Athenaeum*, III, 1

1

The Poetry of Life

'Shelley reawakened in himself the age of faith,' wrote Yeats, 'though there were times when he would doubt, as even the saints have doubted.' Speaking of a fellow poet, Yeats naturally dwells on the wellsprings of his creativity, while a more detached and coolly critical intellect might well feel obliged to confess Shelley's disbelief rather than his faith. Even pious doubt seems hardly characteristic of Shelley, who must often have struck friends and enemies alike as the most irreverent of men. Maddalo's roguish 'If you can't swim, beware of Providence' applies to Julian as much in admonition as in jest.[1] Scoffer at religion, despiser of morals, enemy of authority, atheist, libertine, and republican, Shelley was charged with the most diabolical crimes his age could conceive. It was left to the next generation to sanctify him.

As with most rebels, it is easier for us to see what he rejected than to understand what he would put in its place. Our more liberal era, whose attitudes he and his fellows helped to shape, willingly absolves him of intellectual vice though it remains unclear as to his virtues. We view him as a skeptic, detached from dogma and conventional behaviour, a persistent though sometimes bewildered questioner of all that is and an advocate of some vague ideal that should be. We generously acknowledge in his opinion a considerable degree of qualification and in his poetry an overriding ambiguity. Yes, he condemned orthodox religious belief, but that did not prevent him from pursuing some kind of private mystical vision. He despised the hypocrisy of custom, all the while asserting somehow our moral obligation to virtue. He hated and opposed tyranny, holding up meanwhile the fleeting image of a social order as yet unrealized. It now also appears that, as a skeptic, he took a modest view of the limits of human experience, yet he committed himself to the most consummate aspirations of human desire. The mystery remains how to reconcile his imaginative energy with his very real sense of human limitation.

Yeats thought Shelley's doubt was of a kind shared with saints and philosophers, a disbelief that seeks to establish belief. As belief is always belief *in* something, it follows that Shelleyan doubt (as Yeats understood it) was a means to an end. If he questioned the habits and customs of the past, it was to rekindle a faith in the future. If he denied any certainty about what is, it was in order to allow free play in the realm of possibility. It is only fair to say, then, that he demolished in order to rebuild. His lively imagination, never content, ceaselessly speculated on alternative spheres of existence. Magic, science, and romance blended in his childhood phantasmagoria of an *alter mundus*, another world of mysterious powers that could be unleashed in this world for good or ill. As he grew into adolescent idealism, this model of continual interaction between this world and another took on political form as he became aware of the gap between actual social conditions and human aspirations for political justice. Godwin taught him to unite thought with feeling, and how theory could issue in practice; from Godwin he took his direction but not his mode. His initial forays into practical politics taught him how he could use his gift for language to bring before an audience his vision of a better world. Though he would develop more accomplished techniques, he never abandoned this essential aim. Dedicating himself to poetry, he strove to create increasingly complex and effective verbal structures designed to illuminate this world with the radiance of another purely imagined one. He wrote, then, with a purpose. Throughout the gamut of his varied enterprises there runs a unity of thought and intent that directs his energies: he seeks to establish belief in another, better way of living.

What changes as he grows is not his goal but his method, and his creative development may be charted not by the alteration of his ideas but by the increasingly subtle means through which he sought to communicate them. Shelley's political and philosophical views were set before he was twenty, but it must be admitted that he spent much of the next ten years (a luxury Keats could only wish for) learning to become a poet. That he succeeded with astonishing rapidity is not to deny the tentative and experimental nature of a good many of his poems. Had he attained Wordsworth's ripe old age, how many of the poems we now so treasure might justly be classed as juvenilia? For better or for worse, he was denied the opportunity to outgrow his youthful enthusiasm, but in the interim he mastered his medium.

He lost none of his self-declared 'passion for reforming the world' (J, II, 174) in leaving behind political speeches and visionary agitprop for more cunning modes of discourse. In the process, he discovered how that passion could be disseminated and made universal through poetic form without the sacrifice either of his artistic integrity or of his readers' autonomy. Seeking to share with others a vision of a brave, new world, he pursued strategies that, shunning didacticism, make their appeal at much more fundamental levels of human consciousness. Playing Prospero to our Miranda, he probes in his poetry the very conditions of belief. If he wins our assent, as he has won the assent of generations of readers, it is because, having himself come to grips with the problem of belief, he came to understand how we inhabit language and explored to what extent life could be enriched by verbal means. A tireless experimenter with poetry, he discovered for himself the power of the word to evoke faith.

None of this goes to prove that Shelley was either a saint or a philosopher. His faith was of a different order, and paradoxically grew out of his lack of faith in the established order of either heaven or earth. 'I am a very resolved republican and a determined skeptic,' he boasted to Hogg in 1812.[2] What began as skepticism in religious matters grew to encompass philosophical questions as the scope of his reading widened. Failing to be convinced by Paley, much to the chagrin of his father, and finding in Berkeley only the tendency 'of philosophers to conceal their ignorance even from themselves' (L, I, 316), Shelley was unconvinced by the ruminations of either sages or divines. Plato exerted a stronger appeal, but beneath that madcap episode on Magdalen bridge (when Shelley ventured to interrogate the astonished townswoman's baby on its pre-existent state) lurks his frustration at the inaccessibility of the transcendent realm. Reading Hume's devastating critique of metaphysics only confirmed in Shelley that skeptical bent which led to his ill-judged distribution of *The Necessity of Atheism*. That pamphlet's stated preoccupation with 'the nature of Belief' (J, V, 207) illustrates at an early stage Shelley's fundamental concern with the basis of understanding and action which was to continue throughout his life. It is probable that his grasp of epistemological issues was secured by his study of the *Academical Questions* (1805) of Sir William Drummond, whom Shelley later called 'the most acute metaphysical critic of the age' (L, II, 142). Drummond, a follower and a popularizer of Hume, espoused a qualified skepticism which Shelley referred to as 'the intellectual system.' Drummond agreed with his predecessors that external objects 'exist only as they are perceived' and found in consequence that

experience, as far as it can instruct me, shows me the very limited power of human understanding; and, instead of rendering me confident in my belief, makes me deeply sensible of the uncertainty of all my knowledge. (p. 154)

Shelley gave pride of place to Drummond in his undated *Essay on Life*, where he eloquently describes the vertigo of the skeptic who looks 'down the abyss of how little we know' (J, VII, 196). There is no denying that skepticism was an essential characteristic of Shelley's intellectual constitution, as numerous commentators have shown.[3] Disbelief seems to have been native to him.

Even so, limitation and uncertainty, however useful they may be in ensuring the modesty of philosophers, and even of saints, are not the foremost characteristics of the social reformer. Nor, indeed, can they account at all adequately for a body of poetry marked most forcibly by energy, idealism, and commitment. For Shelley is above all a committed poet, confident in his belief that it is not too late to make a better world. Yet his commitment is not merely to social and political reform – his career is a dedication to language itself, for Shelley is pre-eminently a poet committed to the worth and power of poetry. 'A poem is the very image of life expressed in its eternal truth' (J, VII, 155) is hardly the assertion of a skeptic. Indeed, it is difficult to understand how Shelley could write with any conviction at all if he were a skeptic and no more. To see Shelley steadily and to see him whole requires an approach that will integrate the philosopher, the political activist, and the artist. His creative genius cannot be explained on the basis of so negative a concept as disbelief alone; because his thought is characterized by skepticism it does not follow that his poetry must be marked by incredulity. As a theorist and social critic he could afford to be skeptical, but as a creative being he must have found it necessary to suspend his disbelief. The enigma of Shelley's poetry, then, is not its skepticism but its unremitting testimony to his poetic faith.

What makes this issue so crucial is the way all the tensions of the age converge in Shelley, for in his work idealism and skepticism, revolt and restraint, fiction and truth, art and life contend. So much does Shelley's poetry oscillate between faith and doubt that it has been tempting to allow one to exclude the other. Critical emphasis on either separately, however, produces the by now familiar distortions of the poet on the one hand as ecstatic herald of the absolute and, on the other, as a detached skeptic whose obsession with close metaphysical scrutiny leads to poetic, and personal, collapse. What both views have in common is a focus on the content of Shelley's verse and a conception of poetry primarily as philosophical activity. Their tendency to equate poetry with 'thought' in the restricted sense is the result of a failure, first, to distinguish poetic form from more immediately practical modes of discourse, and, second, to observe the tensions between form and content in his work.

Can we be so certain that the aim of Shelley's poetry was the solution of metaphysical problems? Surely that is too great a burden to place on poetic language, which discriminates itself from philosophical language by its greater freedom to entertain alternative and even contradictory possibilities, and by its abstention from certainty regarding its conclusions. Sidney reminds us that the poet 'nothing affirmeth, and therefore never lieth,' placing poetic language in its own fictional space, outside the demands of historical and philosophical statement.[4] Like music and architecture, poetry is an art to which the categories of true and false simply do not apply. It would be as absurd to try to 'verify' a symphony by Beethoven as it would a poem by Shelley – each has its own validity without requiring reference to anything beyond itself. The locus of literary meaning resides in the mutual implication of reader and author in the experience of the text, not in some transcendental signified outside it. Meaning may be understood with Heidegger to be essentially nexical, an engagement through the medium of language of one consciousness with another. In the case of literary language, that engagement presupposes an agreement to pursue the fictive activity of the imagination through words. Shelley's awareness that poetic meanings are made in consciousness and need extend no farther is at its most acute in his *Defence of Poetry* when he says that 'language is arbitrarily produced by the imagination and has relation to thoughts alone' (J, VII, 133). Far from addressing metaphysical questions, Shelley's conception of language is confined to the conscious presentation of objects in thought, whether real or imagined, which certain philosophers describe as 'intentionality.'[5]

The intentional function of literary language places modest limits on the role of poetry. If the discourse of poetry has no necessary reference to anything beyond itself, we err on the side of caution, if we err at all, when we say that the poem can signify only itself. To ask more of poetry is to wrench it out of its purely linguistic network and to force it to play by the rules of other language games. Literary meaning can never achieve the type of certainty that philosophical, scientific, or even religious discourse aspires to, nor should it. Literary discourse always remains one of uncertainty, for it is a discourse of substitutions, approximations, and analogical possibilities. If, as Wittgenstein warns us, the degree of certainty depends on the language game played, then we can allow poetry the status of hypothesis, of guesses at truth, but not the status of truth itself.[6]

As a writer whose philosophical education had taught him to be 'deeply sensible of the uncertainty of all my knowledge,' Shelley seems an unlikely candidate to be a champion of faith. As a doubter and questioner of all established wisdom, he challenged all the centres of authority on which belief relies. Transcendent authority his skepticism dismissed out of hand; political authority his rebelliousness found intolerable. The authority of tradition and social custom was to him represssive, and personal (especially parental) authority was always arbitrary. With no firm assurance that anything can be taken for truth, faith seems to find no foundation but in whim. Yet Shelley remains committed to a faith in poetry, a faith paradoxically founded on faithlessness in anything but the power of the word. The real story of his poetic career, then, is not a history of the development of his 'ideas' but rather a tale of how he explores, in poem after poem, the multiple potentials of language.

Only gradually does he learn that the problem of authority is one of the many pitfalls that discourse lays for the word-drunk poet. In his earlier works, a skeptical attack on established institutions is accompanied by a naive tendency to project a libertarian ideology in ways that verge on propaganda. The central *poetic* issue raised by his skepticism is therefore very much a question of rhetoric. The language game of his verse either contradicts its principle of uncertainty by usurping the very authority it seeks to challenge, or else it is a vastly more complicated rhetorical game than we have thought, a game whose rules as yet lie hidden to us as they did to Shelley at the outset of his career. It appears that Shelley's dedication to language conceals a problem: it masks a tension between his anxiety over the locus of authority and his persistent though perhaps never fulfilled desire for belief.

Shelley's defiance of religious and political authority is perhaps too well known, for it obscures what is far more pertinent to his life as a poet, his struggle with the very language to which he was committed. By recognizing the 'arbitrary' relation of language to the poetic imagination, he freed subjectivity from one tyranny only to encounter another. Though poetic discourse is a game with a high degree of uncertainty, in so far as it is a game willingly played by writers and readers it involves certain structural conditions. There are rules in the language game of poetry just as there are in all linguistic activities (and in all games), and these rules are prior to the creative consciousness of any one poet. The symbolic order of words, comprising both grammar and myth, is already formed when the literary subjectivity is born into it, as are the systems of genre, form, and convention that govern the very possibility of literary discourse. Just as language is the pre-existent institution through which subjectivity realizes itself, so the forms of literature condition and limit the ways in which that subjectivity can express itself poetically. Neither the imagination of the poet nor that of the reader is completely 'free' – both are caught in what Fredric Jameson calls 'the prison house of language,' where we not so much possess a language but are possessed by it.[7] Because there is no pre-linguistic subject, the life of the imagination must be examined in the light of the rules and limitations that literary discourse imposes on it.

Though freedom of consciousness may be a bourgeois illusion, that does not mean that we cannot achieve a certain authenticity through testing the rules that language imposes on us and perhaps from time to time pushing outward its envelope of limitation. It is in just such a struggle with the limits of language that Shelley is engaged as a writer, and in which he invites his reader to join. Since Shelley was always in an adversarial relation with the existing structures of religious belief, political organization, and social convention, it follows as no surprise that he should adopt a similar attitude to the always already formed structures of language. He worked tirelessly as a poet to undermine and transform the forms and conventions of literary discourse, not always with success, but always seeking to understand more clearly the relationship between belief and our limitations as inhabitants of a verbal universe. As creatures who at once desire to know and suffer anxiety over what can be known, we can learn about our own situation by studying the complex dialectics of Shelley's poetry. His strategies often reflect our common linguistic evasions, but his successes, when they come, show us how we can live in good faith.

More is implied, then, in Yeats' assessment of Shelley than appears at first sight. Faith does not necessarily yield certainty and reassurance. An authentic poetic faith, for example, must include an awareness of the interplay between desire and anxiety in the language game of the text. To focus exclusively on the firmness of Shelley's conscious intentions would be as much a mistake as to concentrate wholly on the sure 'intentionality' of his readers. While neither of these subjectivities can be excluded, they can only be studied profitably when they interact through the medium of the text, where their hopes and fears are subject to order. This particular scene of mental activity must be charted, and its dimensions determined. If any text worthy of being called a text seeks to hide, as Derrida tells us, 'the rules of its game,' then it becomes the function of criticism to disclose those rules by which the text can be played.[8] Such a 'deconstruction' of poetic faith need not be hostile to poetry, nor should it devalue poetry as a human activity to speak of it in terms of games, rules, and orderly play. Taking part in a game, especially a language game, can be a vital affirmation of human value, for as Schiller observes we are most human when we are at play.

The *homo ludens* argument applies as much to the Romantic imagination as it does to literary language. Far from being defeated by the limits of human knowledge and the uncertainty of the cosmos, the Romantics adopted an attitude to imaginative discourse that transcends skepticism. Shelley's faith, like that of his most influential contemporaries, was a faith in poetry, or rather in the unique discourse of poetry. Shelley's skeptical deconstruction of the dogmas of his day did not leave him in despair. Because meanings were not absolute, he did not therefore resign himself to the nullity of words. Words had value for the poet who writes of 'being startled with the electric life which burns within [the] words' of great authors (J, VII, 140). Even so, Shelley cannot be dismissed as a mere enthusiast of language. His passion for the word is qualified by a profound irony that is peculiarly Romantic, for his joy in language is always coloured by an awareness that words are playthings.[9] Perhaps, however, it is precisely Shelley's exuberant sense of play that preserves the authenticity of his poetic voice in the deserts of skepticism. Shelley still speaks to us, and we attend to him, because his poetry still challenges us constantly to stretch our minds.

'Poetry enlarges the circumstances of the imagination,' writes Shelley 'in the same manner as exercise strenghtens a limb' (J, VII, 118). Whether poetry penetrates to truth or is simply the mimesis of what might be seems ultimately of little consequence to him. What matters, he says, is results, not reference; what makes a difference in our lives is not what poetry is but what it does for us. Poetry promotes imaginative vitality, and in doing so it expands ethical awareness.

'Poetry strengthens that faculty which is the organ of the moral nature of man,' he adds, still in the context of the *homo ludens* metaphor (J, VII, 118). It does so because 'the great instrument of moral good is the imagination' and because 'a man, to be greatly good, must imagine intensely and comprehensively' (J, VII, 118). Shelley sees this intimate connection between poetic play, imagination, and the moral life of humankind quite apart from ontological questions. He grounds morality in the exercise of the imagination, an exercise occasioned by a communal participation in the game of the text.

Shelley's motives for writing are therefore never purely expressive. Far from being an exclusively private poet who broods over the nuances of his own consciousness, Shelley is very much a public poet in many of his major poems, directing his discourse outward and concerned more with the minds of others than with his own. Though throughout his poetic career Shelley often vacillated between the public and the private voices, it is in the poems of his public voice that he succeeds most fully in generating that poetic faith for which Yeats revered him. Those poems which invite the participation of the reader in a communal act of faith are poems that recognize verbal discourse as a social phenomenon. The mutual implication of author and reader in the text generates a process by which meanings come to be shared, but this process is a dialogical one in which the 'otherness' of readers' intentions is acknowledged. 'Discourse lives,' writes Mikhail Bakhtin, 'on the boundary between its own context and another, alien, context,' and it is at this boundary that the dialogue between belief and doubt, desire and anxiety, and self and other in Shelley's poetry is conducted.[10] His genius as a poet lies less in overcoming his own skepticism than in creating verbal structures which somehow elicit *in the reader* what Coleridge so ingeniously called 'that willing suspension of disbelief for the moment, which constitutes poetic faith,' A delicate balance of uncertainties, then, is both a cause and an effect of Shelley's poetry, for the poet's own act of faith in his medium calls to the reader across the poetic moment to suspend disbelief and enter into a community of assent. In this enjoyment of the text, the reader accepts the rules of literary discourse and agrees to play the game of signification.

Literary meaning, like other types of meaning, is thus a co-operative venture. That linguistic signs have 'relation to thoughts alone' does not in any way imprison Shelley in his own subjectivity. 'Words and signs,' he tells us, are 'instruments of its [the mind's] own creation' and enjoy the 'capacity of suggesting one thought which shall lead to a train of thoughts' (J, VI, 195). In this way, language ensures that self-consciousness does not arise in isolation. Words are instrumental both in constituting the *alter mundus* of the poet and in 'suggesting' to his audience thoughts of their own. Like a spark which jumps between two charged poles, the word is both a private and a public phenomenon which bridges the gap between selves. The word links the subjectivity of the artist with the subjectivity of the reader in a joyful pursuit of meaning.[11] Poets initiate this creative dialogue, understanding that 'the pleasure resulting from the manner in which they express the influence of society or nature upon their own minds communicates itself to others and gathers a sort of reduplication from that community' (J,VII, 111). Shelley is adamant that the process of sign-making, far from being confined within the isolation of the artist, is a social phenomenon that takes place in the community of speakers and hearers. This dialogical interchange over meaning decentres authorial subjectivity and establishes an intersubjective basis for knowledge which allows an individual to transcend the self and become a social being. 'All knowledge is based on acknowledgement,' says Wittgenstein, and from such mutual assent grow the structures that inform a community.[12] The life of that community is sustained by the intersubjective nature of language which, as an institution, makes co-operation possible. Dialogue is the model of social relations, for it is communication that ensures community. Isolation is always self-imposed. Immersed in language, we dwell in a world of shared meanings which the poet, among others engaged in significant conversation, has helped to construct, and which, perhaps, he can modify.

The social existence of signs suggests that a poet with 'a passion for reforming the world' would do well to begin with a renewal of the language, which after all is what he knows best. For such a person, direct political involvement might prove less desirable than attempting to reshape the meanings which govern our beliefs and actions. The poet is especially well suited to play this pragmatic role. Because language subjects our desires and instincts to rules it can be said to regulate our moral and political lives. As a master craftsman of language, the poet can with his art confirm our beliefs, and thereby affirm the existing structures of social relations, or he can challenge us with new possibilities. In either case, poetry performs a profoundly ethical function; whether its ideology is conservative or revolutionary, it is fundamentally concerned with life and with living. If, as Dewey suggests, beliefs are rules for living, then the poet, who wrestles ceaselessly through his medium with the problem of belief, is dedicated to life. [13] He places art and life in a dialectical relation, for his art does not simply imitate life but acts to re-form it. Understood in the light of pragmatic theory, Shelley's poetry of life (which it will be recalled he defined in practical terms as 'the creative faculty to imagine that which we know, ... the generous impulse to act that which we imagine' [J, VII, 134]) is indistinguishable from political activity.

But how can we extricate ourselves from the traditions and conventions of verbal institutions? The problem with the conception of language as a limiting condition, as always and only an institution that writes us, that possesses us, is that it is ahistorical. It cannot explain how change is possible, how either creative writing or the social fabric can develop and revolutionize itself, as both did in Shelley's time. By 'decentring the subject,' structuralism tried to suppress one of the vital components in the dialectical process of both history and literature. The notion of political activity, as with literary activity, necessitates the existence of an actor, and even if that actor is bound by the script of life he nevertheless strives to make something of the part he plays. Existing conditions and revolutionary consciousness, matter and spirit, must oppose one another, struggle, and interact in order to generate the historical process. Derrida is decidedly a post-structuralist in so far as he allows subjectivity a role in verbal processes. Accused of attempting to 'reduce the I' in discursive events, he responds vigorously: 'The subject is absolutely indispensable. I don't destroy the subject; I situate it. That is to say, I believe that at a certain level both of experience and of philosophical and scientific discourse one cannot get along without the notion of subject. It is a question of knowing where it comes from and how it functions.' [14] Deconstruction, then, need not be inimical to consciousness. When it decentres it does not set out to destroy, but instead seeks to locate subjectivity as an element within the system of discourse and to determine its function. How the subject can function to produce change in literature, however, is perhaps best explained by the dialogical theory of Bakhtin. In his essay on 'Discourse and the Novel,' the latter regards traditional poetry as 'unitary' in its language, excluding the intentions of others in concentrating on its own expressive concerns. Against this highly centred discourse he poses another that reaches out to other discourses and other consciousnesses to interact with them. It is the function of the subject, in Bakhtin's model, to serve as the focus of these centralizing and decentralizing tendencies of language, for, as he puts it, 'every concrete utterance of a speaking subject serves as a point where centrifugal as well as centripetal forces are brought to bear.'[15] In this way, the 'novelization' (in the sense of making new) of literary discourse is carried out.

With this possibility of the renewal of literary language in mind, practical criticism of Shelley's verbal art must turn its attention to the orientation of his text and its functional structure. We may not be able to explain the sources of his poetic genius, but we may observe it in operation. Long ago, T.S. Eliot warned us against the futility of trying to understand a poem by tracing it back to its origins; calling reception by the audience 'the consummation of the poetic process,' he urged us to concentrate instead on the voice of the poet and its direction.[16] Eliot distinguished three voices of poetry. The first is the private voice of the poet, the voice that Shelley compared to that of 'a nightingale, who sits in darkness and sings to cheer its own solitude with sweet sounds' (J, VII, 116). That comparison, taken out of context, may seem to exhaust Shelley's idea of the range of poetry, but in fact Shelley recognizes a public as well as a private function for poetry which he elaborates quite fully in *A Defence of Poetry*. Eliot's second voice, the voice of the poet who addresses an audience, finds its parallel in Shelley's discussion of the epic poet, whose power of utterance causes his creations to be 'copied into the imagination of men' where they become 'as generals to the bewildered armies of their thoughts' (J, VII, 125). In a less imperative mood is Eliot's third voice, 'the voice of poetic drama,' in which the poet's own voice is subsumed in dialogue. It is a voice manifestly public, but communal, in that the poet does not speak *ex cathedra* to his audience but represents his tale through the speech of others. It is characterized for Shelley by 'the dramatic and lyrical poets of Athens' who 'employed language, action, music, painting, the dance, and religious institutions to produce a common effect in the representation of the loftiest idealism' (J, VII, 118–19).

These three voices of poetry, the one private and the other two public in their orientation, correspond to Hegel's discrimination of poetic forms and probably derive ultimately from him. A more succinct summary of these distinctions, however, is provided by James Joyce when he describes the 'three forms' of literary representation in *Portrait of the Artist*:

These forms are: the lyrical form, the form wherein the artist presents his image in immediate relation to himself; the epical form, the form wherein he presents his image in mediate relation to himself and to others; the dramatic form, the form wherein he presents his image in immediate relation to others.[17]

Shelley organizes his own survey of the cyclical development of literary history in the *Defence* according to this scheme of literary forms, and a similar, although circuitous, progression from one to another may be detected in his own literary development. His canon contains examples of poems written in each voice as well as poems which are experiments in their fusion. His growth away from self toward otherness led him to explore the possibilities of dramatic form, the literary form in which 'relation to others' is paramount. In dramatic form, Shelley transcends self and is able to present images 'in immediate relation' to his audience. By subsuming his own voice in that of others, Shelley achieves a text whose orientation is toward readers, absorbing them into its fictional world, and producing that 'common effect in the representation of the loftiest idealism' which fosters intersubjective community among them. Through dramatic form, Shelley reorients his discourse along an affective rather than an expressive path, with the result that his poetry becomes more pragmatic than emotional.

Attention to the rhetorical consequences of literary form leads naturally to an analysis of the functional structure of the text.[18] Shelley's text has a design because, as we have said before, it is meant to fulfil a purpose. That purpose is not to solve metaphysical problems, still less to force on the reader a particular ideology, but to engage the reader in an act of faith. This communal activity of consciousness is conditioned by literary form, however, because each form carries with it certain determinate relations between author and audience that influence the organization of experience. Although form is thus inextricable from ideology, it remains essential to the experience of poetry. Without the order which form gives to content, meaning could not arise. Since the meanings Shelley's poems generate are therefore regulated as much by his choice of forms as by his 'ideas,' a study of his poetic development must include an inquiry into the varieties of order he allows his readers to experience.

Shelley's transcendence of skepticism in his poetry depends upon his ability to weave in the poetic moment a discourse of relationship. Such a relationship is possible because we are all immersed in language, but the constraints of the medium itself give rise to anxiety. Bound by tradition, authority, and convention, the poet strains at the limits of rhetoric to create a poetic discourse that reaches out to its audience but does not bind them in turn in the iron grip of manipulative machinery. The task of the poet is to create a text sufficiently open and uncertain to engage the reader in the play of interpretation, to invite the reader to participate in the endless pursuit of meaning through the play of *différance*. In this task the poet is mightily aided by our desire to know, a desire that it is his function to awaken. Yeats saw most deeply into the essence of Shelley when he said that Shelley's was 'the poetry of desire.' By disseminating his desires, the poet seeks to arouse our own.

The first desire of Shelley was to be heard. He craved an audience, as his envy of Byron's was to show – after all, he could hardly hope to reform the world without first engaging its attention. Because he wrote for others, Shelley's poetry is of course rhetorical, but in the best sense, in the sense of employing the art of language to win the assent of one's hearers. Having learned not to instruct his readers, he developed ever more subtle means of generating conviction in them. He expanded the range of poetic language in his quest for an adequate rhetorical form that would allow him to touch people without violating them. As we watch him grow from oratory into art, we follow his search for forms of dissemination that foster community rather than alienation.

2

Locating an Audience

The story about the optimist and the pessimist is well known. The former, seeing a bottle of whisky, says, 'It's half full,' while the latter, looking at the same bottle, says, 'It's half empty.' Even though both are right, their disagreement springs from a difference of emphasis, and, perhaps, of temperament. It is a salutary reminder of the principle of uncertainty in our judgments to see that the opposite of a true statement may not be a false one, but another true statement.

A similar degree of caution should be observed in critical discussion of works of art. Different approaches provide different perspectives, which in their turn allow fresh meanings to emerge. Criticism of literature should be like turning a diamond in the light, the aim always being to show the gem's many beauties to the greatest advantage. New points of view are always to be welcomed in our quest for the fullest appreciation, and need not exclude others already established.

Now a work of art reveals different facets depending on whether we stress the element of 'art' or the element of 'work.' An emphasis upon the *work* of art lets us see the aesthetic object as a thing made, as an artifact which is the product of human effort. In his *Autobiography*, R.G. Collingwood recalls his early years spent in the company of artists at his family home near Coniston, where Ruskin was a frequent visitor. Watching them at work, he says that he 'learned to think of a picture not as a finished product exposed for the admiration of virtuosi, but as the visible record, lying about the house, of an attempt to solve a definite problem in painting, so far as the attempt has gone.' Scholarship has done much to help us understand the growth of Shelley's poetic thought, and objective criticism has drawn welcome attention to the cohesiveness and beauty of his poetic products, but the process of his poetry, which reaches its fulfilment in the audience, needs further scrutiny. From this point of view, the central problem Shelley had to solve as an artist was the pragmatic one of the relation between means and ends. Understanding the creative act as an attempt to wrestle with such artistic problems of course confines us to the realm of conscious control of materials, but that should be an adequate field for critical inquiry. We naturally remain free to speculate about causes of which the artist is wholly unconscious, such as the muse, neurosis, or the relations of production, but these call into play discourses other than that of literary criticism. There is enough to occupy the critic in the poet's mysterious adaptations of means to ends without delving into origins. Trying to learn why the poem is made as it is poses a sufficient problem.

Regarding the poem as something made focuses what Coleridge called the critical 'act of attention' on design, form, and function. Things that are made are usually made with a purpose, that is, they are designed with some use in mind.[1] Shelley was not the first to ponder the utility of poetry; indeed, some such consideration has always seemed essential to its defence. The Horatian tradition of *prodesse et delectare*, revived by Sidney, has always been such a strong influence in English literature that it should not surprise us to see it still flourishing side by side with an expressive theory of art in the Romantic period. If Abrams was right in seeing the central metaphors of Romanticism as signifying 'the internal made external,'[2] then expression can be only one side of that process, since the externalization of thoughts and feelings through language makes what was formerly private available in a public way. Poems may come into existence by a spontaneous overflow of the poet's emotion, but they do not stop there. If they are successful, they also transmit that emotion to readers, and move us to be gathered up in the poem's fictive world. The creative act, then, becomes a transaction between author and audience through the medium of the text, which, if form follows function, will manifest a structural design that will facilitate that relation. We shall therefore ask not what a poem is or where it comes from, but what a poem does. That functional question is also a formal question, and raises issues of rhetoric that will cast some light on the poet's various strategies in marshalling means and ends.

I

An author's decision to publish should be paid a certain regard. In having his work printed and distributed, he betrays a desire to make con-

tact with a reading public much larger and more various than that intended for a work that remains in manuscript. He cannot be said in so
doing to act on the expressive urge alone, for as Derrida rightly points
out, 'Expressive discourse need not be uttered to the world.'[3] The
privacy of a diary or a manuscript notebook is adequate to the needs of
self-expression, and it was quite properly in the latter that many of
Shelley's briefer lyrics were found. What he himself chose to publish,
however, were works of more elaborate structure and greater variety of
form, in which he was constantly required to think beyond self and
enter into a relationship with others.

The fact that Shelley's actual contemporary audience was minus-
cule does not deny the necessary orientation of his text. Even when his
audience was purely imaginary he nevertheless wrote with another
being in mind, transforming an act of expression into an act of communication. The fictive presence of the other conditions all writing,
but especially that destined for the printed page.[4] The medium of print
makes permanent and reproducible a phase of the artist's creative life
in which he represents himself and his aims to the world. Through it
he continually reaches out to a public beyond his isolation in an effort
to touch them, to satisfy them, to influence them. Despised at first,
Shelley like his fellow Romantics had to form the taste by which he
would be appreciated. He shapes his audience in shaping his text, and
he shapes his text in an awareness of an audience.

The public dimension of Shelley's writing cannot be ignored. It is
true that he consigned a rich store of his private thoughts to paper
which the diligence of scholars and the devotion of his family have
brought to light, but their efforts have not always helped us to see
Shelley plain. The publication of poems from manuscript and fragments from notebooks has provided valuable insight into the range of
thought and feeling found in his published works and the creative conditions in which they grew, and can on no account be excluded from
any assessment of his achievement. Even so, this wealth of material
has tended to obscure the main lines of Shelley's poetry and poetics by
weighting the scale of critical opinion in favour of Shelley the ecstatic
and sometimes melancholy lyrist who felt the expressive urge above
all others. Righting that balance begins with recognizing that the majority of the work he saw fit to publish is not primarily lyrical at all,
but epic, dramatic, and narrative. Many of those which are lyrical are
hardly short swallow-fights of song but instead extended and complex
poetic structures serving more than merely expressive ends. His published lyrics tend to favour the ode and the elegy, poetic species that

lend themselves to public performance and commemorate public occasions. The canon of his published work is that of an author dedicated to social and civil life.

Shelley felt an irresistible urge to publish from his earliest boyhood. He seems blissfully unfamiliar with that almost pathological privacy maintained by most adolescents who write. Indulged by the purse of a doting father, he freely ran up printers' bills while at Eton. He was welcomed by more than one shrewd bookseller as the heir of a gentleman with a large fortune who cared little for mere pecuniary reward. They fed his vanity and printed his books. The young Shelley's healthy self-confidence seems based on a genuine assurance of his creative energy, for it easily survived the drawing of the parental purse-strings. He wrote because he enjoyed it, and published out of sheer bravado.

It was probably not until he entered into correspondence with Godwin that he reflected on his reasons for publishing. Godwin rebuked him for his zeal to appear before the public, sagely warning him with the authority of bitter experience that the man who publishes much when young is likely to have as much to regret later in life. Thus pressed, Shelley rather characteristically replies with a reason of purpose rather than a reason of motive: 'I publish because I will publish nothing that shall not conduce to virtue, and therefore my publications so far as they do influence shall influence to good' (L, I, 259). Though this somewhat begs the question, it reveals an aim beyond mere self-justification. Where Godwin was concerned, Shelley wished very much to appear in earnest.

Nevertheless, Shelley's earliest publications have remarkably little concern with virtue. They are pragmatic in the crudest and most colloquial sense, designed as K.N. Cameron observes to produce 'a quick schoolboy fame.'[5] It seems opportunistic of him to seize upon the popular gothic mode, which even he could not take seriously beyond a certain point. The abrupt collapse of *St. Irvyne; or the Rosicrucian* into narrative equations ('Ginnotti is Nempere,' etc.) shows his impatience with a genre whose limits he had exhausted. Still, while its conventions served his purposes, he revelled in them. *The Wandering Jew* and *Posthumous Fragments of Margaret Nicholson* give ample evidence of his willingness to use, whether in verse or prose, notorious legend and gruesome incident to provoke a response. Judging by his early letters, he enjoyed the adulation of friends who could appreciate his outrageous literary pranks. Indeed, *Zastrozzi* seems to be little else, though it is carried out with such gusto that it is almost readable.

Shelley's gothic novels are propelled by the author's irresistible verbal energy and a titanic display of passion and self-regard on the part of the characters.[6] They are creatures possessed by a single, driving emotion that eventually overwhelms and destroys them, as in the case of Zastrozzi's corrosive hatred and Matilda's compulsive jealousy. Victims of their own ferocious spirits, they find it 'impossible [as Matilda puts it] to overcome the fatal, resistless passion which consumes' them (J, V, 28). It is usually observed that Shelley drew heavily on M.G. Lewis for the gloom and fury of these novels, but it is likely that the monomania of the characters in *Zastrozzi* at least owes something to Godwin, for Zastrozzi's remorseless pursuit of Verezzi puts one in mind of Falkland's unremitting persecution of Caleb Williams. In *St. Irvyne*, however, another strain enters. Woven throughout Shelley's second thriller is a Radcliffian sensibility that binds up the raw emotions of the characters and restrains their excesses.

The better feelings of the characters in *St. Irvyne* are aroused by their responses to three stock themes of the age of sensibility – nature, love, and music. The first two quite properly belong to the sub-plot concerning the sentimental lovers, Fitzeustace and Eloise. Their wooing is conducted under the auspices of the autumnal moon and the evening zephyr, and accompanied by the melody of the nightingale. Under the protection of the devoted Mountfort, they are secure in their love and innocence from the threat of Ginotti-Nempere. He, 'the boldest of the robbers,' is described as 'mysterious and reserved' in marked contrast to Zastrozzi, and it is clear that his power derives from his self-control (J, V, 120–1). Ginotti easily imposes his will on the hapless Wolfstein, who, 'torn by contending paroxysms of passion' (J, V, 137), is no match for his rival's cool determination.

The welter of emotion which Wolfstein introduces into the narrative is soothed only by the music which pervades this book as a thematic leitmotif. Music also provided the few moments of calm in the frenzied *Zastrozzi*, but there it was used primarily by Matilda for purposes of seduction. Here in *St. Irvyne* Shelley introduces music apparently for its own sake, usually in the form of songs that punctuate the narrative. These verses interspersed throughout the text are usually dramatically appropriate to the situation and the character who introduces them. Shelley uses them to give poetic form to Wolfstein's remorse and Megalina's grief, objectifying these emotions so that they can be contemplated. These moments of reflection allow the characters to possess emotions without being possessed by them.

Poetic expression not only brings these characters calm but also checks the fury of others. The effect of music on the robber band is a case in point. Having stumbled into their lair, Eloise channels her fear into song, suspending both her terror and their menace:

She ceased; – the thrilling accents of her interestingly sweet voice died away in the vacancy of stillness; – yet listened the charmed auditors; their imaginations prolonged the tender strain; the uncouth attendants of the stranger were charmed in silence. ... (J, V, 159)

The power of music to charm its auditors is a recurrent Shelleyan strategy which begins to take shape here in these early passages. Later in the book, it becomes the subject of a lively conversation between Mountfort and Eloise. Music, she tells him, 'sublimes the soul to heaven' and is the greatest of earthly pleasures. 'Who,' she asks, 'when listening to harmoniously-arranged sounds of music, exists there, but must forget his woes, and lose the memory of every earthly existence in the ecstatic emotions which it excites?' (J, V, 186–7). Mountfort agrees that music 'is indeed powerfully efficient to excite the interests of the soul'; but he is more equivocal about the value of aesthetic response, for, he says, depending on the auditor, it might 'awaken the powers of grief as well as pleasure.' Nevertheless, they agree that the harmony of numbers has the capacity to affect the soul.

For all its faults, *St. Irvyne* is important because it shows how Shelley struggles with the limitations of the gothic mode. Further, in writing prose, he begins to understand how the power of words is connected with their formal arrangement in verse. Poetic form, imaged in the metaphor of music, disciplines the wild passions of the tale of terror, organizing emotions so that they can be controlled, and conveying their order and harmony to 'the charmed auditors.' It is a music which vibrates in the memory, or as here, in the imagination, whose prolonged effects subtly influence the mind. It is significant that most of the songs in *St. Irvyne* occur in Ginotti's presence, for he is the most controlled and controlling character in the book. It is an unperceived irony, of course, that Ginotti is a villain; it seems that Shelley had yet to sort out the difference between power and virtue. Still the musical metaphor, with all its implications of order and response, was an evocative one for Shelley and was to typify his conception of poetry as he matured.

The lyric impulse thus asserted itself in the earliest of Shelley's works, but it is not to be separated from its connection with larger ends. The songs in *St. Irvyne* give promise of the greater poems Shelley was to write, but viewed in their context they have explicit consequences for the characters, they play a functional role in the plot, and they serve dramatic ends. Ends indeed seem always much more prominent in Shelley's conception of literature than either means or origins. His earliest poetics, though crudely didactic as we shall see, are nevertheless an earnest of his later more refined and sophisticated conception of the *telos* in art.

II

Emerging from the chrysalis of a youthful votary of romance, Shelley wrote that his next attempts at the novel would be 'principally constructed to convey metaphysical and political opinions by way of conversation' (L, I, 25). Presumably, this transition occurrred at about the time when Godwin drew him up short for publishing indiscriminately, and he declared his earnest intention of writing 'nothing that shall not conduce to virtue' in the future. He could view neither poetry nor prose apart from its psychological and political consequences. Even the juvenile *Original Poetry by Victor and Cazire*, alongside of expressive lyrics dedicated to 'the rising tear, the stifled sigh,' contained 'The Irishman's Song,' a provocative political lament which foreshadows his involvement with that oppressed nation's woes and aspirations. And of course the *Posthumous Fragments of Margaret Nicholson*, though in lyric measure, was a political squib that looks forward in both subject and tone to *Queen Mab*.

Political goals were never far from Shelley's mind, even when he was writing poetry. Politics were after all very much part of his life, partly by choice and partly by inheritance. Born into Britain's hereditary governing class, he took his responsibilities to the nation seriously and looked forward to the day when he might play his rightful part in conducting its affairs. At least until the Oxford débâcle, he had been brought up with a view to succeeding his father, as eldest son, in the 'family' seat in parliament. His devotion to public service was almost genetic, a duty that went with privilege. As Mary Shelley was to observe in her notes to *Queen Mab*, her husband was earnest in 'the belief that he should materially benefit his fellow-creatures by his actions' and 'believed that his written thoughts would tend to disseminate opinions, which he believed conducive to the happiness of the human race' (J, I, 166). Far from suddenly becoming a radical, Shelley was raised in a Whig tradition of dissent. His radical opinions were a logical development of his liberal background, and his wish 'to disseminate opinions' through his writings had ample precedent in contemporary political controversy. The advantages of his birth promised a career well-suited to his talents, and he welcomed the burdens of leadership. Expulsion from Oxford, his subsequent alienation from his father, and the consequent loss of his political birthright necessitated a change in tactics, but not in goal. Politics was in his blood. Denied one stage, he would seek another.

Seen in this light, his mission to Ireland might be almost statesman-like had it not proven so futile.[7] True, it was a naive and misguided attempt to enter the public arena, but it nevertheless remains evidence of his acute sense of social mission and political obligation. He acted, as always, with the best intentions. Far from being rash and visionary, though, his concrete political aims were achievable within his lifetime, Catholic emancipation coming in 1829 and the larger goal of Parliamentary reform beginning shortly thereafter. Like many astute politicians, he had an intuitive ability to lay his finger on what would become the leading issues of his age. Irish home rule, though of course coming much later, remained central to political debate throughout the century. Going to Ireland with historically possible goals, then, Shelley embarked on a career of reform that would develop in different modes of action but whose essential thrust would remain unchanged.

In Ireland, though, he hoped to have a practical influence on the course of events. Dublin he thought of as the scene of an impending and momentous change in which he hoped to play a part. If there was to be revolt over the Act of Union, he wished to channel it in a productive direction. 'A crisis like this ought not to be permitted to pass unoccupied or unimproved,' he wrote to Godwin from Dublin, revealing his hopes to seize the occasion thus offered 'of disseminating the doctrines of Philanthropy and Freedom' (L, I, 258, 263). Characteristically, the means of this dissemination was to be the written and spoken word. Although the more ludicrous side of Shelley's activities in Dublin has tended to obscure his practical efforts, it should be remembered that (besides dropping leaflets from a balcony) he addressed meetings, wrote two pamphlets, and was canny enough to seek an interest in a newspaper in order to give wider currency to his views. He was well aware, as he said in a letter at this time, that the press could 'be a powerful engine of melioration' (L, I, 275). He sought every means at his disposal to reach a public and influence their views. In this exercise in practical politics, he turned away from his earlier self-indulgence and directed his creative energies outwards.

Shelley's growing awareness of the social obligations of the word led him to adopt a strategy derived from the progressive liberalism of Godwin, tempered by the civic *caritas* of St Augustine. 'Be free and happy,' he urges his audience in *An Address to the Irish People* (1812), 'but first be wise and good' (J, V, 224). Brotherly love and freedom of discussion he saw as the true foundations of liberty, understanding and verbal exchange the pathway toward harmonious community:

Conversation and reading are the principal and chief methods of awakening the mind to knowledge and goodness. ... Think and talk and discuss. ... The more thought there is in the world, the more happiness and liberty will be there.

(J, V, 224–37)

What is most characteristic of Shelley's radical ideology is a preference for the exercise of mental activity over brute force. His faith in the life of the mind would prove unflagging, and always that life would be conceived, as here, in communal terms rooted in the faculty of language. Shelley need have no metaphysical conception of a supervenient 'One Mind' if he could thus understand intellectual being in terms of social relations and linguistic interaction.[8] For him, mental processes had a vital interpersonal dimension, a reflection of the Enlightenment notion that reason was a social function, exercised on a universal scale. Social life he saw rooted in dialogue and the free interchange of ideas. He seems to have appreciated that subjectivity was not exclusively private, but was institutionalized (and therefore shared) through cultural systems such as language. Reform, therefore, was not purely a matter of individual conscience, but must be undertaken on a social scale. The cultivation of the internal self was not enough; real change could be effected only through altering the intersubjective cultural structures that govern human belief and action.[9] Violence and rebellion must be avoided, but the pursuit of virtue and the cultivation of the public mind that Shelley counselled were to be no less collective and revolutionary .

Shelley developed his principles more subtly in the companion piece he wrote to the *Address*, his *Proposal for an Association of Philanthropists* (1812). Though composed with a more select audience in mind than its predecessor, the *Proposals* shows the same desire to galvanize public opinion at this particular turning-point in Irish history. No solitary crank, Shelley always aimed to promote collective action toward progressive goals. While still at Oxford, he had written to Leigh Hunt proposing the formation of a 'methodical society' consisting of 'enlightened unprejudiced members of the community' who were friends to liberty (L, I, 54). Now, despite his mentor Godwin's misgivings about the wisdom of associations, he persisted in his efforts to weld a social movement 'because,' he writes in the *Proposals*, 'I think that individuals acting singly with whatever energy can never effect so much as a society' (J, V, 256).[10]

Taking the Illuminati and perhaps also Freemasonry as his models, Shelley hoped to create a fellowship of philanthropic individuals who would form a vanguard of social change. From the outset of the *Proposals*, he urges the members of this enlightened cadre to transcend selfish interests and 'seize those ... occasions,' as Shelley had done,

that generalize and expand private into public feelings, and make the hearts of individuals vibrate not merely for themselves, their families and their friends, but for posterity, *for a people*; till their country becomes the world, and their family the sensitive creation. (J, V, 253)

What he calls 'the present state of the public mind in Ireland' is just such an occasion for this universalization of benevolence. By verbally engaging the Irish at this time, Shelley hoped to affect that institutionalized subjectivity, 'the public mind,' by injecting his principles into the debate. If the music of his prose can 'make the hearts of individuals vibrate,' so much the better.

In both these pamphlets, Shelley is keen to infect his reader with the same zeal for the public good that he himself feels. As one might expect in such political addresses, his prose is openly rhetorical, seeking to convince and to arouse his auditors, yet in neither the *Address* nor the *Proposals* does he rant. Each observes a decorum proper to its intended audience. The style of the *Address* he deliberately 'adapted to the lowest comprehension that can read,' as he told Elizabeth Hitchener (L, I, 256), while he wrote the *Proposals* 'in my own natural style' to appeal to his peers. Shelley needn't necessarily have deeply calculated his procedures in these pieces. His schoolboy's acquaintance with the principles of Ciceronian rhetoric was certainly adequate to his purposes.

At first sight, the *Address* seems to defy the oratorical subdivisions of classical rhetoric, consisting almost wholly of an extended *exordium*. However, when it is recognized that the rhetoric of the *Address* is primarily hortatory and so depends crucially on the establishment of the author's *ethos*, the emphasis is understandable. Shelley exploits all the common devices of *attentum*, *benevolem*, and *docilem* to catch the attention of his audience, make it well disposed toward him, and awaken its trust. Only after this lengthy consultation with his audience does he essay his exhortation to them to be temperate and just, and so gain their freedom.

The rhetorical structure of the *Proposals* is much more complex and rigorous, tailored as it is to an audience who may be appealed to in ways other than emotional. Its rhetoric is deliberative, and so follows the traditional articulation of the classical oration. Its *exordium* is very brief, as if it may be dispensed with among like-minded individuals (it is of course directed by a philanthropist to philanthropists). It launches almost directly into a *narratio* giving information on the singular political opportunity that now presents itself. It proceeds to a forecast of the argument (*partitio*), the argument itself (*confirmatio*), the refutation of opposing views (*confutatio*), and a closing peroration in which the discourse shifts startlingly into the second person. Along the way, Shelley allows himself two digressions, one on the nature of government and the other on the errors of the French Revolution. In deference to its audience, the *Proposals* appeals to the reason; *pathos* is restricted to Shelley's use of such figures of speech as personification, metaphor, and the exemplum concerning Jupiter's thunder (J, V, 262–3).

It is vital to see both these pieces as Shelley designed them, that is, as speeches to be delivered before assembled but differing audiences. In their printed form, their audience is a fiction (though an indispensable one), but it should be remembered that Shelley addressed an actual audience on much the same points at the Fishamble Street meeting, where he received a mixed reception. Though the audience hissed when he mentioned religion, they cheered at his denunciations of English tyranny, and his speech had sufficient impact to draw the attention of two Home Office spies to his exploits. [11]

The two pieces, after all, are subversive. Each address is devoted to the same goal, 'the gradual and peaceful regeneration of the world' (J, V, 265), a cause which Shelley was never to abandon. His resolutely non-violent means to this end, however, is to erect verbal structures appropriate to the occasion and his audience, where they may enter and perhaps be somewhat changed. He recognizes, of course, that different audiences have differing requirements. Where the *Proposals* rationally suggests radical reform, the *Address* is written 'to increase, support and *regulate*' the spirit of liberty in Ireland (J, V, 228; italics added). The *Address* is designed not simply to arouse emotion, which would have been irresponsible in the prevailing conditions, but to 'regulate' it. Its exhortations to temperance and wisdom, conveyed in a measured language that reinforces its theme, seek to channel the energy of the Irish masses toward peaceful change. As he had in *St. Irvyne*, Shelley senses the power that arises from self-control and advocates it to his hearers. The *Proposals*, on the other hand, is free to develop within its formal structure, writes Shelley, 'one of the means whose intrumentality I would employ to attain this reform' (J, V, 267). The first aims to awaken in the public mind a desire for justice and freedom, the second to shape the means of satisfying that desire.

The 'instrumentality' (Shelley's word) of language in both the quickening and the restraining aspects of Shelley's program for reform indicates his awareness of its primacy over other means. Language is the fundamental social institution, for it makes shared experience possible. Because intersubjective community depends on language, social reform may justly be expected to begin by verbal means. Language, after all, is not completely determined by outward circumstances; it has a life of its own and may create, as readily as it seizes on, occasions. 'Man cannot make occasions,' Shelley remarks at the opening of the *Proposals*, and then proceeds to give the lie to that statement. 'A recollection of the absent,' he says, 'is a principal source of that feeling which generates occasions, wherein a love for human kind may become eminently useful and active' (J, V, 253). Philanthropy, then, need not await the occasions offered by history – the unique capacity of language to evoke a presence out of absence can create opportunities for the exercise of hope and love. The politician in Shelley seized the occasion of unrest in Ireland to disseminate his ideas, but it was the poet in him that was to go in quest for the discourse that 'generates occasions' by filling absence and vacancy with its own phantoms of difference and trace. [12]

III

The failure of the political process instantaneously to heed his words, as the Red Sea parted for Moses, was naturally disappointing to

Shelley. He learned the hard lesson that humankind could not suddenly be made just and free at the roll of a period, and that the reform
he aimed at was so fundamental as to require the utmost patience. The
collapse of his Irish venture did not, however, divert him from his ultimate aim. As was so often to happen throughout his career, his contin-
uity of purpose was masked by a shift in tactics. Far from abandoning
politics for poetry, he set aside direct address for more subtle modes of
discourse. He was shrewd enough to recognize that imaginative literature is often the most potent vehicle of ideology, a lesson he was familiar with from having read Gibbon and Voltaire. He also knew from his
own experience that fiction engaged an audience more readily than
fact. For some time he had contemplated the merits of combining politics and poetry. *Queen Mab* would be his first serious attempt at that
task.

Shelley was both a prolific writer and a voracious reader. He read
much and he read well, the fertility of his pen being matched by the
sensitivity of his literary responses. An early letter to Hogg records the
profound impression made upon him by Sydney Owenson's *The
Missionary* (1811):

The only thing that has interested me ... is Miss Owenson's *Missionary* an
Indian tale. Will you read it, it is really a divine thing. Luxima the Indian is an
Angel. What pity that we cannot incorporate these creations of Fancy; the very
thought of them thrills the soul. Since I have read this book I have read no other
– but I have thought strangely. (L, I, 107)

Even as a votary of romance, then, Shelley knew the chain-reaction
property of language, its capacity (he would later write in the *Essay
on Life*) 'of suggesting one thought which shall lead to a train of
thoughts.' His desire to share the spellbinding effect of such reading
with his friends is a sign of both sociability and social responsibility. If
a tale of visionary idealism could possibly thrill the soul of the crass
Hogg as it had its own, what might it not do for less worldly readers?
The lessons of his reading experience he applied in his writing.

Like music, imaginative literature might 'sublime the soul' and
awaken human consciousness to higher planes of being and doing. It
could also command an audience in ways that political oration never
could. Imaginative literature need not await historical occasions, but
can generate its own occasion in the process of reading. A verbal struc-

ture that is produced by an act of mimesis differs from one that is a practical act, like the Irish pamphlets, in that one can enter and experience it at any time, quite apart from historical circumstances. In fact, the act of entering it is the occasion of significance, when the reader becomes engaged in the pursuit of meanings. Reception by the reader fulfils the imaginative process, even if, as in *Queen Mab*, the audience is part of the fiction.

Shelley, especially at this stage, did not sing as the solitary nightingale. *Queen Mab* is, as Donald Reiman observes, a rhetorical poem, a work of the public voice like the Irish pamphlets, designed with an audience in mind.[13] It approaches its audience, however, in a more oblique manner. Unlike the pamphlets, it is not a direct address but the mimesis of a direct address. This distinction is crucial, for it marks the difference between a practical and a symbolic act, between artifice and art. The rhetoric of *Queen Mab* is more complex than that of the pamphlets because it is the rhetoric of fiction. It employs devices that, rather than attempting to persuade the reader, invite us to participate in the play of the imagination.

The poem's central device is of course the fiction of Mab's address to Ianthe. The speech of the Fairy Queen is the vehicle of the poem's ideas, but those ideas are here placed in a context of imaginative experience. A narrator at the beginning of the poem makes clear that her speech occurs within the dream of a young woman. Her speech is addressed then not to a waking and reasoning Ianthe but to 'Ianthe's soul.' Just as music 'sublimes the soul to heaven' so the magical power of Mab's speech transports the spirit of Ianthe to a cosmic perspective from which may be viewed the folly of human society and its potential regeneration. Mab's appeal is so irresistible that Ianthe becomes a willing audience for her survey of human history. It is an essential part of the poem's strategy that it should thus inscribe its own audience within the field of its narration. Since Ianthe is meant to be representative of the human spirit, it is obvious that her responses are meant to prompt our own.

Queen Mab succeeds only if we encounter the poem in the spirit of Ianthe. We must enter the world of the poem through her, and share her awakening sympathy for Mab's point of view. What makes this difficult is that Ianthe is cast in the role of a naive pupil to Mab's all-knowing instructor. After listening attentively to a canto and a half of Mab's catalogue of vice, she finally summons the courage to interrupt at the beginning of canto iii:

> Fairy! the Spirit said,
> And on the Queen of Spells
> Fixed her etherial eyes,
> I thank thee. Thou hast given
> A boon which I will not resign, and taught
> A lesson not to be unlearned. I know
> The past, and thence I will essay to glean
> A warning for the future. ...   (J, I, 82)

It is Ianthe's ready acquiescence in the 'lesson' that makes the poem so hard to accept; the role she projects for the reader is far too narrow and passive.[14] Shelley knows the difference between art and life, but he has yet to distinguish between art and propaganda.

Nevertheless, the importance of *Queen Mab* lies less in its artistic value (or rather lack of it) than in what it tells us about Shelley's methods and the limitations with which he had still to struggle. The poem is an openly didactic fiction created by a young genius who had not yet learned the discipline of a poet. Later, he would discover how to incorporate political aims into a poetic structure. At this stage in his career, however, his practice was dominated by a theory as yet unrefined. Writing to Elizabeth Hitchener in 1811, he articulated his earliest poetics and, quite helpfully, noted their source:

My opinion is that all poetical beauty ought to be subordinate to the inculcated moral – that metaphysical language ought to be a pleasing vehicle for useful & momentous instruction. But see Ensor on the subject of Poetry. (L, I, 98)

George Ensor, whose book *On National Education* (1811) made a lasting impression on Shelley, was an Irish radical who championed the utility of education in the cause of social reform.[15] In advancing the proposition that an educated populace is essential to good government, Ensor drew on the authority of the empiricists and Plato, the same body of reading that Shelley had absorbed at Eton and Oxford. The young poet was thus already intellectually inclined toward the poetic theory sketched by Ensor.

In common with Locke and Godwin, Ensor held that the mind is formed by experience, though experience he thought might be beneficially controlled through a selective process of education. From the early books of the *Republic* he adopted Plato's notion of the efficacy of poetry in shaping the young. Believing with an optimism typical of this phase of the Enlightenment that education is the cause of every moral excellence, he argued that 'poetry seems to me the most powerful means for instructing youth, which as Plato says of music, penetrates the recesses of the soul' (p. 263). Shelley had already made the connection between poetry and music by virtue of their effects in his earliest works. The thought that these effects could have moral consequences was, however, new to him.

The moral effect of the arts lies at the basis of what Ensor calls 'preceptive poetry.' His advocacy of the 'irresistible influence' of poetry made waves in Shelley's mind that stretch from *Queen Mab* all the way to the *Defence of Poetry*:

I must inculcate the importance of poetry in consequence of its irresistible influence [wrote Ensor]. Fletcher of Salton says, that his friend affirmed, if he were permitted to make all the ballads in a nation, he was indifferent who made the laws. It was under the impression of the power of song that legislators have used poetry to subdue the savage nature of the people. ... Lycurgus employed the poet Thales to compose odes inviting the Lacedaemons to receive with unanimity and obedience his purposed reformation of their laws.

(p. 283)

Aesthetic experience, then, might pave the way for social reform. If the power of song can embody and disseminate ideology more effectively than the dry legal codes of a nation, then poets may indeed be 'the unacknowledged legislators of the world.'

What Ensor does not explain, and what Shelley could not at this point be expected to understand, is that ideology is conveyed as much by form as by content.[16] Nowhere does he consider the means by which poetry acts upon its hearers. Is the 'irresistible influence' of poetry a result of the words themselves, or of the ways in which they are combined? If the emphasis falls not on the choice of words from the linguistic code but on the relations among words in the syntagmatic chain of discourse, the crucial question for the author is truly one of poetic structure. The form of a literary work, then, even more than its content, is what establishes and controls its relationship with an audience.

Among the ways in which an audience may be oriented to the poem, literary form plays a decisive part. The lyric creates the illusion of overhearing the speaker's innermost thoughts, the epic (and narrative poetry generally) addresses an independent reader directly, while the drama absorbs the spectator into a represented action. *Queen Mab*, Shelley's first serious attempt to find a public voice in his poetry, unfortunately combines and confuses all three. It employs a narrator who establishes the fictional context of Ianthe's dream, but it also brings in the lyric outburst of other, more anguished voices. It has something in common with the visionary epics of Blake (which Shelley is unlikely to have known) and the early productions of Southey and Coleridge, such as *Joan of Arc*, which, as Cameron thought, 'may have inadvertently given Shelley his first lesson in the art of expressing a radical creed in an extended literary medium.'[17] As a dream-vision, however, the poem seeks to absorb its audience into the situation, an illusion enhanced by supplanting the narrator with a dramatization of the Fairy Queen's direct address to Ianthe, the dramatized dreamer. As a dramatic character, Ianthe supplies the reader's role in the poem, manipulating his responses and anticipating his questions. Her role, though, as one might expect in a work whose epic sweep ranges throughout history and the cosmos, is subordinate to that of her guide and preceptress, Queen Mab.

This inequality of roles between speaker and hearer is one of the flaws in the theory of 'preceptive poetry' that Shelley put to the test in *Queen Mab*. Instead of being allowed the delights of discovering for herself, Ianthe is told what to think. Mab's reiterated 'Behold ... behold' directs our attention irritatingly. Her fondness for the imperative mood is matched by the flatly declarative utterances with which she develops the vision. Whether referring to the past, present, or future, her language always indicates some determinate signified that admits of no interpretation. 'From kings, and priest, and statesmen, war arouse'; 'There is no God'; 'happiness / And science dawn though late upon the earth' (J, I, 92, 112, 127) – Mab leaves little to the reader's imagination. Her verbal barrage is interrupted only feebly by Ianthe, who at one point manages to interject the burdened pupil's question, 'Is there no hope in store?' (J, I, 106). But the voluble Fairy, who by this time has totally usurped both the narrator's role and the reader's autonomy, only seizes the opportunity to recapitulate her theme. So thoroughly does the presence of Mab overwhelm the poem that the dramatic illusion of the dream-vision fades away completely. The mimesis of direct address rapidly gives way to a versified sermon in this increasingly 'centred' narrative.

Lest the reader's interest be allowed to flag totally, however, Mab from time to time calls upon other speakers to give testimony. The speech of the Wandering Jew in canto vii provides tactical relief to Mab's lecture, but as a victim of the intolerance she has described he serves naturally to corroborate her observations. The expressively remorseful speech of the conscience-stricken king in canto iii is another instance of this rhetorical strategy of deploying alternate voices throughout the poem to carry Mab's message. Having read his Plato in a typically resistant spirit, Shelley had absorbed the sophist's doctrine that 'speech is a powerful lord' and had learned how to exploit our culture's tendency (which Derrida has exposed at the heart of the *Phaedrus*) to privilege the spoken word.[18] Besides, calling on a variety of characters to speak increases the likelihood that at least one of them will be able to awaken the reader's sympathy.

This device is intensified by the subtle addition of literary resonances to lend authority to these speeches. The language of the king's lament, for example, calls to mind the tragic emotion of Macbeth. Like the ambitious thane, this blood-drenched monarch has murdered sleep:

> Not one moment
> Of dreamless sleep! O dear and blessed peace! ...
> Oh visit me but once, and pitying shed
> One drop of balm upon my withered soul.   (J, I, 84–5)

Throughout *Queen Mab*, Shelley seems to be invoking Shakespearean authority to provide the reader with a context of poetic faith. Observe how the narrator opens the poem with a description of the slumbering Ianthe which recalls Shakespeare's commonplace associating sleep and death. If we can accept this analogy of transcendence in Shakespearean drama, we seem to be asked, can we not also allow it to operate here? And of course the name of the title character herself derives from *Romeo and Juliet*, helping us to recall the banter between Mercutio and Romeo:

ROMEO
I dreamt a dream to-night.
MERCUTIO
And so did I.
ROMEO
Well, what was yours?
MERCUTIO
That dreamers often lie.

ROMEO
In bed asleep, while they do dream things true.
MERCUTIO
O, then I see Queen Mab hath been with you.   (I, iv, 50–4)

Thus naming our preceptress reaffirms the Romantic dreamer's avowal
of the validity of vision and gives her voice a certain authority and
privilege. Referring us to Shakespeare's text is an attempt to establish
that Mab is worth listening to, for she is surely a bringer of truth.
The vision of Ahasuerus is similarly lent credence by a reminiscence at the conclusion of his speech of Prospero's words at the
dismissal of the revels:

> The matter of which dreams are made is
> Not more endowed with actual life
> Than this phantasmal portraiture
> Of wandering human thought.   (J, I, 120)

If we are such stuff as dreams are made on, then Ianthe (and by implication the reader) need not differentiate between vision and reality.
Shelley tries perhaps a little too hard to ease acceptance of his fiction
by sowing such intertextual support throughout his poem and by
dispersing authority among Mab and the other speakers. Like *The
Tempest*, *Queen Mab* is a poem filled with voices in the air; the problem is that they are all mouthpieces for Shelley. Shakespeare and
Prospero are masters of dramatic illusion, but the young Shelley still
had much to learn about his craft. An error of inexperience, his failure
in *Queen Mab* is a failure to sustain illusion and elicit the suspension
of our disbelief.

Shelley acknowledged this difficulty when he felt constrained to
supplement his poem with notes. If it could not stand on its own, then
no amount of apology would justify *Queen Mab*. Nevertheless, it is a
poem that cannot be ignored. It is the pivotal work of Shelley's appren-
ticeship, for in writing it he learned, as he lamely wrote to his publisher, Hookham, that 'a poem very didactic is I think very stupid'
(L, I, 350). Despite all his rhetorical bravura, ideological pedagogy had
betrayed his poem into propaganda. Neither its vocal ethos nor its affective tactics could save it. The poem is an uneasy mixture of lyric
desire for something transcendent, epic apprehension of past defeat,
and an inability to sustain a dramatic here and now. Only the com-
pliant Ianthe can swallow this poem's abrupt swings in mood from the

satire of Mab's jeremiad on civilization to the idealism of its apocalyptic conclusion. These conflicting modes cause the poem's collapse. It was the genius of Blake to find a unique medium in which he
could blend irony and romance; Shelley would spend most of his career
in search of a rhetorical form adequate to the simultaneous creation
and decreation of his poetic vision.

3

A Lyric Turn Within

Shelley's warning to his publisher that he would make his notes to *Queen Mab* 'long and philosophical' and so 'take that opportunity which I judge to be a safe one of propagating my principles' (L, I, 350) is symptomatic not just of that poem's failure to convince but also of a division between thought and life that surfaced at just this time in Shelley's development. Though it was a common Romantic theme, as Geoffrey Hartman has shown,[1] the possibility that consciousness might be at enmity with a happy and healthy existence had not occurred to him before. However, the corrosive effects of his extended analysis of social conditions had taken their toll in alienation, and, in addition, his personal brushes with adversity were enough to convince him that as a philosophic radical he had much to learn about practical human affairs. He now found himself cut off not only from his family but from the vast majority of the people who composed the society he wished to reform. This increasingly intense awareness of estrangement was critical to his conception of himself as a poet, for he could not go on advocating changes for others until he examined what gave him the authority to speak out in the first place. As he could not be sure what he believed without delving into his own nature and that which surrounded him, he turned away from the visionary epic to the more private and self-regarding literary form of the lyric.

The problem of belief for Shelley naturally found its focus in his self-proclaimed 'atheism.' In his long extenuating note to Mab's flat assertion, 'There is no God,' he succeeds not so much in denying the existence of a deity as in showing the lack of proof either to affirm or deny the principle at issue. Confessing that 'we are in a state of ignorance,' Shelley defers the validity of metaphysical hypotheses which presume to explain the mystery of origins. So radical is this deferral that at times he seems to go so far as to distrust the verbal imagination which might invent even a hypothetical God, warning that in numerous instances 'words have been used by sophists ... to hide the ignorance of philosophers even from themselves.' His objection appears to be based on a suspicion that words are too often allowed to have a reference to some determinate entity beyond themselves which they cannot be properly said to have. If Shelley's doubts were so profound that he could consider language itself a deception, he must have been prepared to call into question his very vocation as a poet.

Mary Shelley writes that her husband 'deliberated at one time whether he should dedicate himself to poetry or metaphysics, and resolving on the former, he educated himself for it, discarding in great measure his philosophical pursuits' (J, I, 409). Pinning down exactly when Shelley made his decision for poetry is of course impossible, but it is likely that during the period of introspection following the collapse of his mission to Ireland and the writing of *Queen Mab* Shelley underwent a process of protracted self-scrutiny that eventually issued in his choice. Adrift on a sea of uncertainty, he sought for some firm ground on which he could base his faith in the prospect of a better world. The record of that search is found in *Alastor* and the lyric poems associated with it, the products of this, the most detached and skeptical phase of Shelley's poetic career. It was a time for him of metaphysical and personal crisis, a time when Shelley became preoccupied more with his relation to his own thoughts than with the application of his thoughts to the lives of others.

I

The cleavage between life and poetic vision is the connecting theme of the poems in the *Alastor* volume, which saw publication in 1816. Shelley's increasingly acute perception of the discrepancy between the limitations of human existence and the ideals projected by his imagination generates the ironies and the questions that characterize the shorter lyrics in this collection. It is as if Shelley had reached a creative impasse between the furtherance of virtue and the indulgence of heightened imaginative states. Admitting that his desire for good had been thwarted by the degradation of everyday life in Dublin, he confessed to Godwin that he 'had no conception of the depth of human misery until now' (L, I, 268). His failure to have any impact on the

Mont Blanc grow out of the tensions that render *Alastor* inconclusive; in fact, the recurrence of certain imagistic complexes in each poem suggests how closely linked they were in Shelley's creative development.[6] However, the deliberative fluency of lyric form allows greater latitude than the linear narrative of the earlier poem for the exploration of meanings emergent from symbolic rivers, images of reflection, and the trope of vacancy. These common elements are woven into the verbal fabric of both poems, but in *Mont Blanc* they yield quite a different texture.

The central structuring image common to both poems is the river. In *Alastor*, the young poet's quest for meaning takes him on a journey upstream, on a river whose course recapitulates his ontogeny:

> O stream!
> Whose source is inaccessibly profound,
> Whither do thy mysterious waters tend?
> Thou imagest my life.   (502–5)

Immersed in the flow of time, Shelley regards the stream of life as veiled in a double mystery, that of its origin and that of its end. The question of origins, as we have seen, is central to *Alastor*, but in *Mont Blanc* Shelley puts the matter of origin under 'erasure,' as a concept at once necessary and inexplicable, and then proceeds to explore the consequences of this suspension.

In *Mont Blanc*, the source of the Arve, like the source of the stream in *Alastor* and the source of the Nile later in the century, is the subject of speculation that falls short of certain knowledge. During his visit to Chamounix, Shelley wondered about the source of the Arve but had to be content to note that the glacier-fed river 'rolls impetuously from an arch of ice' (L, I, 498). Though less a revelation than a concealment, this 'arch of ice' poses a boundary to empirical inquiry. Nevertheless, tracing rivers to their origins was a favourite Shelleyan sport, as instanced by the previous summer's excursion up the Thames, though as Charles Clairmont recalled Shelley appreciated that there 'should be no halting-place even there.' The differentiation of things and their origins once allowed, the closure of meaning is endlessly deferred. Beyond the headwaters would be other sources, streams and rivulets, and beyond them others further still, infinite circles in which glaciers, mountain chains, and the atmosphere itself all play a role. The height of land (or a glacier's 'arch of ice') might form a natural point of demarcation, but the water that flowed from it came from the sky above, whose clouds came from the sea below, and so on, as Shelley well knew.[7] It was simply a matter of verbal convention to speak of the 'source' of a river, to denominate a convenient juncture in the endless cycle of natural transformation as a point of origin. Such an arbitrary verbal act is a strategy for coping with the deferral of meaning: we articulate our world linguistically, so as to make it orderly and comprehensible.

Mont Blanc itself is just such a convenient juncture for meaning. As the highest point on the European continent, it may be regarded as the source of all downward motion. Yet when Shelley transforms its topography into words, his attention travels upwards from the base to the peak in a mental struggle to surmount nature. The mechanical energy the mountain lends to the river is in the poem rivalled by the mental energy which the poet infuses into the landscape. Shelley wrestles mentally with nature, trying to turn it back toward its origins, only to discover in the process that the mountain is not an origin but a conventional metaphor for the boundary between what is and what can be known.

Disturbingly, especially to readers like Leavis,[8] Shelley's *Mont Blanc* begins not with the mountain itself but with a metaphorical displacement into a mental context of the river that flows from it:

> The everlasting universe of things
> Flows through the mind. (J, I, 229, lines 1–2)

From the opening of this mental gambit, Shelley approaches an absent cause by way of present and evident effects. In keeping with the empirical doctrines he absorbed from Locke and Hume, he begins by admitting that what can be known are thoughts and never things themselves. Such limitation of knowledge to the contents of the mind is fundamental to what Shelley liked to call 'the Intellectual Philosophy,' which begins with the principle that 'by the word *things* is to be understood any object of thought' (J, VI, 196).[9] This strategy of substitution characterizes the poem's whole approach to the problem of origins. Like the life-stream in *Alastor* whose source is 'inaccessibly profound,' the river of human thought flows from 'secret springs' to blend with the river of 'things' in the mind, for which the Ravine of Arve is a metaphorical substitute. It is an

awful scene,
Where Power in likeness of the Arve comes down
From the ice-gulfs that gird his secret throne.   (15–17)

The force that drives the river of things forward seems no more acces-
sible, no less 'secret,' and somewhat more forbidding, being girded
with ice, than the power behind thought. In any case, the ultimate
'Power' behind both thoughts and things never reveals itself, but is inferred from effects and appearances. The 'Power' that animates this
scene is unperceived by the bodily senses but is apparent to the imagination in the 'likeness of the Arve.' That reality is evident only in
shifting appearance is fundamental to Shelley's philosophical skepticism, but that the imagination can figure forth a conception of reality
by means of metaphorical substitutions and analogical 'likenesses' is
as essential to his poetic faith as it is to our contemporary conception
of poetic language. Mary Shelley once wrote that her husband 'always
looks beyond the actual object, for an internal meaning typified, illustrated, or caused by the external appearance' (J, V, xiii). When Shelley
sees 'Power in likeness of Arve,' he infers from what is present an
analogy for what is absent. This willingness to seek for meanings in
the temporal play of appearances is akin to the view of Wittgenstein,
who once remarked that there is meaning only in the stream of life.[10]
    This willing pursuit of meaning figured in the river carries over into
that other pattern of imagery this poem has in common with *Alastor*,
images of reflection. This repetition of imagery is marked by a significant difference, however, a difference that distinguishes the lively play
of the mind in this poem from the self-destructive quest beyond life in
Alastor. Reflection in *Alastor* was primarily visual and marked the impasse of the visionary imagination. Reflection in *Mont Blanc*, however, is primarily aural and marks the accommodation achieved between nature and the verbal imagination. Anyone who has visited
Chamounix will know that the valley is a natural echo-chamber. The
surrounding peaks rise steeply from the valley floor, creating if not
quite a canyon at least a mountain cleft of vast proportions. This
spacious ravine, through which the glacier-fed river flows, resounds
with the constant uproar of waters. Indeed, Shelley seems to have been
awe-struck as much by the sounds as by the sights of this alpine landscape. 'In these regions everything changes and is in motion,' he wrote
to Peacock; 'the echo of rocks which fall from their aerial summits, or

of the ice and snow scarcely ceases for one moment' (L, I, 500). He tries to capture something of this tumult in the opening section of *Mont Blanc*:

> from secret springs
> The source of human thought its tribute brings
> Of waters, – with a sound but half its own,
> Such as a feeble brook will oft assume
> In the wild woods, among the mountains lone,
> Where the waterfalls around it leap for ever,
> Where woods and winds contend, and a vast river
> Over its rocks ceaselessly bursts and raves.   (4–11)

At the outset, the poem depicts the stream of consciousness as virtually drowned out by the noise of the river. Thought is likened to a 'feeble brook' whose sound is amplified by echoes from the mighty rush of things. Yet the sound of thought is indistinguishable from its context. The sounds of nature are literally 'noise,' in the sense of an irregular and undifferentiated mass of sounds which never resolves itself into a signal. The river 'bursts' and 'raves,' the first verb suggesting only brute material force while the second, though tentatively personifying nature, calls to mind the unintelligible fury of madness. Gradually, however, this welter of energies is resolved into an intelligible message. This transformation of chaos into order is marked by a shift in the metaphors applied to the sounds. The raving ravine of the first section becomes in the second a 'many-coloured, many-voiced vale,' the almost punning repetition of sounds and the alliteration of r's and v's taking a delight in signifiers for their own sake. In Shelley's verbal transformation of the landscape, language begins to detach itself from objective reference as the 'feeble' voice of the mind usurps on the powerful welter of nature. The vale of Arve now resounds not with noise but with voices and echoes of voices whose originals are no longer detectable, a reflective *mise en abîme* in the aural mode, whose cause is 'secret' but whose effect is dizzying.

The putative source of all these effects is spoken of as 'Power' which dwells apart on 'his secret throne.' This disengagement of cause from the effects it is supposed to produce was typical of the deconstruction of metaphysics current in the intellectual climate of Shelley's day. Locke's concept of substance, and, along with it, the 'powers' by which substance produced impressions in our minds, was under constant attack. In his *Essay Concerning Human Understanding* (1690), Locke himself had warned his readers (Book I, chapter 23) that this causal substratum which was the source and original of all reality was a thing 'he knew not what,' and could be regarded as 'only a supposition.' How this unknowable substance could be the cause of all observable effects Locke considered in his chapter 'Of Power' (II.21), where he carefully limits his inquiry; his concern as a philosopher, he says, is 'not to search into the original of power, but how we come by the *idea* of it.' This restriction of knowledge to mental phenomena is consistent with Locke's principle (VI.1) that our knowledge is one of ideas only, not of things or substances.

Locke's deferral of 'the original of power' opened the way for Hume's critique of causality. Hume shrewdly discerned that Locke's 'powers' were never apprehended directly, but were a supposition drawn by analogy from apparent effects. Hume's analysis of the supposed linkage between cause and effect reduces 'empirical metaphysics' to a contradiction in terms by showing that we never actually perceive the 'power' by which one event produces another; all we know is that certain events are 'constantly conjoined' with other events, and that we fall into the habit of expecting one to follow on the appearance of the other. By long use, this habit of the mind becomes a custom, so that our experience of reality is less a product of transcendental entities than of conventional behaviour. As Hume wrote in his *Enquiry Concerning Human Understanding* (1748), this habit or custom of the mind is an indisputable principle of experience in comparison to the shadowy nature of Locke's 'powers':

The bread which I formerly eat, nourished me; that is, a body of such sensible qualities, was, at that time, embued with such secret powers. But does it follow, that other bread must also nourish me at another time, and that like sensible qualities must always be attended with like secret powers? The consequence seems nowise necessary. At least, it must be acknowledged, that here is a consequence drawn by the mind; that there is a certain step taken; a process of thought, and an inference, which wants to be explained.

(Section IV, part 2)

This step, this inference of the 'secret powers' which connect cause and effect, is thus a mental act 'which wants to be explained.'

From this debate in eighteenth-century empiricism, Shelley derived both the vocabulary of 'secret powers' and an appreciation of the mental impetus that pursues them. Though human knowledge is bounded by effects, Shelley sensed that our will to know did not come to rest there. Always seeking 'beyond the actual object for an internal meaning,' he knew that we willingly play a verbal game of analogy and substitution when faced with the prospect of endless deferral. The effects we see are taken as a 'likeness' of their cause, the phenomena of nature read as signs pointing to that which we desire to know. Among the empiricists, the only philosopher with a fully developed theory of signs was George Berkeley. His *Principles of Human Knowledge* (1710) begins from the premise that 'if there had been no such thing as speech or universal signs there never had been any thought of abstraction' (Introduction, 18). Berkeley's view that abstract thought is wholly an artifact of language leads him to criticize the numerous errors that arise from the hasty conclusion that every word stands for a thing. Certain abstract ideas might exist in language and only there. Their being truly depends on their being perceived, and interpreted, in the mind. Hence, Berkeley can explain the relation of cause and effect as a purely semiotic phenomenon:

The connection of ideas does not imply the relation of cause and effect, but only of a mark or sign with the thing signified. The fire which I see is not the cause of the pain I suffer upon my approaching it, but the mark that forewarns me of it. In like manner the noise that I hear is not the effect of this or that motion or collision of the ambient bodies, but the sign thereof. ... Hence, it is evident that those things which, under the notion of a cause co-operating or concurring to the production of effects, are altogether inexplicable, and run us into great absurdities, may be naturally explained, and have a proper and obvious use assigned to them, when they are considered only as marks or signs for our information. And it is the searching after and endeavoring to understand those signs instituted by the Author of Nature, that ought to be the employment of the natural philosopher. (*Principles*, 65–6)

Berkeley's favourite epithet for the deity is 'the Author of Nature,' but his conception of nature as the language inscribed by God for all to read affords the mind an active role. The view that the universe is a vast semiotic system open to interpretation and reinterpretation makes the act of reading nature central to our experience of it.

When Shelley first visited the Ravine of Arve, he did so in the spirit of a reader rather than in that of an author. Thrilled by the alpine scene, he recorded in a letter to Peacock his response in affective terms:

All was as much our own as if we had been the creators of such impressions in the minds of others, as now occupied our own. – Nature was the poet whose harmony held our spirits more breathless than that of the divinest. (L, I, 497)

The spirit is 'held' by the sublime, but Shelley's complex phrasing teases at the notion that this breathless suspension is as much a function of ourselves as of nature. 'All was as much our own' suggests that it is not so much the 'Author of Nature' who authorizes the sublime as the 'reader of nature' who willingly lends authority to the text of the universe. The Ravine of Arve is thus a vast scene of reading, whose meaning and value depend on our perception of it.

Unobserved nature may well contain order, but if so it is a complex organization evident only to itself:

> Thus thou, Ravine of Arve ... thou dost lie,
> Thy giant brood of pines around thee clinging,
> Children of an elder time, in whose devotion
> The chainless winds still come and ever came
> To drink their odours, and their mighty swinging
> To hear – an old and solemn harmony. ...   (12–24)

This harmony is of an 'elder time' than the harmony of the lyric moment in which the poet now reads the text of the landscape. Ascertaining its essential character is the task of other types of discourse, for the centre of the lyric utterance is the self, not the other. The main concern of lyric consciousness here is to come to know its own activity, and to do so it must validate itself in spite of the natural forces that threaten to overwhelm it. This poem enacts a struggle by a mind, which initially regards itself as 'feeble,' to realize its own strength in the act of reading. It is a struggle figured forth in the poet's attempt to think his way upstream on the Arve, and to raise his eyes from the valley floor to the summit of Mont Blanc. This agon reaches its conclusion only when it can be admitted that 'Power' is a thought and not a thing, a reading and not a Being.

This developing awareness of self begins in the second section of the poem with the mention of

> the strange sleep
> Which when the voices of the desert fail
> Wraps all in its own deep eternity   (27–9)

This moment of suspension reveals an absence, a silence of the desert in contrast to the sounds of the alpine scene. In the experience of this absence, it becomes apparent that, with Coleridge, Shelley has been taking the metaphor of 'voice' as a sign of spiritual presence.[11] In *The Friend*, Coleridge develops what he calls the 'Law of imagination' which evokes a presence in absence:

> Even when we are broad awake, if we are in anxious expectation, how often will not the most confused sounds of nature be heard by us as articulate sounds? For instance, the babbling of a brook will appear, for a moment, the voice of a Friend, for whom we are waiting, calling out our own names.
>
> (II, 118)

As a poet, Coleridge had put this law to work in the *Hymn before Sunrise*, which in his own experiment in the sublime mode Shelley was deconstructing. As Thomas Weiskel has shown, the sublime depends on the detachment of the signifier from the signified in order to give free play to language's capacity for generating a presence in absence.[12] In *Mont Blanc*, Shelley frequently detaches words from their supposed referents, thereby displaying the function of language itself in creating the sublime convention. When 'the voices ... fail,' one of the poem's leading metaphors reaches a crisis of signification which leads us to conclude that the only spiritual presence in the poem we can be assured of is the poet's. It is his voice which resonates through nature, reading order into apparent chaos. Abruptly he turns from 'caverns echoing to the Arve's commotion' to himself:

> and when I gaze on thee
> I seem as in a trance sublime and strange
> To muse on my own separate fantasy,
> My own, my human mind, which passively
> Now renders and receives fast influencings,
> Holding an unremitting interchange
> With the clear universe of things around. ...   (34–40)

In this suspension of mere outward sensation, this self-reflective 'trance sublime and strange,' the poet/reader encounters himself.

Within the lyric process, Shelley captures the mind in the act of discovering itself. As yet, it understands itself as operating only 'passively,' but to the extent that it both *'renders* and receives' impressions from without it assumes an active role in generating the sublime ecstasy. In the act of 'rendering' what it receives, the mind transforms random impressions into significant patterns. It reads the chaos of raw sensation (which Shelley calls 'wild thoughts') in terms of its own order, harmony, and meaning:

> One legion of wild thoughts, whose wandering winds
> Now float above thy darkness, and now rest
> Where that or thou art no unbidden guest,
> In the still cave of the witch Poesy,
> Seeking among the shadows that pass by
> Ghosts of all things that are, some shade of thee,
> Some phantom, some faint image ...   (41-7)

'The cave of the witch Poesy' presents an allegory of the way language is used in this poem. Following the examples of Rousseau and Coleridge, Shelley discovers that he can transform the world through language, but in doing so he finds that the thing itself eludes his grasp. The mountain, the Power, remains an inviolate object deferred beyond the reach of discourse. All he can do is search among the verbal traces ('Ghosts of all things that are') for some 'faint image' of reality in the discursive structures he has erected,

> till the breast
> From which they fled recalls them, thou art there!

Thus, the act of reading is an analogy of the act of poesis; both provide an experience of language, not of nature, but it is that which must suffice.

If *Mont Blanc* had been written out of emotion recollected in tranquillity instead of 'composed under the immediate impression of the deep and powerful feelings excited by the objects which it attempts to describe' (J, VI, 88), it might have had a less complex structure. As it is, it records a stream of consciousness that flows back upon itself. *Mont Blanc* is a poem in the tradition of what M.H. Abrams has called 'the greater Romantic lyric,' and as such it proceeds circuitously, advancing by repeatedly elaborating with increasing precision the shift in the balance between mind and nature.[13] Initially, nature predominates, until the mind discovers its own activity. Then in the third and fourth sections of the poem, the mind is depicted in the act of reading and interpreting nature, until the balance shifts back to nature once more when its meanings have been temporarily fixed. An equilibrium is finally achieved in the fifth and concluding section, where imagination is acknowledged as mediating between thoughts and things through its instrument, language.

The third section begins in the mind, in a dreamlike trance between sleeping and waking. Shelley is uncertain whether what he beholds is illusion or reality:

> I look on high;
> Has some unknown omnipotence unfurled
> The veil of life and death? or do I lie
> In dream, and does the mightier world of sleep
> Spread far around and inaccessibly
> Its circles? (52–7)

His state is that in which the imagination plays freely with impressions, combining and associating them in acts of interpretation. Foremost now is the mind's interpretation of nature, not nature itself. The 'feeble' spirit of man is very nearly overwhelmed by natural forms, as it was at the beginning of the poem, but here it quickly recovers and reasserts itself in its conscious activity of 'reading' the landscape:

> Far, far above, piercing the infinite sky,
> Mont Blanc appears, – still, snowy and serene (60–1)

Looking 'on high,' the poet struggles mightily with the mountain, defying its downward forces in an upward leap toward origins. This rising motion of imaginative consciousness, as Gaston Bachelard so wittily conjectures, is a sign of valorization, the mental act of endowing an object with meaning and value, and is an essential gesture of the sublime. [14] Through the deployment of these psychic conventions, the mountain is absorbed into interpretation and the game of the poem is played.

Shelley's act of the mind employs the convention of the sublime to valorize the mountain, lending it through metaphor an ethical value that galvanizes faith. 'Still, snowy, and serene' (61), the peak seems to have little in common with the tumult that flows from it. Rather, it seems a void, a blank, 'a desert peopled by storms alone' (67). It remains mute in the face of the poet's impassioned questions:

> Is this the scene
> Where the old Earthquake-daemon taught her young
> Ruin? Were these their toys? or did a sea
> Of fire envelop once this silent snow?
> None can reply – all seems eternal now.　　　　　(71-5)

The still, snowy, and serene silence of the mountain is yet another instance, and this the most important one in the poem, of absence and detachment from signification. Given this indeterminate silence, it is amazing how the poem can shift so abruptly to an evocation not just of sound but of articulate speech:

> The wilderness has a mysterious tongue
> Which teaches awful doubt, or faith so mild,
> So solemn, so serene, that man may be,
> In such a faith, with nature reconciled.　　　　　(76-9)

Facing the challenge of the absence beyond experience, the poet fills that 'vacancy' of which he has so often spoken with a reading. Poised between skeptical doubt and poetic faith, he chooses a fiction of plenitude over a conjecture of emptiness.

Met only by silence, the imagination arbitrarily reads this ultimate ambiguity as reticence and latency rather than as nothingness. It does so by returning to the poem's familiar metaphorical strategy of the 'voice of nature':

> Thou has a voice, great Mountain, to repeal
> Large codes of fraud and woe; not understood
> By all, but which the wise, and great, and good
> Interpret, or make felt, or deeply feel.　　　　　(80-3)

As the chief sign of spiritual presence, a voice summons our belief in an authority capable of repealing 'large codes of fraud and woe.' It is unnecessary to determine whether this authority resides in divine providence or impersonal material necessity, since what is important is not where it comes from but what it does, not its origins but its ends. We are not asked to understand this authority, which is perhaps after all only a fiction of language, but to suspend our disbelief in its possibility and to trust the good intentions of the reader who 'interpret[s]' the voice in which it seems to speak and makes it felt in our world. The crisis of absence is thus met by a ploy of figurative language in which our tendency to privilege speech provides the occasion for poetic faith.

As if to cleanse of embedded ideology the presence he has conjured up, Shelley devotes the fourth section of the poem to emphasizing its impersonality. In the endless cycle of creation and destruction he observes among the ice-fields, he seems to seek a counterweight to the intense humanization of nature the voice metaphor implies:

> All things that move and breathe with toil and sound
> Are born and die; revolve, subside, and swell   (94–5)

Nature appears in constant motion, engaged in a never-ending process of growth, decay, change, and renewal. On the surface, it seems a chaos, but one churning with fertility. What directs and orders this teeming sea of possibility stands apart from it:

> Power dwells apart in its tranquillity,
> Remote, serene, and inaccessible.   (96–7)

It is as if in this section of the poem Shelley takes for granted the super-abundant energy of nature in order to convey an interpretation of its ambiguity that stresses its temporality. He wishes to 'make felt' an interpretation of nature that reads it, not as informed by a divine teleology, but as manifesting in the temporal flow an endless pattern of creation, destruction, and reconstruction, of which his own poetic process is the prototype. He pushes the always already formed structures of language and conventions of culture to their breaking point, in order to reshape them. Hence, the 'flood of ruin' (107) caused by the glaciers is to be feared no more than the breakdown of a metaphor. The earth will eventually re-form itself into a fruitful landscape, just as the poet will reform those names and signs whose misuse has led to past errors. It is the mind that shapes meanings, can destroy them, and will regenerate them. That Shelley is aware of this potential is demonstrated by his art in this poem, which welcomes what Schlegel called the 'abundant chaos' of nature with the enthusiastic sense of possibility tempered by the skeptical sense of the limits of human knowledge that are essential to Romantic irony.[15] Far from lapsing into despair and gloom at the prospect of uncertainty, he welcomes indeterminacy and joyfully plays its game.

If poesis is the analogue of the act of the mind which organizes the chaos of nature, then it seems that only in attending to the poetic act can the mind come to know its own activity:

> And *this*, the naked countenance of earth,
> On which I gaze, even these primaeval mountains
> Teach the adverting mind   (98-100)

The mind is no longer 'feeble,' or passive, but 'adverting'; reflecting on itself, the mind comes to understand how it formulates meanings like 'Power,' how such concepts organize experience, and how that experience comes to be shared. The poem's discovery is one not of what Wasserman calls 'the transcendent Power' but of the mind's active mediation of reality in perception. To say that *Mont Blanc* reveals the power that resides in nature is only part of the story, for it also shows the power evident in the mind's act of reading the 'Power'; that is to say that the art of *Mont Blanc* not only creates the sense of the 'Power' but also simultaneously decreates the process by which that sense comes to be. The 'reality' figured forth in *Mont Blanc* is what Wallace Stevens calls 'a reality of decreation,' a reality in which, he continues, 'our revelations are not the revelations of belief, but the precious portents of our own powers.'[16]

Shelley's metaphorical strategy in part four of the poem, after all, relegates nature to a raw and brutal status. Glacial impassivity is allowed life only in predatory terms ('The glaciers creep / Like snakes that watch their prey,' 100-1), and the landscape it carves out is described as 'remotest waste' and a 'flood of ruin' (112, 107). There is nothing hospitable to humanity here; in fact, 'The race / Of man flies far in dread' (117-18) from this chaos. The 'adverting mind,' however, it not to be daunted by this encounter with primal forces. Imagination humanizes the world only to the extent that it lends nature a human face, but this 'naked countenance of earth' is yet to be clothed with significance. Nature's countenance is 'naked' both in its mute inarticulateness and in its innocence; that is, nature is at once destitute and exposed, void of meaning in itself but open to acts of interpretation that will conceal its nakedness.

Though mind does not create what Shelley calls 'life and the world,' it does clothe their nakedness by lending them meaning. Shelley expresses this negatively when he writes in the *Essay on Life* that 'the mind cannot create, it can only perceive' (J, VI, 197). In the act of

reading the mind articulates indeterminate being, giving it an existence (as distinct from its essence) in the stream of life. In this process,
imagination plays the leading role in associating ideas according to its
own laws. 'Man,' Shelley wrote,

is not a moral, and an intellectual, – but also, and pre-eminently, an imaginative being. His own mind is his law; his own mind is all things to him.

(J, VII, 165)

The conclusion of *Mont Blanc* seems much less contradictory when
read in the light of Shelley's reduction of metaphysics to psychology. If
law is applied from the internal life to the external world, then the last
lines do indeed sum up the poem:

> The secret Strength of things
> Which governs thought, and to the infinite dome
> Of Heaven is as a law, inhabits thee! (139–41)

Having already established that there is no distinction between
thoughts and things, Shelley now asserts that this 'secret strength'
that pervades the universe is actually the strength of the law that
governs thought. Projected outward, this mental law of the association
of ideas becomes 'as a law' that 'inhabits' the universe, perhaps with a
meaningful pun on 'habit' as a settled tendency of the mind. More important, if our readings of otherness are only products of habit and
custom, then it is the function of the poet to probe and change those
mental habits by reworking the conventions of poetic language.

The final section of *Mont Blanc* recapitulates the movement of the
poem. It begins by, locating 'power' in the outer world, symbolized by
the mountain ('the power is there'), and regarding it as the source

> of many sights
> And many sounds, and much of life and death. (129–30)

This realm, however, can only be depicted in negative terms, whether
of the absence of light or the absence of sound. It is an indeterminate
world of darkness and silence, deferred beyond discourse, inaccessible
to human observation; 'none beholds them there' (132), for the ultimate cause is beyond human knowledge. To our raw senses being is a

nothingness, an unfathomable void of absence and solitude, where 'winds contend silently' and even the lightning is 'voiceless' (134–9). Only an act of the imagination can fill this realm of negation, translating phenomena into human terms and projecting what it guesses from what it knows:

> And what were thou, and earth, and stars, and sea,
> If to the human mind's imaginings
> Silence and solitude were vacancy?   (142–4)

In the end another decreating voice speaks, revealing that the poem's strategies of metaphorical substitution, sublime voices, and daring the abyss were all a part of imagination's game.

The trope of vacancy, which in *Alastor* was the sign of a mental crisis, is thus here renewed in a different context. As in *Alastor*, it denotes absence, whether of a solid underpinning to reality or of human sympathy. In *Mont Blanc*, however, anxiety over negation is allayed by a demonstration of the mind's capacity for supplementation. The mind here seizes on vacancy as an opportunity for the exercise of imaginative free play. Operating according to its own laws, it fills the void with its own 'imaginings,' with fictions that redeem mankind from the threat of nothingness. It is of course a profound irony that these fictions are in themselves a 'nothing,' but this ironic awareness does not rob them of their value as signifiers. Nietzsche, writing in *Beyond Good and Evil*, after all, has taught us how to appreciate the irony of a redemptive fiction:

The falseness of an opinion is not for us any objection to it. ... The question is, how far an opinion is life-furthering, life-preserving. ... Without a recognition of logical fictions, without a comparison of reality with the purely *imagined* world of the absolute and immutable ... man cannot live.

In its conclusion, Shelley's *Mont Blanc* generated a searching Romantic irony by deconstructing the sublime convention and revealing the aesthetic subject whose activity created it. That subject has pushed the signifying process to its limits, where the inadequacy of language to deliver final and fixed meanings betrays an area of experience where words are no longer in control but give themselves up to the control of the imagination.

III

The *Hymn to Intellectual Beauty* puts into practice the theoretical insights achieved in *Mont Blanc*. The *Hymn* welcomes the indeterminacy of ultimate reality as an opportunity for the liberation of human energies in the more proximate realm of temporal existence. If even the structures and conventions of language and culture can be deconstructed to reveal their arbitrary nature, then we are free to attempt to reconstruct those patterns more in accord with our desires of what should be. Having established the proper limits of philosophical and religious claims to transcendent authority, Shelley is faced with the challenge of developing a discourse whose authority rests on a purely subjective basis. Still, the problem remains how to make the authority of the self any less arbitrary than that of the other.

Displacing the locus of 'Power' from the other to the self, from nature to imagination, brought with it a shift in emphasis from metaphysics to ethics in Shelley's thought. His fragmentary writings on metaphysics and morals, probably dating from 1815–16, show how much an interest in what is was giving way to an interest in how we act as his chief preoccupation. In marked contrast to the objective declarations of *Queen Mab* ('There is no God'; 'Necessity! thou mother of the world!'), metaphysical claims are now viewed as a matter of subjective determination. 'Metaphysics,' he writes, 'may be defined as the science of all that we know, feel, remember, and believe' (J, VII, 62–3). Accompanying this move from truth to ideology is a renewed emphasis on rhetoric rather than logic in his discourse. 'The science of words,' he continues, 'must no longer be confounded with metaphysics or the science of facts. Words are the instruments of the mind' (J, VII, 63). Just how those powerful instruments are to be used now becomes the central problem of his poetry.

The *Hymn* commences with the by now familiar gesture of disengaging cause from effect. The 'Power' which underlies life and the world remains elusive and indeterminate. 'Unseen' itself, it nevertheless enters the the temporal world at favourable moments:

> The awful shadow of some unseen Power
> Floats though unseen among us, – visiting
> This various world with as inconstant wing
> As summer winds that creep from flower to flower
>
> (J, II, 59–62, lines 1–4)

Deferred beyond discourse, the 'Power' can be understood only through strategies of analogy and substitution. It is noteworthy that it finds its leading metaphor in the wind, which likewise moves unseen, but whose presence is sensed in the effects that it has on objects.

Since 'Power' itself cannot be understood but can only be perceived in appearances, the poet pursues a series of analogies in order to approximate its nature. This 'Power' is 'like moonbeams,' 'like hues and harmonies of evening,' 'like clouds,' 'like memory of music fled' (5-10). Each of these similes thrown up by that faculty of substitution, the imagination, exhibits two common characteristics which at first seem incompatible, a delicate insubstantiality together with a firm order. The 'Power' has no more metaphysical substance than colours or sounds, yet is possesses a harmony akin to music. Colours and sounds, of course, are phenomena whose being depends on perception, for they must be received by a consciousness before they can be truly said to exist. They must be read, interpreted, and responded to, before they can have their full effect. Their effect depends, too, on their arrangement into a harmonious order. However, since Shelley thought that 'order and disorder are no more than modifications of our own perceptions' (J, VII, 52), their order is a result of an act of the mind.

One of the functions of the imagination, writes Shelley in the *Defence of Poetry*, is to arrange its materials 'according to a certain rhythm and order, which may be called the beautiful and good' (J, VII, 134-5). This identification of beauty with order was an axiom of Greek culture, which Plato simply absorbed as an assumption in a dialogue like the *Philebus*, where Socrates states that 'measure and proportion invariably, I imagine, constitute beauty and excellence' (64e).[17] Shelley qualified the classical equation of order with beauty by his notion that order is a mode of mindedness. It arises within a mental act of organization and depends on an aesthetic perception rather than on a metaphysical entity. Because this order is a phenomenon of the mind in accordance with what Shelley liked to call the 'intellectual system,' the beauty it embodies is truly an 'intellectual' beauty.

Although for Shelley beauty is an aesthetic perception in the mind of the beholder, it nevertheless orients consciousness in the 'unquiet dream' of life. Were the beauty of which Shelley speaks a thoroughly Platonic ideal, it would be constant in our experience, but as an aesthetic response it is but a fleeting perception. Beauty is only significant to Shelley within the temporal flow, its essence as an eternal value being deferred. Characteristically, Shelley seems less concerned

with the mysterious being of beauty than with its various manifestations within our lives. Instead of seeking the eternal Form of Beauty,
then, the *Hymn* is content to commemorate those fleeting moments
in which a multitude of impressions are organized by the mind into the
gestalt Shelley calls 'beauty,' regrets those moments in which it is
absent, but shows (since 'nothing is ever simply present or absent') the
influence those moments have on our 'onward life.'[18] As in *Alastor*,
much of life is led in confusion and loss, in a 'vacancy' which only an
act of imagination will fill. Beauty momentarily illuminates this
darkness, but its passing leaves a void:

> Spirit of Beauty, that dost consecrate
> With thine own hues all thou dost shine upon
> Of human thought or form, – where art thou gone?
> Why dost thou pass away and leave our state,
> This dim vast vale of tears, vacant and desolate? (13–17)

In the aftermath of life's passing stream, Shelley's *Hymn to Intellectual Beauty* is a testament to the persistence of the traces of
aesthetic experience.

Keats evidently had this passage from Shelley's *Hymn* in mind
when he wrote to Bailey concerning those 'Nothings which are made
Great and dignified by an ardent pursuit.' For neither Keats nor Shelley
was beauty the passport to some transcendent world; instead, both
regarded beauty as an aesthetic perception which ennobled this life.[19]
Whether present or absent, its trace could 'consecrate' our life and
thoughts, even though its moments were no more than the imaginings
of the poet who 'gives to airy nothing a local habitation and a name' (as
Theseus so finely says). Even when beauty arises through the mere
play of the imagination, it 'gives grace and truth to life's unquiet
dream'(36), for as an orderly arrangement of ideas it is self-sufficient in
sense and need have no reference to anything beyond itself. In aesthetic experience, we may know nothing more than beauty, but that, as
Keats's Grecian urn tells us, is all we need to know.

Shelley's appropriation of conventional religious terminology in the
poem helps to authorize the role of beauty in making life sacred ('consecrate') and in bestowing a regenerating influence ('grace') upon it. In
the skeptic's random world of 'doubt, chance, and mutability' (31), it
is the only means of consolation, even though it is transitory. In
answer to all our questions about transience, decay, and the human

'scope / For love and hate, despondency and hope' (15-24), there is only silence:

> No voice from some sublimer world hath ever
> To sage or poet these responses given –
> Therefore the names of Demon, Ghost and Heaven,
> Remain the records of their vain endeavour,
> Frail spells – whose uttered charm might not avail to sever,
> From all we hear and all we see,
> Doubt, chance, and mutability. (25-31)

Transcendent otherness has no authority for Shelley. Faced with the mute indifference of a universe in which the voice of God does not speak, the atheist Shelley must turn within. In so doing, he recognizes that our understanding of reality has always depended on verbal conventions, those 'frail spells' of language which conjure up presences by the use and misuse of names and signs. When these verbal devices assume a being apart from the imagination which produced them, they become 'poisonous names' (53) that blight our thoughts and tyrannize over our lives. Only when the verbal imagination acknowledges responsibility for its creatures will humanity be free to control its own destiny. The role of the reformer, then, is first to show the vacancy beyond such words, and signs, and then to replace them with new verbal icons of its own acknowledged making, such as 'Beauty.'

Accepting that all our most cherished beliefs are constituted by the play of the imagination is the sole sure means of human liberation for Shelley. This admission is the commencement of the only authentic way of knowing the reality constituted by language, 'a reality of decreation' (as Steven says) that reveals our beliefs not as false but as 'the precious portents of our powers.' Having skeptically concluded that the rage for truth can never be satisfied, Shelley and those who think like him must rest content with satisfying our rage for order. Though he cannot trace mental events to their origin, he can assure himself of their influence in our life. Words, especially well-ordered words, are powerful, whether they refer to the real or to the purely imagined realm. Whether words denote fiction or fact, they may move us, they my console us, and they may serve 'as generals to the bewildered armies of [our] thoughts' (J, VII, 125). By coming to understand the legitimate functions of poetic language, Shelley was able to return from the private to the public voice in his poetry.

Shelley's public poetry was no mere rhetorical exercise, however, divorced from ethical intentions. He wanted to believe that the power of poetry is not amoral, but is guaranteed to 'influence to good' by its own internal structure. In this view he was aided by a certain Platonic optimism. Intrinsic to the Greek conception of beauty is the view that the order it manifests is akin to the order of the soul, which Plato in the *Republic* calls goodness or justice. As Shelley knew, beauty for the Greeks was a source of both aesthetic pleasure and ethical culture because they believed that an experience of order promotes in us an increase of that orderliness which they regarded as characteristic of the highest good. [20] That 'the good has taken refuge in the character of the beautiful,' as Plato put it in the *Philebus* (64e), was a basic article of Shelley's artistic creed and the principle upon which he would write his greatest poetry. Perhaps Shelley's celebrated Platonism amounts to no more than this, that he adopted the Grecian faith that the beautiful and the good are one. That he wished through his poetry to create the one so as to make the other the rule of life is indicative of his fundamental pragmatism. Though skepticism might prevent him from achieving certain knowledge, he could nevertheless function confidently in the ethical realm by aesthetic means alone.

Stanza four of the *Hymn* makes it clear that in Shelley's mind aesthetic experience and ethical principles were related. The Shelleyan virtues of 'Love, Hope, and Self-esteem' depend on those 'uncertain moments' of mental harmony when beauty provides an experience of order:

> Love, Hope, and Self-esteem, like clouds depart
> And come, for some uncertain moments lent.
> Man were immortal, and omnipotent,
> Didst thou, unknown and awful as thou art,
> Keep with thy glorious train firm state within his heart.   (37–41)

Though beauty has 'unknown' origins, its perception nevertheless is awe-inspiring ('awful'). Here, Shelley characteristically is less concerned with what beauty is than with what it does; in these lines, he pragmatically shifts his emphasis from indeterminate causes to experienced effects. Breathing life into a Romantic myth that would animate successors such as Ruskin, Nietzsche, and Pater, he formulates his belief that man may become godlike ('immortal and omnipotent') through dwelling in beauty. Beauty arouses in man a feeling 'within his heart' that ennobles him, although Shelley is wise enough to know that this feeling is a passing phase bound by the temporal stream of life. Because beauty is perceived in fleeting arrangements of sensory reality, when the constant flow of ideas crystallizes for a moment into perfect order before dissolving again, humankind cannot be entirely perfected nor can eternity be reached by art. Poetry, conceived in the dimension of temporality, is a momentary experience of order, but it remains, as Shelley was to say in the *Defence*, a 'record of the best and happiest moments of the happiest and best minds' (J, VII, 136). So long as it is read, poetry will 'generate occasions' for those moments to be re-experienced. And even though they pass away again, these 'uncertain moments' can 'lend' us those virtues which sustain life in its darker and more disorderly passages.

In a poem which is, as the title suggests, a 'hymn' to a value that is secular in its root sense (pertaining to the temporal world), Shelley typically completes the displacement of religious concepts in terms of human value by strategically humanizing the Pauline virtues.[21] Hope and charity remain unaltered, although Shelleyan 'love' comes closer to Paul's original sense than does 'charity' in its modern, corrupted usage. More important is his replacement of 'Faith' by 'Self-esteem,' a faith in oneself that is essential to Shelley's completely this-worldly aspirations for a redeemed humanity. Self-esteem is a suspension of disbelief in the self, a trust in the imagination which is first nurtured by the exercise of poetic faith. The *Hymn* ultimately locates its centre in the self of the lyric process, but as a song praising an experience which can be shared it transcends the poet's self to embrace other selves in a communal celebration. The *Hymn* is 'impersonal' in Eliot's sense: that is, as a poem that heralds Shelley's resumption of a public voice it offers a trans-personal or essentially social experience.

Stanzas five and six offer a personal example of the principle, evolved in the poem, that aesthetic experience has ethical consequences. The language of this passage is deliberately extravagant in a way that is typically Romantic, adopting as it does the Methodist technique of testimony.[22] Drawing its authority from the intensity of subjective experience, it demonstrates that variety of religious experience known as conversion. It begins with the conviction of sin, primarily the transgression of *Alastor*-like (not to mention Frankenstein-like) curiosity about vital origins which can only be satisfied by the application of 'poisonous names':

While yet a boy I sought for ghosts, and sped
Through many a listening chamber, cave and ruin,
And starlight wood, with fearful steps pursuing
Hopes of high talk with the departed dead.
I called on poisonous names with which our youth is fed;
I was not heard – I saw them not –   (49–54)

The silence with which he was met recalls the 'none can reply' of *Mont Blanc*. Like the lightning that plays about the mountain summit, symbolizing forces beyond discourse, the grave is 'voiceless' (65). Out of this absence, only the poet's voice is heard when he shrieks, inarticulately marking his ecstatic perception of beauty. If the only language available to him is that of religious conversion, it is at least appropriate to the occasion since a similar kind of faith is being generated. It is not a private faith bound within the poet's subjectivity, however, because the occasion of testimony that the hymn generates is meant, as in the forms of Protestant piety that it mimics, to serve as a model for the poetically faithful.

Shelley typically draws also on traditions correlative with the native one. The shriek and the ecstasy are remarkably akin to those of St Theresa, and so is the degree of commitment which follows. The poet dedicates himself to beauty as she did to God:

> I vowed that I would dedicate my powers
> To thee and thine – have I not kept the vow?   (61–2)

Like Wordsworth after the night of dancing in *The Prelude* (IV, 109–38), Shelley emerges 'a dedicated spirit,' but not a mere aesthete. The capacity to appreciate beauty affirms his faith in humanity and fills him with the hope that cultivating this response will nurture others, especially the sympathetic response to human suffering. With Schiller, Shelley shared the Enlightenment's faith that opening the avenue of aesthetic response would pave the way for the moral and political development of the human spirit. His love of beauty, Shelley says, is always connected 'with hope that thou wouldst free / This world from its dark slavery' (69–70). Just as the mental ability to endow Mont Blanc with human value promises the formulation of new 'codes' which will replace those of 'fraud and woe,' so perception of that order called beauty provides models for the reordering of life. Shelley's ideology of beauty is one example among many in an age of

Romantic Hellenism of the optimistic Greek view that the good can take refuge in the beautiful.

The testimony of conversion would be incomplete, and ineffectual as a model for others, without some account of the difference the new faith has made in the life of the convert. In his last stanza, therefore, Shelley speaks of his rededication as a poet. This concluding passage manifests Shelley's unfailing ability to regain control of his emotions, as well as the verbal discipline he is capable of imposing on thoughts which 'words cannot express.' Though at the close of the sixth stanza he comes close to admitting the inadequacy of language to capture the intensity of the moment, he begins the seventh with the thought that the experience richest in meaning in not necessarily that which is most intense:

> The day becomes more solemn and serene
> When noon is past – there is a harmony
> In autumn, and a lustre in its sky   (73–5)

'Solemn' and 'serene,' the adjectives applied to the 'Power' in *Mont Blanc*, are here transferred to the mood itself, completing the transfer of the locus of 'the secret strength of things' from nature to the self. In this reflective mood, he reasserts the potential of aesthetic experience to order the moral life. After the fit has passed, it is the calm assurance supplied to 'onward life' that matters most:

> Thus let thy power, which like the truth
> Of nature on my passive youth
> Descended, to my onward life supply
> Its calm. ...   (78–81)

Whether beauty is a 'truth of nature' or a truth of the self no longer seems to matter. In the last analysis, it is not the source of experience which preoccupies Shelley so much as its quality and its consequences. He is henceforth capable of suspending his own skepticism in favour of 'generating occasions' for aesthetic contemplation and ethical reflection.

When Shelley rehandled this conversion experience a year later, he shifted his emphasis clearly to its moral consequences. In the 'Dedication' to *The Revolt of Islam*, he moves quickly from the emotion felt to the sense of commitment which arises from that emotion:

And then I clasped my hands and looked around –
But none was near to mock my streaming eyes,
Which poured their warm drops on the sunny ground –
So without shame, I spake: – 'I will be wise,
And just, and free, and mild, if in me lies
Such power, for I grow weary to behold
The selfish and the strong still tyrannise
Without reproach or check.' I then controuled
My tears, my heart grew calm, and I was meek and bold.

(J, I, 255, lines 28–36)

The control that is discovered here is the same self-conscious power that pulls the impassioned lyric utterances of the *Hymn* back from emotional excess to a strong and steady public voice. It may even be taken as a metaphor for the control over language which the reform-minded writer must seek. The poet has discovered the precious portents of his own powers; he is bound no longer by 'poisonous names' but by the frail spells of beauty (which he has created and therefore should be able to decreate) 'to fear himself and love all human kind' (84). In that cathartic calm of mind, all passion spent, the worshipper of beauty holds his own imaginative faculty in awe as others 'fear' God.

Having achieved a faith in himself and in poetry, Shelley can resume the challenge of the public voice. He does so in *The Revolt of Islam* somewhat hesitantly, in the manner of Milton in *Lycidas*:

Is it, that now my inexperienced fingers
But strike the prelude of a loftier strain!
Or, must the lyre on which my spirit lingers
Soon pause in silence, ne'er to sound again … ?   (lines 82–5)

Emerging from lyric privacy, he is now prepared once again to address an audience, this time in the 'loftier strain' of the epic. His awareness of just how tenaciously imagination must struggle with the structures of language to create the conditions of meaning, however, makes the lapse back into silence and absence a fearful possibility. He has regained his poetic faith, but he had yet to find a way to manage the power of words.

5

Epic Form

By the time he came to write *The Revolt of Islam* in 1817, Shelley had decided that poetry was to be his preferred mode of discourse. This choice arises out of the lyrics of 1816, for in them he sets aside both philosophical inquiry and public oratory in order to pursue a verbal authenticity that none of the systems of his day, whether metaphysical or political, could afford. In both realms, the prevailing doctrine of circumstances gave priority to things over thought; in philosophy, the popular notion that words are derived from things was the correlative of the political notion that humanity is subject to its environment. By coming to understand language as the instrument of imagination, created for its own use, Shelley detached himself from all the orthodoxies of his day and set a new course toward our own. From the lyrics of 1816 there emerges a poet who consciously tries to seize reality by means of words and for whom, in consequence, the locus of value shifts from the objective order of nature to the symbolic order of words.

Shelley cherished the independence of poetic discourse from the demands of certainty, and understood how words, carefully ordered, could create their own purely verbal realm of being. Having come to know how words mediate between being and knowing, he could allow poetry a function in ethics that he might not be prepared to admit in metaphysics. Even if the fictions of poetry could never be more than hypotheses, they nevertheless exert a powerful influence on human conduct. Poetry, as Arnold was to say, may teach us how to live, even if its imaginative constructions can never be known for truth.

The hypothetical nature of literary language means that poetry is inescapably a pragmatic medium. Its meanings are tested not by the standards of something absolute but by use, or, as Wittgenstein says, in 'the stream of life.'[1] Its meanings depend not on verification but upon a power to persuade, which is to say what should be obvious, that poetry is not a matter of logic but of rhetoric. Now rhetoric, of course, especially in its narrowest sense, was anathema to the Romantics; nevertheless, they admit repeatedly that poetry is an art of persuasion. Blake writes that 'all poets believe that. ... a firm persuasion that a thing is so make[s] it so' and that this 'firm persuasion' can move mountains. Coleridge's concept of poetic faith is not far removed from this, especially in the *Biographia Literaria* when he speaks of

that illusion, contra-distinguished from delusion, that negative faith, which simply permits the images presented to work by their own force, without either denial or affirmation of their real existence by the judgement (ch. 22)

It was on a similar principle of the free-play of poetic fiction that Wordsworth made use of 'the notion of pre-existence' for his purposes 'as a poet' in the *Intimations* ode; the idea had 'sufficient foundation in humanity,' he told Isabella Fenwick, and provided 'a point whereon to rest his machine.' Shelley was by no means alone in his age in believing that conjecture and persuasion were leading elements in poetry. He shared a broadly rhetorical conception of poetry with his contemporaries, regarding literature not as a branch of philosophy or religion but, in Kenneth Burke's phrase, 'as equipment for living.'[2]

As a practising poet, Shelley knew that a 'firm persuasion' was a function of verbal structure. Turning again in 1817 to face his audience directly, he once more sought a rhetorical form to convey his own, and influence their, opinions. To Lord Byron he confided that *The Revolt of Islam* was written

in the same style and for the same object as 'Queen Mab', but interwoven with a story of human passion, and composed with more attention to the refinement and accuracy of language, and the connexion of parts (L, I, 557)

How much he has gained as a poet since *Queen Mab* is evident in the careful attention he now pays to poetic mediation in the new strategy he plots for his return to the public forum. Just as his awareness of the need for human interest ('a story of human passion') reflects his wish for popular appeal, so his emphasis on 'accuracy of language and the connexion of parts' suggest a renewed concern with form. Embodying his ideal of a better world in the form of an epic and heroic narrative, he hoped, as he told a prospective publisher, 'to speak to the common and elementary emotions of the human heart' (L, I, 563). However, despite his appeal to human emotion and his attention to the functional structure of his text, he was betrayed by his adoption of epic form itself. His experience with *The Revolt of Islam* was to provide a lesson crucial to his development, that poetic faith is mediated by literary form as much as by symbols and signs.

I

The Revolt of Islam is unquestionably a poem of Shelley's public voice, and provides the clearest evidence of any poem in his canon that he could sing in accents other than those of the nightingale when he wished. His epic is a poem unmistakably written with an audience in mind, and consequently is the most rhetorically aggressive of all his works. Abandoning direct address for the creation of an imaginary world where the revolutionary process can take shape, the poem far surpasses *Queen Mab* in the subtlety of its art. Instead of preaching, it tries to engage the reader in an imaginative experience. Inviting his reader from the outset to share in an intentional act, Shelley transcends lyric privacy and seeks to make poetry a social discourse.

As the poem opens, Shelley struggles out of his visionary seclusion to deliver his fiction of a new social origin to a public that has been disillusioned by other initiatives. The collapse of the French Revolution into empire and reaction has cast his generation into despair, but he will make one more attempt to scale the traditional mountain of vision:

> When the last hope of trampled France had failed
> Like a brief dream of unremaining glory,
> From visions of despair I rose, and scaled
> The peak of an aerial promontory,
> Whose caverned base with the vext surge was hoary;
> And saw the golden dawn break forth, and waken
> Each cloud, and every wave: – transitory
> The calm: for sudden, the firm earth was shaken,
> As if by the last wreck its frame were overtaken.
>
> (J, I, 257, canto i, 1–9)

The instability of these opening lines, where 'the golden dawn' quickly gives way to 'the last wreck' of apocalyptic violence, is characteristic of the poem as a whole, and seems to derive from a fundamental conflict between static idealism and the temporal exigency of the historical process. In the first canto of the poem, Shelley seems to try to arrest the flow of time by inviting his reader to follow him into a visionary space. The appeal to the reader is overt in the third stanza:

> Hark! 'tis the rushing of a wind that sweeps
> Earth and the ocean. See! the lightnings yawn   (i, 19–20)

These imperatives draw our attention to the strange sight of 'An eagle and a Serpent wreathed in fight' (i, 67), probably a rather crude emblem for the clash between empire and revolt.[3] The wounded serpent is eventually gathered to the bosom of a mysterious woman, whose appeal to the reader is rather more indirect. She invites Shelley to hear the tale that lies behind this portentous spectacle, thus piquing the curiosity of the reader who eagerly accompanies a somewhat disingenuous Shelley into his world of artifice.

The methods which Shelley adopts in the first canto are reminiscent of those of Coleridge, his master, who in *The Rime of the Ancient Mariner* employs the wedding guest as a model to guide the reader through his role in the poem. Like the wedding guest who 'cannot choose but hear,' the Shelleyan narrator 'could not choose but gaze' (i, 46) at the epic struggle in the heavens, whose approach is described in terms exactly paralleling the arrival of the ghost-ship in Coleridge's poem:

> A speck, a cloud, a shape, approaching grew,
> Like a great ship in the sun's sinking sphere
> Beheld afar at sea, and swift it came anear –   (*Revolt*, i, 52–4)

> A speck, a mist, a shape, I wist!
> And still it neared and neared:
> ... that strange shape drove suddenly
> Betwixt us and the Sun.   (*Rime*, 153–76)

Persistent imagery of chasms, rivers, and fountains in both this first and the concluding cantos show the extent to which Coleridge was still in Shelley's thoughts a year after Switzerland. These striking

echoes of the verbal landscape of *Kubla Khan* come to a focus in the
description of the earthly paradise Laon and Cythna awaken to after
their execution:

> And round about sloped many a lawny mountain
> With incense-bearing forests, and vast caves
> Of marble radiance, to that mighty fountain.   (xii, 163–5)

The boat which at the end of the poem transports them to 'The Temple
of the Spirit' recalls the vehicle which at the beginning conveys
Shelley to those celestial regions to hear their tale. There it was described as 'a boat of rare device' (i, 199). The rare devices of Shelley's
narrative framework function similarly to convey the reader into a fictive world.

Perhaps Shelley relies so heavily on Coleridge in establishing his
narrative frame because he feels the need to work just such a Kubla-
like 'miracle of rare device' as his predecessor had. After all, what the
two Coleridge poems have in common is less their subject matter than
their technique, and technique seems to be what Shelley is most
deeply indebted to Coleridge for in *The Revolt*. Shelley seems intent
on establishing a locus of vision for his tale, and entices his reader into
this world of artifice by attempting to transfix him with a sort of verbal
hypnosis. In the preludial first canto, the Shelleyan narrator hath his
will, so much so indeed that the critical reader may wonder whether
we are likewise meant to listen like the three years' child. Whether
Shelley succeeds in winning our rapt attention by these devices is certainly arguable, but it seems likely at least that he is trying here to
adapt to his own uses proven techniques for authorizing the discourse
of his tale. In short, we are being asked to suspend our disbelief.

Shelley's debt to Coleridge has been noted in general terms by other
readers.[4] What needs to be appreciated more specifically is the way in
which the Coleridgean conception of a 'negative faith' that delights in
illusion (as distinct from delusion) lies at the root of Shelley's
rhetorical art. As a literary artist, Shelley firmly believes that a fiction,
given the proper conditions, can be more compelling than a fact, indeed can make facts and bring them into play in our lives. Shelley's
own experiences with art taught him that the experience of art, though
at bottom based on illusion, was itself a fact which has consequences
that shape our being and influence our doing; and Shelley dedicates his
art to generating those 'occasions' on which aesthetic experience gives
free play to the exercise of the imagination.

The exercise of the imagination was, as has been seen, essential to the moral life in Shelley's view, and it was no less essential to political life. For one to whom politics was but a branch of morals, it was natural to see poetry as an instrument of social as well as personal improvement. The problem for Shelley, as for all political poets, was how to draw a firm line between art and propaganda. In attempting to puzzle out the moral intentions of Shelley's art, Carlos Baker has defined the characteristic tactic of Shelley's public poetry: 'The aim is to re-create in the reader feelings analogous to those which inspired the author, and thus to convert him to the author's way of thinking through activation of his imagination.'[5] The discourse of poetry does not instruct the reader directly in any particular ideology. Instead, it uses its affective powers to arouse readers and animate their imaginations in sympathetic identification with those principles and emotions that rule in the author's breast. The aim of poetry, then, becomes less to convey ideas than to engage the reader in an act of the sympathetic imagination.

This pragmatic poetics receives its first full-scale formulation in the preface to *The Revolt of Islam*. His success, Shelley writes, is to be measured not by the poem's truth to nature but 'by the effect which I shall produce upon those whom I now address' (J, I, 244). Throughout the preface he emphasizes this adaption of means to ends. 'It is the business of the Poet to communicate,' he says, 'to awaken,' and even 'to excite.' Nevertheless, his claim that his poem is 'narrative, not didactic' seems to indicate a wish to move beyond crude rhetorical assaults on the audience. Putting Ensor's 'preceptive poetry' firmly behind him, he seeks a gentler approach; he now intends, he says, to teach through delighting:

I sought to enlist the harmony of metrical language, the ethereal combinations of the fancy, the rapid and subtle transitions of human passion, all those elements which essentially compose a Poem, in the cause of a liberal and comprehensive morality. (J, I, 239)

Shelley here is very candid about his methods. The pleasures of poetry will serve moral and political ends, but they will do so through neither coercion nor deception. Instead, they will be employed in an attempt to awaken an audience from lethargy and apathy.

The metaphor of arousal which dominates Shelley's poetics at this stage is probably a result of his awareness that his mission as a poet in

1817 was to reanimate latent forces in a dormant and inert society. In the aftermath of the Congress of Vienna, *The Revolt of Islam* is a poem meant to test the readiness of the reform-minded portion of the public for a renewal of political engagement:

> It is an experiment on the temper of the public mind [writes Shelley], as to how far a thirst for a happier condition of moral and political society survives, among the enlightened and refined, the tempests which have shaken the age in which we live. (J, I, 239)

For all its radical message, this poem, which Shelley calls 'my first serious appeal to the Public,' does not seek to mould its audience but simply to locate one. The reference to 'the enlightened and refined' presupposes a restricted audience already receptive to the work's ideology and techniques, but who because of historial circumstances have disengaged themselves from the political process.[6] The poem is not a call to mass action; rather, the experience of reading it is meant to 'generate occasions' in which a self-selected group of readers may rouse themselves from despair and disillusionment.

In declaring his intention 'to awaken public hope, and to enlighten and improve mankind,' however, Shelley makes it clear that he has by no means abandoned the revolutionary's role. Though he is no longer willing to play an active part in practical politics, he does not waver in his conviction that art is action. His commitment to poetry as the most effective means of social discourse at his disposal is inseparable from a belief that the poem can be a political act. If he prefers to represent rather than to inform, to show rather than to tell, he no less wants to communicate. He simply acknowledges the way in which poetry operates when he adopts the rhetorical strategy of the fictional tale, in which ideology is given human and concrete form. 'The essential attribute of Poetry,' he says in the preface, is 'the power of awakening in others sensations like those which animate my own bosom' (J, I, 244). This reproduction of mental and emotional states in others is the means by which poetry acts to transmit the poet's inspiration. As an artist committed to social change, Shelley is less interested in conveying doctrine and ideas than he is in disseminating his own imaginative state of mind and making it the rule of life. The flaw in this approach, however, is that, by locating 'the power' exclusively in the words of the poet, Shelley can achieve only the insemination of meanings and not their true dissemination.[7]

In pursuit of his aims, Shelley takes Milton and Homer as his models and epic as his efficient poetic form. Speaking of Milton's poetry in his essay *On the Devil, and Devils*, Shelley evolves a theory of the epic not far removed from his own practice in *The Revolt of Islam*. His comments show that Milton could influence his Romantic heirs in formal matters as well as in mythic ones:

He [Milton] mingled as it were the elements of human nature, as colours upon a single pallet, and arranged them into the composition of his great picture, according to the laws of epic truth; that is, according to the laws of that principle by which a series of actions of intelligent and ethical beings, developed in rhythmical language, are calculated to excite the sympathy and antipathy of succeeding generations of mankind. (J, VII, 91)

Shelley's definition of 'epic truth' is very much in keeping with the lessons learned in his lyric reflections of 1816. The 'truth' of poetry is primarily ethical and centred in humanity, rather than metaphysical and transcendent. It cannot be verified, but its influence may be felt in the 'sympathy and antipathy' it excites. The heroic figures of epic poetry are larger than life, but their value resides in how they affect us rather than in their truth to nature. This 'high mimetic mode,' as Northrop Frye calls it,[8] trades in ideals rather than reality, although the perfected human models it projects are still subject to the demands of verisimilitude; it advances its fictions with full confidence in the reader's poetic faith in order, in the words of Shelley's preface, to 'excite in the reader a generous impulse, an ardent thirst for excellence' (J, I, 240). This attraction toward excellence is Shelley's criterion of artistic success, which he finds typified in Homer:

Homer embodied the ideal perfection of his age in human character; nor can we doubt that those who read his verses were awakened to an ambition of becoming like to Achilles, Hector, and Ulysses; ... the sentiments of the auditors must have been refined by a sympathy with such great and lovely impersonations until from admiring they imitated and from imitation they identified themselves with the objects of their admiration. (J, VII, 116)

This moral mimesis on the part of the audience is simply the obverse side of the epic's exalted aesthetic mimesis. It is one of the ways 'in which poetry acts to produce the moral improvement of man,' as Shelley writes in the *Defence*, and illustrates how poets of the second, epic voice of poetry become 'as generals to the bewildered armies of [men's] thoughts' (J, VII, 117, 125).

That poetry arouses in the reader an imaginative sympathy which enlarges and refines the human spirit is a concept which comes to fruition in the *Defence of Poetry*, but its roots are evident in Shelley's struggle to find a public voice. From his own experience as a reader, he knew the value of established works of art in providing cultural models and patterns of human behaviour. Poets, he writes in the *Defence*, have 'created forms of opinion and action never before conceived,' but their influence works primarily through the aesthetic rather than the didactic mode because 'it is impossible to feel them without becoming a portion of that beauty which we contemplate' (J, VII, 125, 128). Becoming what we contemplate was a fundamental tenet of Shelley's aesthetic credo, and accounts for his repeated returns to the public voice. Above all, he strives to create beings of the imagination that call his readers to a nobler way of life.

Our identification with heroic figures and our adoption of 'forms of opinion and action' projected by literary artists is the result of an imaginative response to a beauty that irresistably absorbs us to itself. In the process, we become like the objects of our imagination, enlightened, refined, and beautiful. Significantly, the notion that we become like what we contemplate takes shape during this crucial transitional year of 1817, and probably grows out of Shelley's experience in writing *The Revolt*. Among the fragments that make up the unfinished *Prince Athanase*, which Shelley worked on at Marlowe at the end of the year, we find lines describing how the prince's kind old teacher grew into wisdom:

> With soul-sustaining songs, and sweet debates
> Of ancient lore, he fed his lonely being; –
> 'The mind becomes that which it contemplates,' –
>
> And thus Zonoras, by forever seeing
> Their bright creations, grew like wisest men.   (J, III, 139)

That the mind becomes like what it contemplates is a recurrent principle in Plato. For instance, in the sixth book of *The Republic*, Socrates wonders how it is possible for us *not* to imitate the things which we admire:

By seeing and contemplating things which are well ordered and ever unchangeable ... we surely imitate these things and make ourselves most like to them. (500c; Rouse's translation)

This notion is not exclusively Platonic, however, and offers one of many instances in which Shelley found a happy correspondence between ancient and modern thought. It is of course a fundamental principle of empiricism that the mind can know nothing but what it experiences through the senses, and hence only through the contemplation of objects does the mind come to be stocked with ideas which resemble those objects. The empirical version of mental affinity is put succinctly by Thomas Paine at the end of the first part of *The Rights of Man*:

It is the faculty of the human mind to become what it contemplates, and to act in unison with its object.[9]

It is perhaps welcome to lay to rest the persistent notion that Platonism and empiricism were in violent conflict in Shelley's thought in favour of the view, which this instance illustrates, that Shelley was frequently able to entertain both philosophies simultaneously when their doctrines were found to coincide. In this case, especially, Platonism can be seen to supplement empiricism in a crucial way: empiricism teaches that we become like what we contemplate, while Platonism provides the important moral qualification that it is best for us to contemplate (and become like) those things which are beautiful and orderly.

The belief that humankind has a mental affinity for beauty extends from here throughout Shelley's major works. It is a recurrent theme, for example, in *Prometheus Unbound*:

> As a lover or a camelion
> Grows like what it looks upon,
> As a violet's gentle eye
> Gazes on the azure sky
> Until its hue grows like what it beholds   (J, II, 258)

The characteristically Hellenic identification of beauty with order, however, provides Shelley the bridge between aesthetics and ethics. The 'measure and proportion' which 'invariably constitute beauty and excellence' in the *Philebus* (64e) are exemplified in the structural proportions of literary form and in the metrical measure of verse itself. We are aroused and excited into 'sympathy and antipathy' not only by the content of a work of art but by its form as well. When that form is beautiful and orderly in a high degree, the work of art according to Shelley's theory may have profound social consequences. In the concluding lines of Shelley's lyrical drama, Demogorgon advises us

> to hope till Hope creates
> From its own wreck the thing it contemplates.   (J, II, 262)

Even when the work projects only the phantoms of hope and desire, the form of the work regulates and disciplines those passions into a force productive of social good.

The role of metrical language in the creation of 'epic truth' was essential to Shelley's faith in poetry as an instrument of social regeneration. From his earliest days in Ireland, Shelley was convinced that in the struggle for political justice words were superior to physical force. This view is echoed in the poem, where the lines 'Great is the strength / Of words' (iv, 156–7) point the way to the thematic heart of *The Revolt of Islam*.[10] Laon and Cythna, the protagonists after whom the epic was originally named, are revolutionaries whose greatest skill is oratory, and their activities in the poem provide a curious parallel to Shelley's own. This correspondence has more often than not led to biographical interpretations of the poem, although it is probably more accurate to say that in *The Revolt* the poem provides an interpretation of the poet's life rather than the other way round. Indeed, it is not too much to claim that in *The Revolt* Shelley explores the teasing relation between art and life in terms of a dialectic between language and revolution. Language, especially in the form of the highly wrought and impassioned speeches of Laon and Cythna to the populace, shapes the revolution, but the power by which words can unleash revolutionary violence has a way of turning upon language and distorting it. In giving radical ideology poetic form in this work, Shelley is able to examine the interrelation between the two.

The careers of Laon and Cythna typify the role of the reform-minded poet in society. Labouring under tyranny, they each quite separately discover a gift for language that gives shape and definition to their hopes and desires for a better world, and that, more importantly, allows them to communicate their passion for reform to others who are prepared to assist in its realization. Repelled by the inhuman conditions under which his countrymen suffer and inspired by tales of previous civilizations more just and free than his own, Laon resolves to 'arise and waken / The multitude' (ii, 118–19). His aspirations not only find expression but also evoke the response considered by Shelley as 'the essential attribute of Poetry':

> These hopes found words through which my spirit sought
> To weave a bondage of such sympathy,
> As might create some response to the thought
> Which rules me now – and as the vapours lie
> Bright in the outspread morning's radiancy,
> So were these thoughts invested with the light
> Of language: and all bosoms made reply.   (ii, 136–42)

Laon, like every great poet whom Shelley admired, has discovered the power of the word. 'The light of language' rivals nature and gathers 'all bosoms' into a society that far surpasses primitive atomism in its potential. This awakening of the spirit by means of language Shelley sees as indispensable to every revival of civilization. 'Dante was the first awakener of entranced Europe,' he wrote in the *Defence*; 'He created a language, in itself music and persuasion, out of a chaos of inharmonious barbarisms' (J, VII, 131). The poet's first duty is to shape a language, but that language bequeathed to subsequent generations may shape the future.

Typical of Shelley's attitude to language in his comment on Dante is his insistence on the one hand on its rhetorical dimension ('persuasion') and on the other on its autonomy from nature, which he likens to music. Like music, language is an independent human artifact 'arbitrarily produced by the imagination' and further, like music, language is susceptible of special internal organizations of its own signs which are their own justification, as Cythna discovers during her imprisonment:

> And on the sand would I make signs to range
> These woofs, as they were woven, of my thought;
> Clear, elemental shapes, whose smallest change
> A subtler language within language wrought:
> The key of truths which once were dimly taught
> In old Crotona. ...   (vii, 280–5)

The reference to Pythagoras ('in old Crotona') once again links language to music as keys to unlock hidden significance. The 'subtler language' of both music and poetry detaches the auditor from nature and immediate circumstances; it replaces the world into which we are cast with a world that projects desirable possibilities, which in turn illuminates the world of our experience, awakens us to the potential of alternative ways of being, and binds us together in our pursuit of them.

The affiliative power of language is an important sub-theme sewn among the threads of meaning in *The Revolt*. Although they speak quite independently, Laon and Cythna both rely on the same material metaphor to capture their sense of the effects of metrical language. They both compare the language of their speeches to the process of weaving. Cythna orders signs 'to range / These woofs, as they were woven, of my thought' and Laon speaks of his efforts to employ words 'to weave a bondage of such sympathy' between himself and his audience. The analogy with weaving suggests both the intricate texture of language and the network of relationship which this 'subtler language' fabricates among human consciousnesses. Each individual who apparently suffers alone in fact is enmeshed in a web of words which connects him to others. This interrelationship can have both positive and negative results, depending on whether language is seen as an instrument of affiliation or of bondage. People suffer because 'their will has wove / The chains which eat their hearts' (iv, 231–2). These sad victims, like those imprisoned by Blake's 'mind-forged manacles,' have not grasped that language is in their power and that therefore they are trapped in a net that might be woven otherwise. Through their mastery of language, Laon and Cythna teach their fellow humans about new patterns of social organization; these awakened and enlightened auditors become capable of freeing themselves from old habits and reweaving the social fabric. Discoursing of justice and liberty, we learn, 'Earth's children did a woof of happy converse frame' (v, 579). In this way, Shelley translates into vivid metaphor the Godwinian principle that freedom of discussion is indispensable to the regeneration of society.

Practical instances of the way in which carefully ordered words can galvanize persons to benevolent deeds abound in the poem. Early in their career, Cythna recalls one such for Laon's benefit:

> I remember now,
> How once, a slave in tortures doomed to die,

> Was saved, because in accents sweet and low
> He sung a song his Judge loved long ago,
> As he was led to death.   (ii, 362–6)

This parable of the power of metrical language to forestall brute force is reminiscent of the way in which Eloise charms the bandits with her song in *St. Irvyne*. Shelley's long-standing faith in the capacity of poetry to renovate the world here finds eloquent expression in Cythna's words:

> All shall relent
> Who hear me – tears, as mine have flowed, shall flow,
> Hearts beat as mine now beats, with such intent
> As renovates the world; a will omnipotent!   (ii, 366–9)

The music of her speech will not only sweep away opposition, but will also harmonize the intentions of others with her own. This boast is fully borne out late in the tale after Cythna has explored the inner space of consciousness during her imprisonment in the symbolic cave where she learned to arrange signs into a 'subtler language.' Rescued by sailors, she employs her eloquence to persuade them to join in the struggle for liberty:

> They came and questioned me, but when they heard
> My voice, they became silent, and they stood
> And moved as men in whom new love had stirred
> Deep thoughts. ...   (vii, 366–9)

Repeating a by now familiar Shelleyan strategy, her voice summons them both to forbearance and to action. After her speech in praise of liberty and brotherhood in the next canto, the sailors swear to be free and firm in the pursuit of justice. Their oath shakes the very foundations of the world:

> The very darkness shook, as with a blast
> Of subterranean thunder, at the cry;
> The hollow shore its thousand echoes cast
> Into the night, as if the sea, and sky,
> And earth, rejoiced with new-born liberty,
> For in that name they swore!   (vii, 244–9)

There is no more optimistic assertion than this in Shelley's poetry of the omnipotence of 'names and signs.' With such might ranged around them, it is astonishing that Laon and Cythna's revolution in the Golden City fails.

II

The failure of the revolution inspired by Laon and Cythna is entangled in the inadequacies of *The Revolt of Islam* as a poem. Its structure is puzzling in its complexity, its narrative line contradicts itself, and its form proves unequal to Shelley's rhetorical demands. Because the activities of Laon and Cythna display an analogy with those of the revolutionary rhetorical poet, we can detect in their errors a corresponding failure on Shelley's part. Yet it is out of this failure that Shelley learns to be the poet of the Italian years whom we admire so much. How the writer of *Queen Mab* and *The Revolt of Islam* became capable of such subtle and complex works as *Prometheus Unbound, Ode to the West Wind,* and *Adonais* is the problem to which we must now turn our critical scrutiny.

Although Shelley has been much praised for his lyrics, we have seen that he repeatedly sought a larger canvas on which to work. This ambition to succeed in the larger forms is very much connected with his need to communicate. His frequent returns from lyric privacy to the public voice is indicative of his desire to contact an audience, a motive which at a deeper level shows his increasing tendency (evident in the careers of Laon and Cythna) to make poetry a political art.[11] Shelley never created art for art's sake. He drew upon the autonomy of language to create purely imagined models of existence intended to evoke the reader's assent, and through that assent to shape the beliefs and values of his audience. His exploration of the major literary forms is the history of his search for a discourse that would change the world.

Whether epic form could fulfil his aims is the real creative problem of *The Revolt of Islam.* In this poem, he erects a verbal structure about the use of verbal structures for political purposes, so that the poem often seems to be a comment on itself. But because he creates a work of such baroque complexity, it seems less to engage the reader than to imprison us. The frame of the poem, which is often taken to be its saving grace, deserves some of the blame here. Shelley devotes the whole of the first canto to projecting himself into the role of an apocalyptic narrator, only to relinquish this prophetic stance to Laon's retrospective account of a failed revolution. This shift of voice in the poem abandons anticipation for a fixed historical past that severely confines, if it does not wholly exclude, the entertainment of possibilities.

The submersion of the original epic narrator is one of the chief flaws of the poem because it makes him unnecessary baggage and calls into question the function of the narrative frame. Indeed, the failure of the narrator ever to actually resume his own voice in the twelfth and final canto shows just how dispensable he has become. His role in the first canto is that of a vehicle. With him we are conveyed to an imaginative space where the story of Laon and Cythna can be told, and through him we behold the emblem of the poem, the Eagle and the Serpent wreathed in fight. If we take this emblem, as we are invited to do, at face value, it imposes a vastly oversimplified interpretation on the historical events the poem depicts. Whether we see the eagle as the symbol of imperial tyranny or as representative of all that is noble in the human spirit, whether we see the snake as a cherished symbol of satanic rebellion or as the sneaking servant of evil, the Manichean confrontation of good and evil they inevitably suggest to many readers is a serious distortion of the complex human tragedy the poem actually unfolds.[12] In this respect, the frame masks the poem's meanings rather than giving them free play.

The presence of the narrator serves merely to create another mask, as distinct from a persona, the effect of which is to further muffle the poem's impact. Given the narrative form of the poem, we can only receive a deep impression if its tale comes across as the heartfelt testimony, given by the participants themselves, of experiences and feelings they have actually undergone. Though a reader might disagree with the views expressed, the poem's authority as sincere testimonial would at least have immediacy. What *The Revolt* gives instead is layer upon layer of reported speech. The narrator will recount how he heard Laon recount his adventures, much of which includes Laon's account of Cythna's account of her adventures. Not only does the intimidating multiplication of inverted commas make it difficult for the reader to determine exactly who is speaking at any given point, but this nesting structure causes the action to recede so far into the past that it can have little connection with the future, much less with the reader's present. Hence, the 'occasion' of reading the poem only serves to distance the audience from the revolution, rather than to involve them in the aspirations which the participants are trying to project.

The narrator's essential function in the first canto seems limited to providing a bridge between the historical world and the allegorical realm of immortal spirit from the midst of which Laon speaks. The narrator could be regarded as a device to cue the reader's responses to Laon's discourse if indeed the narrator ever chose to comment on, or even react to, Laon's history. But he doesn't, unlike Coleridge's wedding guest, who at least awakens 'a sadder and a wiser man' from the experience of the Ancient Mariner's tale. The failure to exploit the narrator to instruct the reader's response is one of the missed opportunities of the poem, unless the very passiveness of the narrator in listening to Laon is meant to serve as a model. After all, since we are listening to an immortal revolutionary hero, perhaps a hushed awe is the only proper response for us lesser beings. In giving way to the narration of Laon the narrator transcends himself only to privilege another, equally limited, voice. By deferring to Laon, the narrator provides an unfortunate model for the way the reader is expected to defer to the author in this poem.

The privileging of Laon's voice in the poem depends only partly on the narrator's deference to him, for it also derives from the peculiar eminence from which he speaks. The narrative frame operates to remove the action of the poem to an other-wordly plane, a realm of perfected being disjoined from the imperfections of the human life Laon and Cythna have known. Transported to a static glory outside the dynamic of the historical process, they dwell in 'a Temple of the Spirit' located beyond the verge of 'nature's remotest reign' (i, 433, xii, 366). From its description, this Temple of the Spirit is also apparently a Palace of Art. The 'fretwork' of its 'ivory stair,' its 'roof of moonstone carved,' and its adornment with sculpture and paintings (i, 453-9, 473-5) all suggest a world of the highest human artifice. Furthermore, verbal parallels already noted with the Xanadu of *Kubla Khan* reinforce the sense that this is, in all senses, an artificial paradise. The problem is that this paradise of the artist's vision is irreconcilable with life on earth. A poem dedicated to the 'epic truth' of ethical and intelligent human beings in action finally collapses into Laon's confession that value resides ultimately only beyond life:

> and we did know,
> That virtue, though obscured on Earth, not less
> Survives all mortal change in lasting loveliness.   (xii, 331-3)

Reading the poem through the frame has led some readers to conclude that Laon and Cythna are heroic martyrs to a lost cause. [13] But that is to admit that the ideal and the real are necessarily incompatible, and that art can never serve life. The world of Laon and Cythna's struggle, represented by their tale, and the world of aesthetic vision, represented by the frame, are alternate perspectives then, not complementary ones. This basic split in the poem is concealed only to the extent that Shelley has been successful in creating a structure which lends authority to Laon's voice. As a martyr transposed to some sort of secular heaven he enjoys a privileged perspective; however, the authorization of his voice becomes a dubious force in the poem when the ironies of his career as a revolutionary prophet begin to assert themselves.

Just as the poem as a whole fails to integrate art and life, so the tale of Laon and Cythna's experiences in the revolutionary struggle ironically exposes the gap between rhetoric and ideology. Because it depicts the relation between poets and their audience when engaged in revolutionary action, the main body of the poem can be seen as Shelley's own objectification of the poet's role in effecting social change. By following this tale where it leads him, Shelley begins to distinguish art from propaganda and establishes for himself the tragic consequences of the failure to keep them apart.

Close examination of Laon's tale reveals a sub-text of tragedy that calls the optimism of the narrative into question. His story generates ironies of which he is only imperfectly aware, but which Shelley himself puts into perspective. If this perspective had not been obscured by Shelley's attempt to give Laon narrative authority, the poem would have given us a clearer picture of the fate of the tragic hero. The tragic waste of Laon's very considerable talents in a lost cause, his ignorance of himself and his consequent commission of a tragic error (hamartia), and the peripeteia of his fortunes would all be more evident in a work of dramatic rather than narrative form.

The ironies of Laon's fate turn upon the dialectic between language and revolution in the poem, an interaction whose dual aspect is represented by the doubling of the protagonist as Laon and Cythna. Cythna's career as a revolutionary poet repeats that of Laon, but hers is a repetition with a difference, a difference figured forth in the poem as a difference in gender. Like the visionary maid in *Alastor*, Cythna appears at first to be merely a reflection of her male counterpart; however, during her period of imprisonment, when she is isolated from Laon's influence, she begins to develop a female identity of her own. Her growing self-awareness is connected with the development of her 'subtler language,' which allows her to throw off her traditionally passive feminine role and become active in the rescue (on at least two occasions) of Laon from the impasse into which his masculine leadership role has led him. It is as if, while apart from Laon, Cythna comes to understand for herself what feminist theory now proposes, that the world of meanings has been encoded by men to enhance their power, that she must reject the inherently masculine rhetorical discourse of dominance and submission, of leaders and followers, and that she must encode her own meanings and develop her own discourse. [14] In the poem, she comes to embody an understanding that persuasion and rhetoric are acts of aggression and forms of dominance constructed by males. Through her, Shelley can glimpse the need to seek a discourse that is less hierarchical and authoritarian than the prophetic mode; through her, he can reach toward a discourse that is communal and co-operative, one that respects individual autonomy and invites participation in a collective vision without compulsion or coercion. At this important juncture in a life dedicated to reform, Shelley comes face to face with the prospect that of all the institutions which oppress humanity, the most fundamental may be that encoded within language itself. Because the symbolic order as it exists is a patriarchal order, he must devote his attention to language itself and try to develop a poetic mode that moves away from a metaphorically 'male' preoccupation with inseminating ideas toward a more 'androgynous' *dis*-semination of imaginative states.

Cythna's experience therefore represents an ideal alternative (as yet unrealized in Shelley's work) to the tragedy of Laon; her 'subtler language' may be seen as a union of male and female discourses characterized by Dante as 'music and persuasion,' in contrast to the more aggressively masculine rhetoric of Laon. Laon's oratory is too often modelled on the very relationship of dominance and submission which he is rebelling against – the people follow when he speaks 'as general to the bewildered armies of their thoughts.' The goal of Cythna's discourse, on the other hand, is best described by Julia Kristeva's term 'jouissance,' a totality of enjoyment working through the signifier. 'Our only chance to avoid being either master or slave of meaning,' says Kristeva, 'lies in our ability to insure our mastery of it (through technique or knowledge) as well as our passage through it (through play or practice). In a word, jouissance.' [15] It is under Cythna's auspices that language is shown to be essential in creating the network of relationships that helps to reweave the social fabric. It is under Laon's generalship, however, that the bloody revolution ultimately rends the society of the Golden City, Argolis, and with its violence reveals what is problematic about Laon's language.

Laon's attitude to his role as revolutionary poet parallels the urge felt by Shelley in the preface to 'awaken' and stir up the slumbering sources of discontent in society. In marked contrast to the metaphor of weaving, Laon eschews analogies of artifice and images his intent in more elemental and apocalyptic terms:

> I will arise and waken
> The multitude, and like a sulpherous hill,
> Which on a sudden from its snows has shaken
> The swoon of ages, it shall burst, and fill
> The world with cleansing fire. ...   (ii, 118–22)

This analogy with volcanic eruption is, as G.M. Matthews has shown, characteristic of the way in which Shelley often envisions social change.[16] Such a violent and purgative explosion is not the exclusive means of transforming society, as the imagery of weaving suggests, but it may well be the necessary though tragic result of repressing those forces which seek reform. Volcanic eruption is an accurate imagistic projection of the consequences of socio-psychological repression, for it points toward the devastation that must ensue from such an expression of mass fury. Laon's readiness to unleash such ungovernable powers is especially ironic in the light of what he later learns about the desolation that Pestilence and Famine visit upon the earth in the aftermath of civil war. Furthermore, Laon displays a fatal hubris when he claims in the same breath to be the one still centre around which the whole upheaval will come to revolve:

> ... it must, it will –
> It may not be restrained! – and who shall stand
> Amid the rocking earthquake stedfast still,
> But Laon? on high Freedom's desert land
> A tower whose marble walls the leagued storms withstand!
> (ii, 122–6)

Laon's confidence is centred in the arrogance of his masculine ego. He sees the revolution as depending exclusively on him and his words, but fails to see that this self centredness is in fact a very grave flaw. Sadly, it is too late when Cythna warns him against this 'dark idolatry of self' (vii 192).

The elemental images associated with revolutionary upheaval are also applied to the rebellious multitude who, roused to action by Laon's oratory, invade Argolis and overthrow the tyrant, Othman. So fierce and unreflective are they that Laon is scarcely able to restrain their passion for vengeance. They rush around the fallen tyrant 'like the rush of showers / Of hail in spring' and their demand for retribution is imaged as 'the gathering of a wind' (v, 255–6, 372). Laon manages to calm them at last, and they agree to spare the tyrant for the moment.

Laon becomes increasingly aware that the forces he has 'awakened' are less in need of being roused than restrained. On the night before the town is taken, he keeps like Henry V a lonely vigil and reflects on the inner battle raging among the patriots:

> Oh, what a might
> Of human thought was cradled in that night!
> How many hearts impenetrably veiled,
> Beat underneath its shade, what secret fight
> Evil and good, in woven passions mailed,
> Waged thro' that silent throng; a war that never failed! (v, 13–18)

Laon's observation is a signal admission that the conflict between good and evil is primarily internal to human ethical consciousness rather than an external clash of opposed social forces. What Laon has bestowed on the patriots is an armour of 'woven passions,' instead of the ideal of 'a woof of happy converse' advanced in Cythna's name. He has helped to create a repressive shell beneath which a 'secret fight' of emotions continues to rage.

In his haste to play the revolutionary's role, Laon has allowed his discourse to be corrupted by its own verbal power. Where Cythna would play the healing role, he plans a strategy of attack. Though he begins by wishing his words 'to weave a bondage of such sympathy' as would overcome all opposition, he ends by forging the shackles of 'woven passions' that exclude love and forgiveness. Laon falls into the bondage of his own rhetorical strategy when he adopts a language that betrays the anti-martial ideal he pursues:

> I drew
> Words which were weapons; – round my heart there grew
> The adamantine armour of their power. ...   (ii, 175–7)

It is a tragic irony that Laon would try to make love the rule of life with 'words which were weapons' rather than with Cythna's 'subtler language.' Encased within the armour-plate of his words, he is prepared for conflict rather than for reconciliation. Though he prefers words to physical force, he makes a tragic error in choosing to wield language as a weapon rather than as a delicate instrument of human regeneration.

The effects of Laon's tragic choice are not felt immediately; instead, he initially establishes those principles he will finally be forced to violate by the inner dynamic of his own rhetoric. In the first phase of the revolution, liberation, Laon is successful in preventing violent conflict. His willingness to give his own life in non-violent confrontation so impresses the tyrant's soldiers with the moral superiority of his cause that they join the patriots in their march on the now defenceless city:

> Lifting the thunder of their acclamation
> Towards the City, then the multitude,
> And I among them, went in joy – a nation
> Made free by love; – a mighty brotherhood
> Linked by a jealous interchange of good   (v, 118–22)

Though bound by love and goodness, the multitude threaten to burst all restraint when, reaching the Imperial House, they come upon the forsaken tyrant. Giving vent to their elemental passion, the multitude demand his death, but Laon is able once again to show them the high road:

> The sceptred wretch then from that solitude
> I drew, and of his change compassionate,
> With words of sadness soothed his rugged mood.
> But he, while pride and fear held deep debate,
> With sudden guile of ill-dissembled hate
> Glared on me as a toothless snake might glare:
> Pity, not scorn, I felt. ...   (v, 217–23)

This return of love for hate is of course the essence of Christian morality. Shelley always had a high regard for 'the moral saying of Jesus Christ,' even if he rejected the transcendent implications of what he called 'the mystery ... which surrounds them' (L, I, 265). Laon, though not a follower of Christ, is devoted to what Shelley calls in his *Essay on Christianity* 'the profound wisdom and the comprehensive morality of his doctrines' (J, VI, 227), and it is on the basis of the forgiveness of one's enemies that the new commonwealth is to be established. The terms of Cythna's festal ode echo the ethical standards Laon espouses:

> Scorn and Hate,
> Revenge and Selfishness are desolate –
> A hundred nations swear that there shall be
> Pity and Peace and Love, among the good and free! (v, 489–92)

The superiority of love over hate and of pity over 'scorn' and revenge is the creed the patriots would establish and live by, were they not inhabitants of a world where power and the patriarchal emotion of 'patriotism' alike oppress them.

The verbal interplay of words like 'pity' and 'scorn,' and of concepts like forgiveness and revenge, generates another ironic sub-text in the poem through which Shelley comments on the hamartia of the revolutionary poet. Under pressure of external attack in the second phase of the revolution, reaction, Laon is finally swept up in the violence tragically unleashed by his own words. Shelley knew the French Revolution as history and not, as the elder Romantics did, as experience; consequently, he could reflect on it as an accomplished process and contemplate its meanings. He certainly knew how many of those involved in it had betrayed their ideals. A revolutionary hero viewed from a post-revolutionary perspective, Laon provides a fictional model of what went wrong. When foreign powers seek to restore the old regime, as they attempted to during the French Revolution, and as they finally succeeded in doing after the Congress of Vienna, the resolve of even the best breaks down. The restoration of Othman is no exception. The patriot's cry 'to arms! to arms!' is a natural reaction to an external threat, but it is a betrayal of the non-violent ideal Laon has laid down. Unfortunately, even Laon himself is unable to resist the urgency of the situation. In his panic, he lapses into the very 'scorn' he has condemned:

> these alarms
> Came to me, as to know their cause I leapt
> On the gate's turret, and in rage and grief and scorn I wept!   (vi, 25-7)

Acting according to his instincts rather than with his whole being, Laon embraces the very opposite of his ideals. He stirs the crowd 'with loud cries of scorn' (vi, 69) and now sees his forces inspired by 'deliberate will' (vi, 77) without the restraint of love and the discipline of virtue. The irony of the outcome is bluntly driven home in the description of how 'Myriads flocked in love and brotherhood to die' (vi, 90). Swept away in the violence, Laon finds that 'like the rest I grew desperate and unaware' until he confronts in the midst of battle

> how ugly and how fell
> O Hate! thou art, even when thy life thou shed'st
> For love   (vi, 137-9)

Laon's experience shows how easily in the stream of life one meaning can turn into its opposite.

The subversion of an end by its means, the corruption of love by hatred and of pity by scorn, are the supreme ironies of *The Revolt of Islam*. Nevertheless, in these ironies lies the tragic wisdom derived from the peripeteia of Laon's fortunes. If it is true that human beings learn through suffering, then in the catharsis provided by this poem the reader may share the insight offered in the dedication 'To Mary,' which Shelley wrote after he had completed his 'summer task' of learning to write a public poetry:

> Now has descended a serener hour,
> And with inconstant fortune, friends return;
> Tho' suffering leaves the knowledge and the power
> Which says: – Let scorn be not repaid with scorn.
>
> (Dedication, 73-6)

Though Laon never comes to know himself, there is reason to believe that through the labour of transcribing his tale Shelley gained considerably in self-knowledge. By penetrating the tragedy of Laon's fate, Shelley exorcizes the worst aspects of his public persona. No longer will he wield words as weapons, having discovered that he cannot do so without becoming their victim himself. In the few years that lie ahead, he will learn how to cultivate the 'subtler language' of poetry that subjects desire to the discipline of words. No longer will he have the vanity to put himself (or someone very much like himself) forward as the centre of a discourse which seeks to convey an ideology. He has learned that the most valuable kind of transcendence is self-transcendence because he has discovered that the evil he battles is as much in himself as it is in external circumstances.

Of all the ironies of ends and means in a poem, surely the greatest is the way Shelley's epic of revolutionary love and life betrays itself through violent hatred and death. Something in the writing of the poem itself seems to take charge of Shelley's initial lofty intentions, twisting the epic from 'the *beau ideal* as it were of the French Revolution' he proclaimed it to be into a tale of defeat and tragic martyrdom. It might be said that the epic's traditional association with the subject matter of martial heroism was at odds with Shelley's attempt to use that form to convey his non-violent and anti-martial ideology, were it not that both Milton and Blake succeeded in adapting the epic to accommodate tales of moral heroism.[17] Instead, the problem Shelley faced in *The Revolt of Islam* seems to have more to do with form itself than with content. The relationship between author and audience which literary form imposes differs as the form differs. Goethe's description in his essay *On Epic and Dramatic Poetry* of the epic poet as 'a rhapsodist ... surrounded by a circle of listeners quietly following with rapt attention' suggests just how form may be regarded as the true bearer of ideology.[18] Shelley's democratic and co-operative ideology is at odds with epic form itself, and with the determinate relations between author and audience that are a function of epic form. The mimesis of direct address, the authorization of a privileged voice, and the consequent passivity of the 'rapt' audience are the characteristics that make the epic an authoritarian form. This magisterial relation of dominance and submission is a concomitant of the prescriptive and descriptive discourse of the epic. It depicts already accomplished events and transmits meanings ready-made to readers who must either accept or reject them. This categorical imposition disallows the open text necessary for dissemination and violates the principle that the conditions of meaning require the activity of the reader as much as the activity of the author. If Shelley is to touch his readers without violating them, he must turn to a literary form that encourages their participation and minimizes his own patriarchal and authorial dominance. In the drama, Shelley was to find a form harmonious with his ideology, a form that allowed a dialectic interchange with the audience, inviting them to engage in the imaginative activity of a cooperative venture to reshape the world.

6

Dramatic Form – Tragedy

For both Hegel and Joyce, drama was the highest form of poetry. Though they might disagree on which was the more primative form, lyric or epic, they concurred in seeing drama as the culmination of a cultural process that moved away from the individual and toward society. The connection between the flowering of the drama and a society's reaching a cultural peak is insistent in Shelley's *Defence of Poetry*: 'The drama at Athens, or wheresoever else it may have approached to its perfection, ever co-existed with the moral and intellectual greatness of the age' (J, VII, 121). Whether he thought that the creation of drama would be a sign of the social enlightenment of his age or whether he actually believed that achievement in the drama might hasten the age's attainment of perfection, his gravitation toward dramatic poetry is the logical consequence of his commitment as a public and political poet.

Nevertheless, Shelley's adoption of dramatic form is as much pragmatic as it is ideological, for it grows out of his developing awareness of the inadequacies of lyric and epic forms to his poetic needs. The lyric allowed for the exploration and expression of his inner life, but its concerns remained too uniquely private. The epic enabled his public voice to project the social ideas he aspired to, but it entailed an authority and enforced a didacticism which as an artist he abhorred. Above all, he craved a literary form through which he could communicate his enthusiasm to others without imposing on them the force of his own personality. How he found this ideal rhetorical vehicle is perhaps best described again in the words of James Joyce:

The dramatic form is reached when the vitality which has flowed and eddied round each person fills every person with such vital force that he or she

122 The Poetry of Life

assumes a proper and intangible aesthetic life. The personality of the artist, at first a cry or a cadence or a mood and then a fluid and lambent narrative, finally refines itself out of existence, impersonalizes itself, so to speak. The aesthetic image in the dramatic form is life purified in and reprojected from the human imagination. [*Portrait of the Artist as a Young Man*]

Because dramatic form allows for the communication of a 'vital force' while decentring the powers of the poet's subjectivity, it makes possible the dissemination of an 'aesthetic life' in which the reader or spectator participates as an equal. In dramatic form, Shelley transcends himself and thus achieves the only sort of transcendence that is authentic, a transcendence toward others engaged in a co-operative social life.

I

As Michel Foucault has argued, every institution has its own unique discourse embedded in it, a discourse which at once defines and delimits its subject matter and the mode of its operation.[1] It is instructive to think similarly about types of literature as institutions, especially when we consider their functional dimension. Each literary form (and mode) has a distinct discursive strategy which functions to circumscribe the options it can present and to determine its relations to its audience. Because of what it can exclude as much as what it includes, form is the critical factor in literary discourse.

The severe limitation of the reader's role in epic discourse is a case in point. The strategy of epic narrative is a strategy of power, a strategy which authorizes a speaker or speakers and orders listeners in a ritual passivity, like that so well described by Goethe. The reader's role in the conventional epic is that of faithful recruit, in keeping with that form's traditional martial ideology. Even when the epic seeks to replace the warrior's heroism with moral triumph, the reader is too often given the role of disciple to some bearer of the word. Because it excludes the active participation of the reader in formulating meanings, epic form is aggressively rhetorical. Epics aim to convince, to stir, and to inspire their readers 'as generals to the bewildered armies of their thoughts.' To surmount the limitations of didacticism and to accommodate the autonomy of his reader, Shelley requires an interactive or 'dialectical form,' a form which employs a discursive strategy that distinguishes itself from crude rhetoric by seeking less to convince than to disturb the reader, and unsettle his or her conventional expectations.[2]

The notion that literary forms have an exclusionary aspect began to take shape in the aesthetic theory of Shelley's own day. Hegel elaborated his discrimination of epic, lyric, and dramatic forms in a discussion of their peculiar characteristics. Because epic relates events that are already past and at a certain distance from us, its narrative has a certain detachment and equanimity. Lyric and drama, however, relate events as immediate and present; the latter gathers us into its emotion while the former brings people and actions vividly before the mind in actual representation. Lyric and drama, therefore, lend intense presence to what the epic must regard as absent. Furthermore, according to Hegel, epic can give no glimpse into the inner life of individuals nor can it depict immediately their external interactions:

There is no scope in epic for the heart-rending cry of passion, or the outburst of the inner soul pouring forth in song for the sake of self-revelation alone. Epic poetry spurns no less the life of dramatic dialogue where individuals converse on the basis of their present situation, and the chief aspect is always the characteristic interchange between the dramatis personae. ...[3]

From what Hegel says, it may be inferred that lyric and drama differ from one another in a way that we may call ideological. The lyric is a fundamentally personal and subjective discourse whose sole aim may be merely expressive of the artist's inner being. The fact that *it* may gather us into the artist's passion serves to indicate that lyric places its priority on the self rather than the other. Lyric form bears the ideology of individualism, and it is perhaps because of this that Shelley was prized as a lyric poet by nineteenth-century bourgeois taste. The drama, on the other hand, is a public and 'objective' discourse, in which the author's individuality gives way to speech itself, that is, to dialogue and the dialectical interaction of others. The drama is an essentially social form of literature, and bears with it the ideology of communal participation.

Closer to home, native British aesthetics had already formulated the principle that the work of art requires the imaginative participation of its audience. Coleridge's reflections on 'the willing suspension of disbelief' were doubtless familiar to Shelley by this time, since his wife records in her *Journal* that he read the *Biographia Literaria* virtually hot off the presses in the latter part of 1817. The concept of a 'negative faith' that delights in the play of illusion was taken a step further by Charles Lamb, who linked the problem of belief with dramatic form in his essay 'Stage Illusion.' Though it was published too late for Shelley to have read, it suggests a parallel to a line of thought which Shelley could have developed for himself. Lamb writes that our pleasure in dramatic illusion depends on the 'secret connivance' of the audience, on what he describes more fully as 'a tacit understanding with them [which] makes them, unconsciously to themselves, a party in the scene.'[4] Shelley did not require Lamb's prompting to appreciate that dramatic illusion calls forth the activity of the audience, for the principle had been firmly established a generation before by Samuel Johnson, who pointed out in his *Preface to Shakespeare* that 'the delight in tragedy proceeds from our consciousness of fiction.' The view that dramatic form involves a process of socialization for the audience as well as for the characters was very much in the air during the Romantic period.

Shelley was certainly alive, then, to the potentials of dramatic form before he came to read August Wilhelm Schlegel's *Lectures on Dramatic Art and Literature* (in John Black's translation of 1815) during his journey to Italy in 1818.[5] Schlegel's influence on Shelley might be regarded as crucial to his search for literary form were it not for the persistent impression that Shelley read theoretical works only to confirm what he had already come to suspect out of his own practice. Certainly, though, it can be said that Schlegel provides us with a useful theoretical explanation for what Shelley tried to accomplish in dramatic poetry. Schlegel's analysis parallels the Hegelian distinctions among the three forms, but his discussion of dramatic form in both its historical and theoretical aspects explores dimensions of the drama Hegel can only suggest. Chief among these is the concept of drama as a social form. From the very opening pages where he considers what is fundamentally dramatic, he begins his analysis of drama from an ethical perspective. He launches his discussion from the Aristotelian assumption that life is action, asserts intermediately that 'the highest object of human activity is man,' and concludes that only in the drama do we see represented man in action. In the drama, he says, we behold how the moral, intellectual, and emotional influences which human beings exert on one another 'decidedly determine their reciprocal relations' (pp. 21–2). Although depiction of this social dynamic is the true stuff of drama for Schlegel, it need not simply record life as it is lived but may sketch models of life as it should be lived. Tragedy, especially, assumed in Schlegel's theory an ideal status, for it endows its characters 'with heroical grandeur, a dignity more than human, and an ideal beauty' (pp. 62–3). Because, as he says, such drama 'affords us a renovated picture of life,' it may be considered the highest poetry of life seen in both its actual, its moral, and its political dimensions.

The social function of drama was not confined for Schlegel to what it depicted but extended to how it operated. In drama, according to his theory, the members of the audience are not mere passive beholders of a represented social interaction but enter into a dialectical relation with the society they see depicted. The imaginative acitivity of the audience is encouraged by the peculiar 'rhetoric' of dramatic form, whose effect on the audience is to unify and to socialize:

The object proposed [in dramatic representation] is to produce an impression on an assembled crowed, to gain their attention, and to excite in them an interest and participation. This part of his business is common to the poet with the orator. ... The orator and the dramatic poet find means to break down these barriers of conventional reserve. While they transport their hearers to such scenes of mental agitation, that their external signs break involuntarily forth, every man perceives in those around him the same degree of emotion, and those who before were strangers to one another, become in a moment intimately acquainted. The tears which the orator or the dramatic poet compels them to shed for persecuted innocence, or a dying hero, make friends and brothers of them all. The effect produced by seeing a number of others share in the same emotions, or an intense feeling which usually retires into solitude, or only opens itself to the confidence of friendship, is astonishingly powerful. ... The powerful nature of such an engine for either good or bad purposes has justly, in all times, drawn the attention of the legislature to the drama.
(pp. 31–5)

It is just this recognition of the rhetoric of drama that has caused social theorists from Plato to Rousseau to distrust the drama, and tyranny to ban it. The authorities are well aware that in any semi-literate society the drama is a vital and effective medium of communication. If it is true that whoever controls the media controls society, then the work of the dramatist has inescapable political implications.

As a poet rather than a propagandist, however, Shelley was attracted to the drama not so much as a vehicle for ideology as for its dialectical form. The idea that drama could allow others to overcome 'conventional reserve' and share in 'an intense feeling which usually retires into solitude' pointed the way out of lyric isolation. The spirit of solitude which had haunted Shelley since *Alastor* could be banished by dramatic form. The thought that drama is a sort of communal dream, a sharing of private myth through ritual enactment, must have occurred to Shelley. Northrop Frye has shown how differently drama and lyric project myth: lyric form expresses private myth as dream, while dramatic form makes myth public through ritual.[6] Now Shelley would be very ineffectual indeed as a myth-making poet if he had no way of sharing his myth with others. Shelley's adoption of dramatic form was the practical artistic consequence of his mythopoeic mode, the strategy by which he solved the creative problem of poetic narcissism, and the instrument by which he made poetry a social discourse. Discovering drama's potential for creating intersubjective community, Shelley found 'an engine' (Schlegel's term) for reforming the world through the generation of shared visions.

Lest Shelley be thought to have been attracted more by abstractions than by experience, however, it is well to remember that during the latter part of 1817 and throughout 1818 he was an assiduous reader of dramatic literature and a frequent theatre-goer. In company with Leigh Hunt or Thomas Love Peacock, Shelley and Mary would often attend performances in London during the Marlowe days, although Peacock recalls that Shelley's decided preference was for the musical stage rather than for 'legitimate' drama. Still, Peacock was deeply impressed by 'his absorbed attention to Miss O'Neill's performance of Bianca in *Fazio*,' and thought it likely 'that she was always in his thoughts when he drew the character of Beatrice in the *Cenci*.'[7] It is evident from his letters that he designed the role of Beatrice specifically for Eliza O'Neill, and was disheartened to learn that the Covent Garden directors refused even to let her see the manuscript because of its apparently unsuitable subject matter. He was at least canny enough about the theatre to nominate Edmund Kean for the part of the Count (L, II, 102–3). Nevertheless, his real fondness was for the Italian opera, to which Peacock introduced him in 1817. Characteristically, as a poet of social sympathies, Shelley's attention focused as much on the behaviour of the audience as on what took place on stage; Peacock remembers how his friend enjoyed the fellowship of 'the quiet decorous audiences, of whom Shelley used to say, "It is delightful to see human beings so civilized." '

Shelley's experience of drama on the printed page was far wider than his attendance at actual performances and it is worth noting that an upsurge in his reading of dramatic literature coincides with just the period we are considering. In the spring and summer of 1817 (according to Mary's *Journal*), he was deeply immersed in Spenser's *Faerie Queene*, no doubt as a means of keeping up the discipline of the Spenserian stanzas in which he wrote *The Revolt of Islam*. By August, however, when his 'summer-task' of composition was nearing its end, he began to pick up Sophocles' *Oedipus Rex*. His reading of Greek drama intensified over the next year, as he turned on his travels to Aeschylus, Euripides, and Aristophanes. Meanwhile, he was reading a good deal of Beaumont and Fletcher, some Ben Jonson, and had renewed his acquaintance with the plays of Shakespeare. 'What would the human race have been if Homer, or Shakespeare, had never written?' he asked Byron in 1816 (L, I, 507). Travelling on the continent two years later, his observations of the rack and ruin of European civilization brought him face to face with the transience of the plastic (as distinct from the verbal) arts:

Books are perhaps the only productions of man coeval with the human race. Sophocles and Shakespeare can be produced and reproduced forever. But how evanescent paintings, etc. must necessarily be. ... The material part indeed of these works must perish, but they survive in the mind of man, and the remembrances connected with them are transmitted from generation to generation. The poet embodies them in his creation, the systems of philsophers are modelled to gentleness by their contemplation, opinion (that legislator) is infected with their influence; men become better and wiser, and the unseen seeds are perhaps thus sown which shall produce a plant more excellent even than that from which they fell. (L, II, 53)

Shelley's understanding of how print disseminates imaginative energy came immediately out of his experience as a reader. As he turns to sow 'unseen seeds' of his own after this fallow year of 1818, he gives voice to the spirit which breathes in the *Ode to the West Wind*, and indeed in all of the public poetry of his Italian years.

Another less well known book that may have helped open Shelley's mind to drama was Lamb's *Specimens of English Dramatic Poets*, which Shelley read in 1817. Lamb's selections gave Shelley access to previously obscure plays by Shakespeare's contemporaries, and it was perhaps the reading of Lamb's collection that inspired him to explore further the works of Beaumont and Fletcher, and of Jacobean dramatists like John Webster. Indeed, Stuart Curran's detection of some 'momentry resemblances' between *The Cenci* and Webster's *The White Devil* becomes less speculative when it is realized that one of the passages from Webster's tragedy that Lamb chose to reproduce is the famous trial scene of Vittoria Corombona.[8] Indeed, in her strong-willed defiance of judges whom she regards as hypocrites and in her unremitting protestations of innocence, Beatrice at her own trial has much in common with Vittoria. Lamb deliberately chose such passages, less for their poetic merits than for their projection of intense passion. In such displays of feeling, Lamb thought, the moral nature is most exposed:

My leading design [he writes in his preface] has been to illustrate what may be called the moral sense of our ancestors. To show in what manner they felt, when they placed themselves by the power of imagination in trying situations, in the conflicts of duty and passion, or the strife of contending duties.

(*Works*, IX, 2)

It is in the spirit at least of Lamb's preface that in the next year Shelley undertook to dramatize the story of the Cenci family. Representing the moral sense of his characters in action and interrelationship, Shelley wrote *The Cenci* (as he himself confessed) in the attitude of 'one whose attention has but newly been awakened to the study of dramatic literature' (J, II, 73).

II

Shelley seems to have understood the exigencies of dramatic form by the time he came to write *The Cenci*. He knew that the conventional drama of his age favoured realism in both presentation and subject matter, so that he welcomed the opportunity to dramatize events that had an actual historical basis because it enabled him to meet the demands of contemporary taste rather than to pursue his own visionary 'apprehensions of the beautiful and just' (L, II, 96). In his dedicatory epistle to Leigh Hunt, however, he also acknowledges the demand of the form for the exclusion of the author: 'I lay aside the presumptuous attitude of an instructor' is an expression of great personal awareness as well as a considerable triumph over the less attractive aspects of the poet's public persona. Later, in the *Defence of Poetry*, Shelley would admit that in the case of poets with definite moral aims 'the effect of their poetry is diminished in exact proportion to the degree in which they compel us to advert to this purpose' (J, VII, 118).

Certainly by 1821 Shelley had grasped the way poetry operates. He knew that unlike moral philosophy and political rhetoric 'poetry acts in another and diviner manner':

It awakens and enlarges the mind ... Poetry enlarges the circumference of the imagination by replenishing it with thoughts of ever new delight, which have the power of attracting and assimilating to their own nature all other thoughts. ... A poet therefore would do ill to embody his own conceptions of right and wrong, which are usually those of his place and time, in his poetical creations, which participate in neither. By this assumption of the inferior office of interpreting the effect, in which perhaps after all he might acquit himself but imperfectly, he would resign the glory in a participation in the cause.

(J, VII, 117–18)

Poetry thus 'acts to produce the moral improvement of man' neither by preaching nor by teaching, but by providing the imagination (that great instrument of moral good) with 'ever new delights.' Shelley firmly believed that this exercise of the imagination was indeed 'the cause' of heightened moral sensibility, the capacity for sympathy being enlarged by aesthetic pleasure. Poetry, therefore, should not aim at immediate moral and ideological impact; instead 'it administers to the effect by acting upon the cause.' And far from being a mere aesthetic hedonist, Shelley was aware that 'pleasure in its highest sense' could not be separated from pain:

Sorrow, terror, anguish, despair itself are often the chosen expressions of an approximation to the highest good. Our sympathy in tragic fiction depends on this principle: tragedy delights by affording a shadow of the pleasure which exists in pain. (J, VII, 132–3)

His success in conveying this paradoxical tragic pleasure is confirmed by George Bernard Shaw's remark, on seeing *The Cenci* produced for the first time, that 'Shelley and Shakespeare are the only dramatists who have dealt in despair of this quality' (*Our Corner*, June 1886). Above all, it was the play of the mind that Shelley sought to encourage with his art; that even the most serious drama may be called a 'play' seems in concert with the recreative metaphors Shelley so often employs in his discussion of aesthetic effect.

Seen as a work of art, then, *The Cenci* recreates, re-creates, and at the same time decreates. Shelley's drama is of course based on actual historical circumstances with which he became acquainted through an archive manuscript.[9] His re-creation of the events there recorded, how-ever, was dictated by artistic purposes rather than a desire for histor-ical accuracy. Removing them from life into art, Shelley knew, would require a poetical transformation of the Cenci family:

The person who would treat such a subject must increase the ideal, and diminish the actual horror of the events, so that the pleasure which arises from the poetry which exists in these tempestuous sufferings and crimes may mitigate the pain of the contemplation of the moral deformity from which they spring. (J, II, 70)

In this passage from his preface to *The Cenci*, Shelley seems to be feel-ing his way toward what Nietzsche in *The Birth of Tragedy* would later articulate as 'that Apollonian illusion which saves us from the direct identification with. ... Dionysiac tendencies.' Both looked to the delight and discipline of art to redeem the self-destructive fury of human existence. We must acknowledge *The Cenci* as, in Shelley's words, a 'tragic fiction' before we can experience the pleasure to be derived from its depiction of excruciating pain.

What Shelley means by 'the poetry which exists in these tempest-uous sufferings,' then, cannot be the simple addition of verse to other-wise inarticulate cries of torment but the whole process of mimesis by which they are conveyed. That Shelley's conception of mimesis was no crude theory of imitation is made clear by his reflections in the preface to *Prometheus Unbound*, which he was writing about this time. Admitting that poetry is a mimetic art, he goes on to qualify the term by associating mimesis with the act of creation. His under-standing of the term recalls the Aristotelian conception of mimesis as 'combination and representation':

Poetical abstractions are beautiful and new, not because the portions of which they are composed had no previous existence in the mind of man or in nature, but because the whole produced by their combination has some intelligible and beautiful analogy with those sources of emotion. (J, II, 173)

This stress on 'the whole' produced in the process of poetical respresentation shows how in Shelley's aesthetics mimesis was insep-arable from poesis. Because poetry 'reproduces all that it represents' (J, VII, 117), an Aristotelian bias toward the poet as maker rather than mere Platonic imitator is fundamental to Shelley's poetics right through to the *Defence of Poetry*; there, the poet does not hold a mirror up to nature, nor does he reflect the Platonic Forms – instead, he shapes a brilliant and complex surface which transforms what it reflects, and holds up in his work of art 'a mirror which makes beautiful that which is distorted' (J, VII, 115).[10] At least since the poems of 1816, Shelley regards the poetic act as a tranformation of the annals of what is called reality into an 'intelligible and beautiful analogy' of reality which exists beside our life in order to supplement and illuminate it.

This freedom of the poet to transform events imaginatively, to read the annals of history and pursue meanings which others have not seen in them, is precisely what Beatrice is denied. Whether this incapacity results from a flaw in her character or from the circumstances in which she finds herself enmeshed, it equally is a function of the discourse of tragedy to exclude alternative possibilities and to cut off the tragic protagonist from life-saving choices. Agamemnon has no real alternative but to sacrifice his daughter at Aulis; not to do so would be to relinquish his lot (*moira*) as king and commander. Oedipus has no choice but to pursue the murderer of the previous king; not to do so would be to deny not only his own intense curiosity but also his more important role as saviour of the city. Similarly, Beatrice is a prisoner of her society's conventional views of power and authority. She seems unable to defy the always already formed structures that limit her freedom and so compulsively repeats a pattern of behaviour dictated by tragic necessity. Seen in this light, her experience is a parable of the poet trapped within the confines of the institution of tragedy. Writing *The Cenci*, Shelley confronts for the first time the possibility that modes of literature possess exclusionary aspects as much as forms do.

The established moral interpretation of Beatrice among critical readers is that she confuses vengeance with justice until in the end she becomes tragically little better than her father.[11] But on an even more fundamental level her tragedy is the failure of her imagination to develop a reading of events consistent with life – she finds only a single, fixed meaning in what happens to her and so finally destroys herself like her father. She seems incapable of interpreting her experience in any other way than according to models already authorized by the existing social structure and the men around her who support it. In his preface, Shelley deplores her confinement within this restricted moral code:

Undoubtedly no person can be truly dishonoured by the act of another; and the fit return to make to the most enormous injuries is kindness and forbearance, and a resolution to convert the injurer from his dark passions by peace and love.

Revenge, retaliation, atonement, are pernicious mistakes. If Beatrice had thought in this manner she would have been wiser and better; but she would never have been a tragic character. (J, II, 71)

Far from expressing the condescension of an idealist, this comment points directly to the necessity that makes Beatrice a tragic heroine. Sadly oblivious to alernative possibilities, she slides ever more deeply into what it is given to her to contemplate.

The single most influential model for behaviour in her experience is her father. That Count Cenci is one of the earliest explicit depictions of the sadist in English literature only serves to remind us that Shelley is after all a contemporary of the 'mad' Marquis. While characters such as Cornwall might perform an isolated sadistic act like the blinding of Gloucester, Shelley is very much a creature of his times in being able to project the whole psychological complex that motivates such a character. Cenci is one whose total existence is defined by a conscious lust for cruelty:

> I rarely kill the body, which preserves,
> Like a strong prison, the soul within my power,
> Wherein I feed it with the breath of fear
> For hourly pain.   (J, II, 80)

He cannot understand human relationships based on anything but power, and thus he becomes an apt Shelleyan symbol for the correspondence between paternal and political tyranny echoed in the play by the Pope (the Holy Father) and by God. It is thus not just patriarchy which is the oppressive force in the play, but the pervasive conception (which the age of revolution yearned to change) that all human relationships must of necessity be based on a pattern of dominance and submission. Cenci's tyrannical oppression of his family reaches its dreadful climax in the violation of his daughter. Beatrice, however, makes her fatal error in embracing this same ideology of power and authority as her own. By taking revenge and killing her father, she usurps the paternal power of the state and of God, playing out a hubris which is a tragic reflection of her father's megalomania.

But, it will be asked, how can Beatrice act other than she does? The answer, which has already been given by Shelley, is that in the tragic universe of the play she cannot. Tragedy, like any institution, involves a structure of exclusion. What the tragic discourse of Beatrice's world excludes is any alternative to the prevailing ideology of patriarchal power. In her spirited denunciation of her father in the first act, she shows herself to be the only character with sufficient courage to resist him:

> What, although tyranny and impious hate
> Stand sheltered by a father's hoary hair?
> What, if 'tis he who clothed us in these limbs
> Who tortures them, and triumphs? What, if we,
> The desolate and the dead, were his own flesh,
> His children and his wife, whom he is bound
> To love and shelter? Shall we therefore find
> No refuge in this merciless wide world?
> O think what deep wrongs must have blotted out
> First love, then reverence in a child's prone mind,
> Till it thus vanquish shame and fear! O think! (J, II, 87–8)

Her appeal is powerful both in its rhetoric and its logic: her words place the onus on her hearers to respond with understanding to her quite just claim that parental authority does not carry with it the privilege of violence and abuse. Colonna and Camillo are deeply affected by what she says, but are too intimidated by Cenci's power to take the initiative. Yet there seems to be hope in the power of her words, as her mother points out:

> ... you have ever stood
> Between us and your father's moody wrath
> Like a protecting presence: your firm mind
> Has been our only refuge and defence. (J, II, 92)

It is vital to the strategy of 'age's firm, cold, subtle villainy' that the Count knowingly attacks the integrity of his daughter's 'firm mind' when he assaults her. Once that firmness is shaken, she truly can find 'no refuge in this merciless wide world' apart from the reassertion of her unnerved will.

The play then depicts an internecine struggle between two wills. There can be no doubt about the firmness of Cenci's resolution when he says that 'my revenge is as the sealed commission of a king' (J, II, 87). Monster though he is, he has at least the virtue of utter candour, which makes him at once both villainous and veracious. His frank admission of the true motives on which he acts reveals the extent to which authority is based on force in the tragic universe of this play. He openly rejoices in the deaths of his sons and offers numerous explicit threats that leave no doubt about what he plans to do. Repeatedly, he unmasks the ideology of power and lust that governs his world of church, state, and family, but in doing so he enables us to decreate the legitimacy of Beatrice's revenge. Beatrice's first speech in the play, 'Pervert not truth,' erects a standard to which she can never measure up, for it indicates a determinate signified set at defiance by the moral ambiguities of her experience. Her devotion to plain speaking and her rejection of hypocrisy, evident once again in her further rebuke of the devious Orsino, 'You have a sly equivocating vein that suits me not' (J, II, 81–2), after all ironically allies her with her father as an advocate of true speech. One must grudgingly agree with Count Cenci when he says 'I speak the sober truth,' for his every utterance is absolutely consistent with his villainy. Ironically, it is Beatrice who evades the 'sober truth' when she engages in a mystification of her own responsibilities by denying any complicity in her father's murder. She is unwilling to admit that the authority for her vengeance derives from the same sources drawn upon by her father. Her rationalization of her deed is a discourse of self-deception, which can unfold itself in the service of her will to truth only on the condition that it conceal its real service to desire and power. By pursuing what she calls 'truth,' she attempts to mask her motives not only from her accusers but from herself. The fate of Beatrice Cenci illustrates a dilemma which Shelley, as a poet, was just beginning to face, that the authority of the self is no less arbitrary than the authority of the other.

As an artist, Shelley must throw off the shackles of the tragic mode, just as Beatrice must transcend her pain, her shame, and the sort of individuality that patriarchy has imposed on her. Unfortunately Beatrice is a heroine who lacks the 'subtler language' of a discourse beyond tragedy. She does not welcome indeterminacy, but acts instead in the certainty of her rectitude, and hence limits and destroys herself. She succumbs to an ideology that reposes authority in the individual alone. So accustomed is she to attribute patriarchal authority to the men in her world that when she is betrayed by them she usurps an authority for herself that is no less relentless and oppressive. She does not struggle, as the creative being must, with the established forms and conventions of her time. She gives expression to her will and the absolute objects it defines, just as her father does. It is her tragedy that

her will to truth abets the perversion of her own proclaimed standards
and assists the triumph of her father's will to power. And it is perhaps
what Foucault calls the 'vocation of exclusion' embedded in the institution of tragedy that prevents her from remoulding her will in accord
with something other than the patriarchal model. [12]

The firmness of Beatrice's mind gives way, just as her father had
planned. She enters at the beginning of Act III in a wild and disturbed
state verging on madness. Earlier, she had assured her mother 'You see
I am not mad; I speak to you' (J, II, 91). Now fearing 'I am mad beyond
all doubt,' her disrupted speech is a sign of her disordered spirit:

> Pah! I am choked! There creeps
> A clinging, black, contaminating mist
> About me ... 'tis substantial, heavy thick,
> I cannot pluck it from me, for it glues
> My fingers and my limbs to one another,
> And eats into my sinews, and dissolves
> My flesh to a pollution, poisoning
> The subtle, pure, and inmost spirit of life!   (J, II, 102)

Cenci has achieved his ambition, as expressed in his curse on his
daughter in the fourth act, that 'she will become ... what she most
abhors' (J, II, 120). Indeed she must follow the script her father has
prepared for her, for she can read no other meaning in it than the one
he intends.

The ironic degeneration of Beatrice's character is depicted not only
by her dramatic utterances but also in the highly organized patterns of
imagery which Shelley, following the example of Shakespeare, carefully threads throughout his text. [13] Two of the most prominent refer to
the hardening of the sensibility necessary to the performance of the
play's outrages, and the clash of good and evil, indicated by the interplay of light and darkness. Count Cenci, of course, is so inured to evil-
doing that he defies all guilt. When Camillo suggests that he must be
'most miserable,' he replies:

> Why miserable? –
> No. I am what your theologians call
> Hardened. ...   (J, II, 79)

The central tragic irony of the play is that in order to deal with him in
the way they have chosen his children too must harden their hearts. In

136 The Poetry of Life

urging on her brother Giacomo the necessity for revenge, Beatrice fatally falls into the lexicon of her father:

> Let piety to God,
> Brotherly love, justice and clemency,
> And all things that make tender hardest hearts
> Make thine hard, brother. (J, II, 114)

Speaking in her father's terms has caused Beatrice to betray her own upright principles, and this twisted reasoning which perverts virtue in the service of vengeance is a sign of the gradual corruption of her soul. Later, expressing the firmness of her resolution, Beatrice compares herself to stone:

> Consequence, to me
> Is as the wind which strikes the solid rock
> But shakes it not. (J, II, 130)

In order to fight fire with fire, she has in fact had to become like what she most abhors. Having developed this rock-like hardness of spirit, she realizes too late the power of her father's words to make her coldly inhuman like himself:

> 'Tis past!
> Whatever comes, my heart shall sink no more.
> And yet, I know not why, your words strike chill. ...
> I am cut off from the only world I know,
> From light, and life, and love, in youth's sweet prime.
> You do well telling me to trust in God,
> I hope I do trust in him. In whom else
> Can any trust? And yet my heart is cold. (J, II, 152)

Spoken as she prepares to meet her death, this speech represents Beatrice's anagnorisis in the tragic structure of the drama. Beatrice comes to know what she has become, and her awareness of her diminution as a human being is what makes her a tragic heroine. The irony of the drama's imagistic sub-texts allows us to chart Beatrice's development and to decreate her self-mystifications. In the final analysis she is not like her father: her tenderness to the remaining members of her family and her consciousness of her own defeat mark the distinction between a villain and a tragic figure. Poised between a languge that controls her and a troubled awareness of its consequences, Beatrice remains a figure of irreducible ambivalence.

Her realization that she is 'cut off ... from light, and life, and love' is a poignant reminder of the triumph of evil in this play. In his second-act speech resolving on his course of villainy, Cenci identifies himself in terms of both the drama's key image patterns. First, he decides to retreat to 'That savage rock, the Castle of Petrella,' a fit refuge for one so impervious to human feeling. Next, he invokes the pervading darkness that is her element:

> The all-beholding sun yet shines; I hear
> A busy stir of men about the streets;
> I see the bright sky through the window panes:
> It is a garish, broad, and peering day;
> Loud, light, suspicious, full of eyes and ears;
> And every little corner, nook, and hole,
> Is penetrated with the insolent light.
> Come, darkness! Yet, what is the day to me?
> And wherefore should I wish for night, who do
> A deed which shall confound both night and day?
> 'Tis she shall grope through a bewildering mist
> Of horror: if there be a sun in heaven
> She shall not dare to look upon its beams,
> Nor feel its warmth. Let her then wish for night.   (J, II, 95–6)

Momentarily cowed by the light of day, Cenci reasserts a monstrous will that defies all categories of good and evil. However, his wish that darkness should finally swallow up the light represented by his daughter is horribly fulfilled. It is her innocent brother Bernardo who finally perceives the tragedy of Beatrice's end:

> O, life! O, world!
> Cover me! let me be no more! To see
> That perfect mirror of pure innocence
> Wherein I gazed, and grew happy and good,
> Shivered to dust! To see thee, Beatrice,
> Who made all lovely thou didst look upon –
> Thee, light of life – dead, dark!   (J, II, 154)

Having become distorted herself, Beatrice no longer can make all who gaze upon her example beautiful and good.

It is impossible to separate the character of Beatrice from the consequences she suffers. Her firmness, which initially is admirable, is ultimately her undoing, for once she resolves on vengeance she carries it out ruthlessly. Deprived of her self-esteem by her father's brutality, she becomes another one of the self-destructive characters of the play, whom Giacomo describes as 'scorpions ringed with fire / What should we do but strike ourselves to death?' (J, II, 98). But we can never overcome the enigma of Beatrice's character. The outrage done to her is certainly sufficient justification in most minds for the revenge she takes. Her vulnerability and the state to which she is reduced after she has been raped make her eminently pitiable, and who has insufficient sympathy with her to say that in similar circumstances we should not react in the same way? In his preface to the drama, Shelley astutely predicted the audience's inevitable involvement with her dilemma:

It is in the restless and antomizing casuistry with which men seek the justification of Beatrice, yet feel that she has done what needs justification; it is in the superstitious horror with which they contemplate alike her wrongs and their revenge, that the dramatic character of what she did and suffered, consists.

(J, II, 71)

Though we are sympathetic to Beatrice, her crime remains fearful. Indeed, her circumstances are precisely calculated to produce the effect of catharsis, engaging the audience's emotions and purifying them in self-recognition.

Shelley recognized in the story of the Cenci family 'a light to make apparent some of the most dark and secret caverns of the human heart' (J, II, 70). When he mentions this effect of the tragedy in his preface, he refers as much to the spectators as to Beatrice herself. Having discovered in tragic drama 'a capacity of awakening and sustaining the sympathy of men,' he was in a position to prove in practice his developing theory of the sympathetic imagination. William Hazlitt, in his *Essay on the Principles of Human Action* (1805), taught a whole generation how the imagination could leap beyond the self to sympathetic identification with the suffering and joys of others.[14] Hazlitt argued that if the mind can imagine its own future well-being it can imagine the well-being of another in the present:

The imagination, by means of which alone I can anticipate future objects, or be interested in them, must carry me out of myself into the feelings of others by one and the same process by which I am thrown forward as it were into my future being, and interested in it. I could not love myself, if I were not capable of loving others.

On the premise that 'our sympathy with the feelings of others [is] always imaginary,' Hazlitt elevated the imagination into one of the leading principles of human action and probably suggested to Shelley just how the imagination could become the great instrument of moral good. Certainly Hazlitt found that this moral philosophy carried with it an implicit poetics, and he applied them in his *Lectures on the English Poets*, which he began to deliver in 1818, just as Shelley was in London preparing to leave for Italy. In his lecture 'On Shakespeare and Milton,' Hazlitt remarks:

The objects of dramatic poetry affect us by sympathy, by their nearness to ourselves, as they take us by surprise, or force us upon action, 'while rage with rage doth sympathize'; the objects of epic poetry affect us through the medium of the imagination, by magnitude and distance, by their permanence and universality.

Had Shelley, who was much in Hazlitt's company at this time, heard these ideas, he would have been well prepared to comprehend Schlegel's observations on dramatic form.

Whether or not Shelley was influenced in his view of the imagination by Hazlitt, he certainly believed that 'a man, to be greatly good, must imagine intensely and comprehensively; he must put himself in the place of another and of many others; the pains and pleasures of his species must become his own' (J, VII, 118). This maxim is at once a principle of morality, a reminder of the need for self-transcendence in poetic creation, and a model of the reader's activity. During the Italian years, Shelley's desire to improve his audience changes its mode from the inculcation of dogmas and rhetorical aggression to inviting the engagement of their sympathy, encouraging the exercise of their imagination, and striving to enlarge their understanding. For the Shelley who wrote *The Cenci*, 'the highest moral purpose aimed at in the highest species of the drama, is teaching the human heart, through its sympathies and antipathies, the knowledge of itself' (J, II, 71). Two years later, Shelley would reiterate in the *Defence of Poetry* the principle evolved in writing *The Cenci*, that 'in drama of the highest order there is little food for censure or hatred; it teaches rather self-knowledge and self-respect' (J, VII, 121). That the sympathetic imagination could be an instrument for the achievement of that self-knowledge 'in proportion to the possession of which knowledge, every human being is wise, just, sincere, tolerant, and kind' (J, II, 71) Shelley knew from his own experience of tragedy:

The tragedies of the Athenian poets are as mirrors in which the spectator beholds himself, under a thin disguise of circumstance, stript of all but that ideal perfection and energy which every one feels to be the internal type of all that he loves, admires, and would become. The imagination is enlarged by a sympathy with pains and passions so mighty, that they distend in their conception of capacity of that by which they are conceived; the good affections are strengthened by pity, indignation, terror and sorrow. (J, II, 121)

In the *Defence of Poetry*, Shelley achieves a very sophisticated version of the doctrine that we become what we contemplate when he links imaginative growth to the effects of tragic catharsis. It is not so much that we copy what we behold, but that in the act itself of beholding our imaginations are stretched and our feelings are exercised.

Tragic catharsis, however, while it draws the audience together in a shared emotional and imaginative response, promotes an ambivalent reaction which is congruent with the undecidability of Beatrice's character. On the one hand, Beatrice is sympathetic; her wrongs cry out for justice to be done. On the other, Beatrice's act is repellent; the killing of a parent violates some of our most instinctive taboos. We at once pity her shattered being and condemn her ruthlessness and deceit. Her plight is pitiable but her response to it inspires fear and even some degree of loathing. It has to be said that the convention of catharsis in tragedy cuts two ways, for pity is attraction and fear is aversion, so that in our response to tragedy we are moved both toward the text and away from it. Sympathy draws us toward the tragic protagonist at the same time as our judgment must lead us to distance ourselves from his or her actions. Tragedy awakens us to human vice and error and to evil in the world, but as in Beatrice's case, it excludes alternative visions. The discourse embedded in the institution of tragedy makes circumstances seem irresistible and things as they are overwhelming. It is absurd in the extreme for anyone to expect

Beatrice to behave other than she does, given the world her drama projects. Such a world is not an exhaustive interpretation of reality, but it must nevertheless be contemplated. As Shelley remarked to Byron, 'it is well for us to know what we should avoid no less than what we should seek' (L, II, 358).

That literary discourse does not exclude the projection of other, better worlds in addition to the tragic universe of *The Cenci* is clear from *Prometheus Unbound*. Critics have often remarked on the thematic interrelationship of the two plays, as well as on the complementarity between the characters of Beatrice and Prometheus.[15] Certainly, Beatrice fails where Prometheus succeeds, in forgiving the oppressor, in returning 'peace and love' for even 'the most enormous injuries,' and in avoiding the tragic consequences of scorn and hate. 'Cut off ... from light, and life, and love' by her own pursuit of a determinate justice, Beatrice never has the chance to entertain the alternatives that Prometheus grasps. Having no access to an alternative discourse, Beatrice locks herself into tragedy by embracing the ideology of vengeance embedded in the prison-house of her father's language. Because she dwells on past wrongs, she is a prisoner of the givens of her experience and becomes what she contemplates only in the empirical sense. Her world is never illuminated by an alternative vision, an ideal such as Prometheus represents to which she can be assimilated and by which she can grow. Such alternatives to tragedy are explored by Shelley in the form of the lyrical drama. Finding himself trapped like Beatrice within the confines of the tragic convention, Shelley has the creative vitality to resist its limitations by bringing into play the discourses of other modes.

While the two plays are thematically related, it is possible that they are also pragmatically two sides of the same coin. Where *Prometheus Unbound* was written with 'the more selected classes of poetical readers' in mind, *The Cenci* was 'calculated to produce a very popular effect' (L, II, 116–17). When he offered them together to Ollier in 1819, he distinguished *The Cenci* from its more esoteric counterpart by describing the tragedy as 'of a very popular character' (L, II, 111). He confided to Peacock that he was 'exceedingly interested in the question as to whether this attempt of mine will succeed or no' and assured his publisher that ' "Cenci" is written for the multitude, and ought to sell well' (L, II, 102, 174). Even though he asked Peacock to withhold his name from the directors of Covent Garden, he did so convinced that his authorship would make *The Cenci* anathema, and that therefore anonymity was 'deeply essential to its success' (L, II, 102). It is possible that he courted popular success with *The Cenci* in order to establish himself as a force in the theatre, proving with it that he could command an audience. As he unfolded to Peacock his plan for his play's production in London, Shelley made quite clear that he would admit authorship only if it were a success, 'and use the celebrity it might acquire to my own purposes' (L, II, 102). Those purposes may have included the presentation of other, more daring plays, for which *The Cenci* was to prepare the way. It is at least likely that *The Cenci* was meant to help create an audience that could appreciate *Prometheus Unbound*, to challenge the imaginations of play-goers surfeited with the comedy of manners and what Wordsworth called 'sickly and stupid German Tragedies.' Knowing that *Prometheus Unbound* was 'a drama, with characters and mechanism of a kind yet unattempted' (L, II, 94), Shelley may have seen *The Cenci* as an opportunity to familiarize a potential audience with the unsettling effects of his dialectical form.

III

Shelley seems to have regarded tragedy as 'the highest species of the drama' even as he struggled to break its bounds. His esteem for tragedy is quite orthodox for one so immersed in classical literature, though it is well to remember a distinct preference for tragedy in modern drama prevailed among his contemporaries. Charles Lamb chose most of his *Specimens of English Dramatic Poets* from tragic rather than comic drama on the grounds (explicitly stated in his preface) that since tragedy presents scenes of passion and serious description it is 'more nearly allied to poetry.' Nevertheless, Shelley's admiration for Shakespeare helped show him the way to dramatic modes other than the tragic. Shelley was astute enough to have seen that the world of tragic convention was the world of the established order he had struggled against all along. He needed an alternative mode to project what Yeats called his 'heart's desire of a world,' a world where people were not confined by circumstances and the established symbolic order but could realize their best aspirations.

Shelley was a tireless poetic experimenter who strained at the limits of the drama of his day in ways that later in the century would eventually revitalize dramatic form.[16] The elaborate imagistic sub-text by which we can chart Beatrice's tragic development highlights Shelley's preoccupation with the inner life as the focus of drama, a focus on the inner dynamics of character, indeed, which had not been seen on the British stage since Shakespeare wrote *Hamlet*. Throughout the century that psychological drama would be the province of prose fiction, but Shelley had seen in dramatic form itself an instrument of social change superior to the novel. Having for so long shown us what to avoid, drama in Shelley's hands would now show us what we should seek, and not only show us but engage us in a dialectical participation with a text that defeats our conventional expectations of dramatic realism and challenges us to reformulate the meanings by which we live.

Signs that Shelley could not be content with the limits of the tragic mode are evident in the unfinished manuscript of *Charles the First*, which he urged Mary to write in 1818 and later took up himself. Though Shelley's allegiances would hardly make him likely to favour the monarchy in the Civil War, he had a certain respect for Charles. Medwin writes (p. 342) that in that struggle Shelley looked upon Charles as a martyr and Cromwell as a hypocrite and a tyrant. It is possible that Shelley saw in Charles the potential to be a tragic hero, and there are indications in the fragment we have that Shelley was developing him as such. Shelley depicts Charles as wholly admirable in his willingness to restrain the church and in his reluctance to take revenge on Scotland:

> Oh, be our feet still tardy to shed blood,
> Guilty though it may be! I would still spare
> The stubborn country of my birth, and ward
> From countenances which I loved in youth
> The wrathful Church's lacerating hand.   (J, IV, 156-7)

His sensitive response to the masque performed in his honour reveals yet another facet of Charles's best self, for it shows him to be a man of imagination. We do not know how Shelley would have depicted Charles's fatal flaw, for the manuscript is incomplete; but he may well have considered Charles's irresolution in allowing the execution of Strafford a fundamental expression of weakness in his character. Certainly Charles is a man who perceives a better way, but follows a worse.

That better way is espoused in the play by the king's fool, Archy. Charles's undertaking in the second scene that 'I will make my Fool my conscience' promises him an alternative to the tragedy of his reign that Beatrice sadly lacked. Shelley was of course familiar with the role of the fool in *King Lear*, and he also had read Schlegel's commentary on his dramatic function. In the *Lectures on Dramatic Art*, Schlegel calls the fool Lear's 'wisest counsellor' and writes of the fool's 'warning raillery' that 'it is well known that they frequently told such truths to princes as are never now told to them' (pp. 205, 145). Charles appreciates that his fool can be a source of insight, for in his play with words the fool weaves a subtler language than that of conventional wisdom:

> his words, like arrows
> Which know no aim beyond the archer's wit,
> Strike sometimes what eludes philosophy.   (J, IV, 149)

Through this verbal play, Charles says, Archy is able to weave a texture of illusion that creates another world of alternative possibilities:

> He weaves about himself a world of mirth
> Out of the wreck of ours.   (J, IV, 149)

The verbal parallel with the conclusion of *Prometheus Unbound* is not accidental, for his ability is akin to that of Hope which 'creates / From its own wreck the thing it contemplates' (J, II, 262). Archy's activity is a counter-parable to Beatrice's defeat; he is the artist who strikes forth from the margins of sanity and convention toward new discursive possibilities.

Archy's function in the play is symbolized by the opening scene's masque and its capacity to generate redemptive illusion. The ability of such ceremony to transform humdrum and even baleful reality is the drama's first theme:

> 1ST CITIZEN
> What thinkest thou of this quaint masque which turns,
> Like morning from the shadow of the night,
> The night of day, and London to a place
> Of peace and joy?
>
> 2ND CITIZEN
>   And Hell to Heaven.   (J, IV, 141)

The masque not only remakes a chaotic world into its own image but also provides its spectators with refreshment and renewal:

> – 'tis like the bright procession
> Of skiey visions in a solemn dream
> From which men wake as from a Paradise,
> And draw new strength to tread the thorns of life.   (J, IV, 141)

Fantasy does not provide escape, then, but rather a form of imaginative recreation which revitalizes the human spirit so that we may return to the struggle of existence with restored vigour. So Hampden, Pym, and other rebels have glimpsed another ideal than that of power, by which they seek to renew social life. Archy compares their project of an ideal commonwealth to 'Gonzalo's in the play,' calling to mind *The Tempest*'s world of fantasy. Both Archy and Prospero are familiar with the motives of illusion in promoting new forms of subjectivity. Tragically, however, Charles is better suited to play Prince Hamlet than Prince Ferdinand.

Though Charles must eventually fall from power and face death, the role of his fool grows too large in the play for the focus of the drama to remain on the tragic hero. Archy's alternative vision deconstructs the tragic vision in *Charles the First*, confirming the observation of I.A. Richards that 'tragedy is only possible to a mind which is for the moment agnostic or Manichean. The least touch of any theology which has a compensating Heaven to offer the tragic hero is fatal.'[17] Archy is a representative of Shelley's faith in language to remake the world. In Shelley's canon, the wise fool stands as an emblem pointing the way from tragedy to the ideal vision of comic romance.

7

Dramatic Form – Comedy

Though Shelley had found in dramatic poetry the dialectical form through which he could best engage an audience, he now encountered in the modes of drama the severe limitations of their respective conventions. If as a dramatic author he could operate only within the already formed structures of tragedy and comedy, then he was in danger of admitting the loss of his own creative control to institutions which overpower the writer and, in a sense, write themselves. What Mikhail Bakhtin has called the 'unitary discourse' of conventional drama began to assert itself most insistently at this stage in Shelley's development, and posed an obstacle to his aims. Ever the rebel, however, Shelley would not allow his faith in poetry to wane without a struggle, even though it be an agon with the restrictions of the very means by which he sought to liberate humanity.

Bakhtin's theory brings an historical consciousness to bear on the supposed fixity of structures and helps to account for the phenomenon of development and change in literary culture. He points out that 'a unitary language is not something given but is always in essence posited – and at every moment of its linguistic life it is opposed to the realities of heteroglossia.'[1] It is his view that authors who have 'novelized' literary discourse have done so by promoting a dialectic between conventions and counter-conventions. These counter-conventions, which he calls 'heteroglossia' or alternative languages, are found at the boundaries of conventional systems where, according to Bakhtin, discourse can be truly said to live and grow. Only by the constant collision of an established structure with other ways of being and doing found on its fringes can social and cultural life avoid ossification and renew itself. Thus Shelley sought to control literary modes that threatened to control him by searching at their margins for elements of heteroglossia with which to oppose their central and most over-whelming tendencies. This dialogical strategy is most evident in Shelley's experiments with comedy during his first years abroad.

The year 1818 was one in which Shelley gathered his forces. Taking up residence in Italy, Shelley breathed in the larger and more varied cultural atmosphere of the continent, rife with theory and rich in prac-tice. There he not only gained perspective on familiar works of liter-ature from his own nation but also vastly expanded his mental world by further reading in those works of European literature which his improved facility in modern languages now made possible. Shelley, whose tastes had always ranged beyond the boundaries of his own nation, now became a truly cosmopolitan person, and in the process gathered together those heteroglot materials that helped him resist the limits of convention.

Another factor which shaped his growth during the Italian years was the frequent company of Lord Byron. Shelley had always found his relationship with Byron extremely stimulating, but now that friend-ship was to become more complex and take on some of the nature of a rivalry. Byron was the most famous author in Europe, a man who could command a vast audience, but who seemed to Shelley to have nowhere to take them. Measuring himself against Byron, Shelley came to a deeper understanding of his vocation as a poet. Byron was the liv-ing illustration of resistance to established norms, but now Shelley found it necessary to resist him. Shelley's agon with Byron is dialogism in action.

I

At the somewhat drowsy conclusion of the *Symposium*, Socrates is glimpsed trying to convince Aristophanes 'that the same person is able to compose both tragedy and comedy, and that the foundations of the tragic and comic arts were essentially the same' (J, VII, 220; cf. 223d). Their discussion arises naturally from the occasion, for Shelley under-stood this dialogue to have been set among the celebrations connected with Athens' annual drama competitions. It is an apt commentary, too, on Shelley's growing interest in the drama, both ancient and modern, at this time. He began his translation of the dialogue during July 1818, 'in despair of producing anything original,' as he confided to Godwin (L, II, 22). Trying to find his creative bearings again after his

epic venture of the previous year, Shelley repeatedly found his attention drawn to the drama. Armed with the precedent of Shakespeare,
who excelled in both, Shelley was to prove out Socrates' claim that the
same artist could compose both tragedy and comedy.

Although Shelley would come to see how comedy could coexist
with tragedy, he seems at first to have regarded tragedy as the only
mode for serious drama and to have despised the popular comedy of his
day. His prejudice against comedy may have been influenced by the
severely contracted range of comedy in the eighteenth century, which
sustained the Restoration conventions of social realism and moral
licentiousness. His friend Peacock, who undertook to cultivate
Shelley's dramatic taste prior to his departure from Britain, was
mystified by his companion's aversion to comedy. On one evening,
Shelley was restless throughout a performance of School for Scandal
and commented acidulously on 'the withering and perverting spirit of
comedy.' Later, when Peacock tried to arouse his admiration for a
finely written passage in Beaumont and Fletcher's Rule a Wife and
Have a Wife satirizing a woman hobbled by age and a lazy maidservant,
Shelley's reply was indignant:

There is comedy in its perfection. Society grinds down poor wretches into the
dust of abject poverty, till they are scarcely recognizable as human beings; and
then, instead of being treated as what they really are, subjects of the deepest
pity, they are brought forward as grotesque monstrosities to be laughed
at. (Memoirs, p. 46)

Certainly Shelley hated comedy that appealed to the worst side of
human nature. For him, drama that depicted the corrupt state of manners (even with satirical intent) only served to confirm the existing
state of society. His judgment on School for Scandal is characteristic of
his strictures on the comedy of manners:

I see the purpose of this comedy [he told Peacock]. It is to associate virtue with
bottles and glasses, and villainy with books. (Memoirs, p. 45)

Shelley could sense something pernicious in the appeal of the reckless
Charles Surface and in the unmasking of his seemingly bookish
brother.

From his experience of the theatre, Shelley was aware of the severe
limitations of prevailing comic convention, but from his reading and

his friendship with Byron emerged a broader sense of what the comic mode could accommodate. Where tragedy reveals a structure of exclusion, allowing no acceptable alternative in the dilemmas it poses for its protagonists, comedy seems often to turn upon a series of choices where alternatives are equally possible. Tragedy is perhaps less open to heteroglossia than comedy is, for at the boundary where tragedy is exhausted comedy itself awaits with all its possibilities. As the existence of tragicomedy indicates, comedy lies on the margin of tragedy and constantly threatens to undermine its gloomy sense of necessity with the thought that things might be otherwise. Shelley's growing sense that tragic circumstances might be alleviated by the free play of possibilities is evident in *Julian and Maddalo*, a poem that dramatizes alternative viewpoints on an essentially undecidable central figure.

Shelley called the poem 'A Conversation,' but in doing so he pointed less to the vernacular register of its language than to its dramatic form. Neither is *Julian and Maddalo* a 'conversation poem' in the Coleridgean sense, where an isolated speaker pursues a monologue that leads him from alienation to recovery and relation. Instead, Shelley's poem is manifestly a dialogue in which the monologue of yet a third speaker becomes the subject of debate. The poem then becomes a conversation between two subtle but contrasting personalities who in essence dispute the significance of a speech by a third rather enigmatic character, much as Claudius and Polonius mull over Hamlet's strange behaviour. What Northrop Frye would call its 'radical of presentation,' then, is distinctly dramatic in its use of dialogue and dramatis personae.[2]

Julian and Maddalo is best understood as a decentred poem which thrives on the tolerance of conflicting points of view and gathers its significance from their play off one another. None of its speakers is an authoritative voice, not even Julian, whose speeches open and close the poem. Though Julian certainly espouses the meliorist views so dear to Shelley, he and Maddalo are equally baffled by the riddle of the madman. Also, Shelley makes it clear that because (in the delicious understatement of the preface) 'Julian is rather serious' he may not fully appreciate the ironic perceptions of his interlocutor. As a matter of fact, Shelley deliberately says that the validity of Julian's point of view, as well as that of the other characters in the poem, is something that 'the pious reader will determine.' The significance of the Maniac, especially, is displaced into the reading process, where his 'unconnected exclamations,' says Shelley, may be read according to 'the text of every heart' (J, III, 117–8). Like any good dramatist, Shelley retreats behind the scene he has created and invites his audience to judge for themselves the spectacle his characters offer.

As always, however, our judgment is prompted by Shelley's verbal strategies. Far from surrendering the possibility of meaning in this poem, Shelley employs the arts of literary discourse in order to condition our experience of it. One of these means is the ethos of the poem, which depends on the analogy between music and poetry so often prominent in Shelley's works. Perhaps because Shelley's visual imagery is often dazzling if not always pellucid, critical attention has been distracted from the prevalence of auditory imagery in his greatest works. Apart from *Prometheus Unbound*, the other major poem in which Shelley carefully crafts an imagistic soundscape that governs the world of the poem is *Julian and Maddalo*.

This technique relies not so much on the deployment of particular resonances in the verse as on the creation of various patterns of associated sounds which become signs whose differentiation generates potential meanings. For example, in *Julian and Maddalo* the two worlds of the madhouse and the Venetian lagoon are identified with contrasting sonorities. The harsh clang of the 'hoarse and iron tongue' of the madhouse bell characterizes a dissonant world where

> the clap of tortured hands,
> Fierce yells and howlings and lamentings keen,
> And laughter where complaint had merrier been,
> Moans, shrieks, and curses, and blaspheming prayers
> Accosted us.   (J, III, 185)

The more orderly and (one would like to think) saner world of Count Maddalo and his riding companion is equally defined by gentler sounds, by the civilized counterpoint of their conversation and the harmonious lapping of the waves on the Lido:

> And, from the waves, sound like delight broke forth
> Harmonizing with solitude, and sent
> Into our hearts aereal merriment.
> So, as we rode, we talked. ...   (J, III, 179)

The riders' measured speech is somehow akin to the rhythmic hoof-beats of their mounts, for they are men in control of their passions and their words as the babbling inmates of the madhouse, their reason overthrown, are not.

Harmonious sound, in the forms of music and metrical speech, lend significance also to the speech of the Maniac. Maddalo has charitably supplied the unfortunate with books, flowers, and instruments of music; when first seen the madman is seated at a piano, a music book open before him. On entering the asylum, the disputatious friends had 'heard on high, / Then, fragments of most touching melody, but looking up saw not the singer there'; his unseen presence is reminiscent of Shelley's skylark, who 'singing still dost soar' beyond the range of the human eye until only the 'shrill delight' of his disembodied song can be heard, an apt allegory of the decentring of authorial subjectivity. Like that of the skylark, the Maniac's song evokes a presence in the midst of absence, allowing for the play of uncertainty. Though it cannot be traced to its source, this song has profound effects, both on its hearers and on the singer himself. 'Madness' does not always hold him in thrall; moments of lucidity are lent by the song, for under the influence of his music the Maniac's thoughts seem more organized, and he even has a calming effect on the others. Hearing his song, the raving inmates of the madhouse are 'beguiled / Into strange silence' – Maddalo comments:

> And those are his sweet strains which charm the weight
> From madman's chains, and make this Hell appear
> A heaven of sacred silence, hushed to hear.   (J, II, 186)

Similarly, Milton describes the songs of the devils after Satan's departure:

> Their song was partial, but the harmony ...
> Suspended Hell, and took with ravishment
> The thronging audience.
> (*Paradise Lost*, II, 552–5)

Music, like the mind, is its own place and can create, like poetry, its own conditions. Once the song ceases, however, its spell is broken and chaos reasserts itself as we hear 'the din / Of madmen, shriek on shriek begin.' While the Maniac tells his melancholy tale, 'the loud and gusty storm / Hissed through the window' (J, III, 186–7), an auditory objective correlative for the disordered state of his mind which constantly threatens to engulf his moments of lucidity and self-control.

The significance of his speech lies less in what he says than in the fact that he can speak at all, unburdening his troubled mind and gaining respite, however briefly, from madness, in the formal conditions of verse. In giving, as he says in his soliloquy, 'a human voice to my despair' (J, III, 187), he works through feelings of bitterness and resentment until he can arrive at some momentary resolution of them. It would appear from what he says that he has been disappointed in love, but, surmising from what he mentions about his boyhood devotion 'to justice and to love' (J, III, 189) that his passions have been engaged by objects not merely personal, we may conclude that his deep melancholia stems from a total frustration in achieving his desires and a consequent disillusionment with both human beings and causes. His better nature has been overwhelmed by a tide of hostility and recrimination, which he can only feebly resist with his broken phrases. His resentment finds its focus in the woman who apparently once loved and then betrayed him; a deeply sensitive being, he sees in her desertion of him a symbol for the failure of all his hopes. *Alastor*-like, he sees in vengeful love the source of the disturbed emotions he feels:

> It were
> A cruel punishment for one most cruel,
> If such love, to make that love the fuel
> Of the mind's hell; hate, scorn, remorse, despair.   (J, III, 191)

Curiously, the vocabulary of moral failure which helped deconstruct *The Revolt of Islam* permeates the Maniac's speech. It is as if Shelley here paints a picture of what Laon might have become had he not had the good luck to be elevated to the heavens at the right moment. Consumed by 'hate' and 'scorn,' the Maniac suffers a nervous exhaustion that condemns him to acedia.

He rouses himself from his torpor long enough, though, to make an abreactive speech which climaxes in his mimic forgiveness of the beloved:

> Alas, Love!
> Fear me not ... against thee I would not move
> A finger in despite. Do I not live
> That thou mayest have less bitter cause to grieve!
> I give thee tears for scorn and love for hate.   (J, III, 193)

The Maniac's return of love for hate and tearful understanding for scorn provides a thematic bridge between *The Revolt of Islam* and *Prometheus Unbound*. He seems to tell us that the demon within must first be cast out before we can make a heaven of the hell of this world. His words also echo the ethical imperative of *The Cenci*, that 'revenge, retaliation, and atonement are pernicious mistakes.' But because *Julian and Maddalo*, like Shelley's tragedy, is a 'sad reality' (cf. L, II, 96 and 246), temporal necessity reasserts its dominion as the Maniac's song comes to a close. Finally, the pitiful madman must 'let / Oblivion hide his grief':

> the air
> Closes upon my accents, as despair
> Upon my heart – let death upon despair! (J, III, 193)

Like the poet whose words are subject to the temporal process, he must eventually surrender unto time. The Maniac is a metaphor for the poet of uncertainty, who speaks as if in acknowledgment of the fragility of his own discourse. But, so long as he speaks, and speaks in measured tones, he can resist closure and 'generate an occasion' for the experience of order, hope, and self-control.

In both his sensitivity and verbal struggle with what would overwhelm him, the Maniac has something in common with the poet. Julian senses this affinity when he remarks,

> The wild language of his grief was high,
> Such as, in measure, were called poetry. (J, III, 194)

If he is a poet figure, then the plight of the Maniac can also be read (as it is by Maddalo) as a warning about the risks of cultivating the imagination. In opening himself to the aspirations and sorrows of humankind, the poet makes himself a lightning-rod for emotion which may overcharge and destroy him. The Maniac's picture of himself as a raw 'nerve o'er which do creep / The else unfelt oppressions of this earth' (J, III, 191) vividly suggests the extent of his vulnerability. This morbid sensitivity was considered a characteristic symptom of mania, as Michel Foucault has pointed out, and it may be that Shelley was deliberately adopting a contemporary clinical term in denominating his protagonist a 'Maniac.'[3] However this may be, Julian still marks the slim difference between the madman and the poet by a single word, 'measure.'

Measure is a concept common to both music and poetry, and suggests art's mastery of the temporal process of life through the imposition of order. Now order is precisely what the thoughts of the Maniac lack, until, that is, he expresses them musically. The power of music to discipline human psychology, which was well known in Shelley's day, is a prominent theme of *Julian and Maddalo*. Those who suffered from mania, in fact, were thought to respond especially well to the calming effects of music. Julian, ever the optimist, dares to hope for 'a cure of these with patience and kind care, / If music can thus move' (J, III, 185). In giving measured human voice to his despair, the Maniac at least achieves a degree of control over his turbulent emotions and enjoys a cathartic relief from his pain. Where to Julian the Maniac's speech offers hope for eventual recovery, to Maddalo the catharsis it provides is merely evidence of the agony humankind is condemned to suffer:

> Most wretched men
> Are cradled into poetry by wrong,
> They learn in suffering what they teach in song.   (J, III, 194)

Both men concur in seeing the speech of the madman as an expression of his tribulation; where they differ is over the significance each attaches to his song. The dramatic dialogue in which they engage serves as a model of a reading process in which each interprets the text of the Maniac's music according to his 'heart's desire of a world.'

At the beginning of the dialogue, Maddalo offered the madhouse to Julian as 'the emblem and sign / Of what should be eternal and divine' (J, III, 182). To Maddalo the asylum is of course an ironic symbol for man's hopes in this world; but to Julian, who thinks that 'it is our will / That thus enchains us to permitted ill,' mental collapse 'is not destiny, / But man's own wilful ill' (J, III, 183–4). These alternate interpretations of the significance of the madhouse indicate the poles of the disagreement between Byron and Shelley over the relation between poetry and human destiny. Maddalo's understanding of the motives for poetry is essentially tragic: poetry is the expression of the tormented soul. Julian's, on the other hand, is essentially comic and redemptive. For him, poetry is the discourse of the madman redeemed and disciplined by the order, measure, and regularity symbolized by music. That Julian can foresee a comic resolution to the potentially tragic situation of the Maniac is suggested by his encounter at the end of the poem with Maddalo's daughter. Impressing him as being 'like one of Shakespeare's women' (J, III, 195), she tells him of the rumoured reconciliation of the lovers. Perhaps it can be said that Maddalo's daughter signifies the potential for comedy in every tragedy, although it is a type of comedy that Shelley fears 'the cold world shall not know.' The outcome of the Maniac's sorrows remains finally unresolved, an open text to be read by each human heart.

II

Shelley devotes much of his creative energy to warming the world to an appreciation of his special sort of comedy. Having weighed his open comic vision against the determinate closure of Byron's tragic pessimism, Shelley comes to the conclusion that poetry ought to be fundamentally therapeutic. This resolution is not only an ethical determination but also an answer to a psychological need, for with Charles Lamb, among others, Shelley regards poetry not as an illness but as an attempt at cure.[4] The poetry of Shelley's major phase seeks to achieve sanity in the pursuit of ideals, and to establish the authenticity of the language of desire. Shelley's poetic language is not rant nor is it evasion, but an experience of order that disciplines, even while it stimulates, desire. Its measure masters time, and its highly wrought structure of signifiers exerts a salutary influence on the attentive consciousness that is not soon dissipated. This understanding of poetic language, its nature and function, Shelley would put into practice in *Prometheus Unbound*.

As Julian is to Maddalo, so *Prometheus Unbound* is the comic counterpart that awaits at the edge of Aeschylean tragedy. It is the antidote to the the despair of *The Cenci*'s tragic discourse, but to function as such it must employ a discourse which turns its back on conventional comic realism and the world of historical time. This abstract and non-representational discourse, though characteristic of Shelley's imagination, was a source of disagreement between him and Mary. Her 'Note on The Cenci' is the most enthusiastic of her commentaries on Shelley's major poems. She thought the play 'the finest thing he ever wrote' and wished him 'to write again in a style that commanded popular favour.' Her regret that he did not take her advice is barely concealed:

But the bent of his mind went the other way; and even when employed on subjects whose interest depended on character and incident, he would start off in another direction, and leave the delineations of human passion, which he could

depict in so able a manner, for fantastic creations of his fancy, or the expression
of those opinions and sentiments with regard to human nature and its destiny,
a desire to diffuse which was the master passion of his soul.   (J, II, 158)

It was perhaps the sole uncongeniality in their marriage that Shelley
could never share his wife's exclusive taste for the realistic in art.
Shelley shunned realism in favour of 'fantastic creations' precisely
because his views on 'human nature and its destiny' did not accord
with existing standards – he always desired more than was already
formed in this world. He could not be content with realism's devotion
to the typical or the ordinary because his ideology demanded the rejection of established norms and the creation of new modes of being and
acting. Ideology and imagination were connected for Shelley, because,
while tales of human passion served to confirm for him our confinement by circumstances, the prospects of human destiny could only be
imaged in those 'fantastic creations of his fancy' that Mary failed to
appreciate. Next to the language of 'sad reality,' Shelley posited
another language of desire; this and other 'heteroglossia' make up the
textual fabric of Prometheus Unbound.

   This fantasy of 'human nature and its destiny' is the most characteristic poem Shelley wrote. Deliberately leaving behind 'delineations of
human passion,' Shelley's lyrical drama projects imaginative objects
that bring to life 'those opinions and sentiments with regard to human
nature and its destiny, a desire to diffuse which was the master passion
of his soul' (J, II, 158). Mary Shelley's shrewd comment on her husband's foible effectively highlights the ruling passions of his poetic
career – desire and diffusion. His wish for a better world was folly so
long as he nursed it in isolation, where his sanity was vulnerable to the
spirit of solitude; but in attempting to disseminate that desire through
measured words, he used communication as a means to overcome
alienation and shape social consciousness. If it is foolish to prefer
words to weapons and persuasion to force, then it is at least a harmless
folly that Shelley indulged.

   The folly of Shelley's language in Prometheus Unbound, at least
from the viewpoint of the cold world, is its detachment from determinate signification. Prometheus Unbound is a play of signs and sign-
making, a play of 'sense' independent of 'reference,' to borrow Frege's
distinction once again. None of the events in Shelley's elaborate fiction refers to historical time, nor do his characters stand for specific
concepts. Of the two types of literary discourse open to Shelley, tales

of human passion such as *The Cenci*, with their necessary historicity and reliance on circumstance, were far less congenial to his special talents than tales of human destiny, which looked to the future rather than to the past, a future which, being in its very nature hypothetical, allows for the entertainment of hypothetical conditions. Rather than recounting the past, describing the present, or predicting the future, Shelley's was a prospective discourse whose essential nature was to be hypothetical and fundamentally uncertain.[5] Because human destiny can only be imagined, can only be an object of consciousness whose being is not yet in existence, it can become an object of attention only through discourse itself, particularly a discourse whose language is 'arbitrarily produced by the imagination.' This prospective discourse differs from prophecy because it is ironic toward the whole process of signification in its disavowal of all claims to truth or reference. Shelley's literary discourse is an originary activity that forms the objects of which it speaks in the process of sign-making, gives those objects free play for the benefit of his audience, and has consequences for human life.[6]

A measure of the uniqueness of Shelley's undertaking in *Prometheus Unbound* was his determination that it should stand apart from his other works. He informed his publisher, Ollier, of his wish that the drama and *Julian and Maddalo* should not be printed together because the two 'would not harmonize'; the latter represented 'a *sermo pedestris* way of treating human nature' (L, II, 196), a prosaic or ordinary discourse on mankind, in contrast to the equally Horatian *fictum carmen* of the lyrical drama (see *Ars Poetica*, 95 and 240). The 'new created song' of *Prometheus Unbound* observed a quite different decorum from that observed in the rhetoric of *Julian and Maddalo*, which aims at description rather than prescription. As Shelley told Hunt in his dedication to the poem, *Julian and Maddalo* presented a 'sad reality,' while *Prometheus Unbound* is described in its own preface as 'a beautiful idealism of moral excellence' (J, II, 174). Shelley's lyrical drama may be distinguished as one of those 'dreams of what ought to be, or may be' rather than a picture of what is; as such, it participates equally in uncertainty and possibility, for all its tentativeness exerting an influence on the imagination of the reader. The play is baffling to many, and teasing to others, but it is dismissed only by those who demand of a literary text that it deliver up ready-made meanings and fixed principles.

A guide to the appreciation of *Prometheus Unbound* can profitably begin with an exploration of the vast array of intertextual analogues to this creation that help define it as a variety of comedy. The literary analogues to the work display the formidable range of Shelley's knowledge and taste, for they are found in classical, British, and continental sources. It becomes plain from pursuing them that Shelley's whole outlook was formed as much by his experience of art as by his philosophical and political reading. From this experience he gathered the heteroglossia that enabled him to transcend the conventional comedy of his age.

At first sight, the comic tradition may appear quite foreign to Shelley; Julian is, after all, rather serious. Nevertheless, it is vital to a just estimate of *Prometheus Unbound* to understand it as an essentially comic poem, or, more precisely, as representative of a certain kind of comedy that had become marginalized in Shelley's day. Struggling to define the comic genius of Shakespeare, John Dover Wilson differentiated two distinct strands in the line of comic tradition.[7] One, evident in the 'comical satires' of Ben Jonson and the neoclassical drama of Molière, derives from Roman New Comedy and is handed down through the Restoration stage to Wilde and Shaw. It is a realistic and critical comedy that scrutinizes prevailing manners and morals and offers a picture of existing social reality for the judgment of the audience. Its characteristic device of irony appeals to the intellect of its audience, asking them to discriminate, for example, hypocrisy from truth or vanity from worthiness. Certainly, this variety of comedy has been predominant in the British tradition, although plays like *Twelfth Night*, *As You Like It*, and *The Tempest* do not fit neatly into its scheme. Certain of Shakespeare's comedies, argues Dover Wilson, require the recognition of a second comic strain in the British tradition. It is this marginal sort of comedy, found on the boundaries of tragedy and romance, that Shelley brought to bear in *Prometheus Unbound*.

It is apparent that Shelley found the critical and ironic mode of comedy uncongenial to his temperament. His contemptuous dismissal of Sheridan's *School for Scandal* is perfectly consistent with the notion that other comic modes may coexist beside the comedy of manners. Shelley nevertheless did experiment with ironic comedy, if only in its extreme form of satire. His parody *Peter Bell the Third* and his burlesque *Swellfoot the Tyrant* show that he was at least capable of exercising a sense of humour, even though a somewhat malicious one. The rancorous and slightly spiteful quality of these two works shows how the ironic mode called forth the worst side of Shelley's character (surely, calling Wordsworth a 'moral eunuch' betrays a narrowness and lack of generosity uncharacteristic of Shelley at his best). While *Peter Bell the Third* at least is somewhat redeemed by the spirit of playfulness so essential to Shelley's art, the same cannot be said for the rather repellent satire of *Swellfoot*. Nevertheless, *Swellfoot the Tyrant* deserves attention both as another Shelleyan experiment in dramatic form and an example of what Shelley had finally to reject in both comedy and his art in general. *Swellfoot* is also important for pointing to the classical roots of Shelley's conception of comedy and for showing the inadequacy of satire to Shelley's artistic purposes.

Swellfoot the Tyrant has received very scant critical attention, perhaps justifiably. The bitterness of its tone, the clumsiness of its allegorical machinery, and the crude avowal of its message all conspire to make it repugnant as a work of art. Its tenuous relation to the Oedipus legend resides primarily in the impact of an oracle upon events. 'Choose reform or civil war' is the blunt message of the prophecy which the leaders of church and state hasten to forestall by making a scapegoat of Swellfoot's queen, as Castlereagh had done to Queen Caroline in order to divert attention from the need for reform in England. The reduction of the principal characters to pigs and the play's working definition of 'Piggishness' as 'religion, morals, peace, and plenty' make contempt the primary emotion evoked by the play. Thematically, it treats with derision such social ills as corruption in high places, the evils of class exploitation, and the unjust distribution of wealth, all of which are allegorized in the Worship of Famine:

> Those who consume these fruits through thee grow fat,
> Those who produce these fruits through thee grow lean.
>
> (J, II, 344)

The chief characters, denizens of a Shelleyan rogue's gallery of reaction, are easy targets. Mammon, the arch priest of Famine, is probably Malthus, while Purganax, chief wizard and upholder of 'the glorious Constitution of the Pigs,' is likely Castlereagh; their depiction of the populace as 'the Swinish multitude' owes as much to Burke's contemptuous use of that phrase in his *Reflections on the Revolution in France* as it does to the pigs of San Giuliano. In any case, the chorus of pigs at the fair of San Giuliano were merely a mnemonic intermediary, as they put Shelley in mind of Aristophanes, whose chorus of frogs led by a process of 'one ludicrous association suggesting another' to the composition of this 'political-satirical drama on the circumstances of the day' (J, II, 350). As such, Swellfoot is a closed text whose determinate satirical references leave little to the imagination.

By pursuing the ironic mode to an extreme in Swellfoot, Shelley betrays his deepest commitment as a poet. This vicious satire is a step backward for him; not simply a regression to the rough agitprop of Queen Mab, it represents a failure of imaginative energy and moral vision reminiscent of Laon's collapse into self-destructive rhetoric. The visionary mode of Queen Mab offered at least some counterweight to what he despised most about monarchy and Christianity, but encountering in satire no checks to bitterness and cynicism he tips the balance precariously toward despair. In the hands of an author less an idealist than Shelley satire can, of course, be a potent weapon, but it was thoroughly uncongenial to his particular temperament. For him the satirical mode could only give rein to the very scorn and self-hatred which destroyed Laon, drove Beatrice to vengeance, and unbalanced the mind of the Maniac. As Shelley worked them out, tragedy and satire could only pillory vice, and so became creative blind alleys. Seeking always a mode that could animate virtue, he was dedicated less to criticizing error and abuse than to generating in his audience a self-esteem that could overcome scorn, and a faith that could replace despair.

If Swellfoot has any value at all, it is that in reminding us of Aristophanes it points toward the Old Comedy of Athens as one of the models for the dramatic mode that Shelley adopted in Prometheus Unbound. For all its broad satire, Old Comedy possessed a dimension of fantasy which allowed for the free play of the imagination. Imaginative activity was encouraged by two characteristic elements of Old Comedy, its use of allegorical action simultaneously to develop an idea and further the plot, and the choric parabasis which, like romantic irony, shatters the illusion of reality when it invites audience participation in the dramatic process.[8] Reading Schlegel's Lectures, Shelley would have found praise for this dramatic mode based on a discrimination not far removed from the sermo pedestris/fictim carmen distinction of Horace: the Old Comedy of the Greeks, wrote Schlegel, was 'entitled to the appellation of the genuine poetical species; and the new comedy ... is a falling off into prose and reality' (p. 191). What appealed to Schlegel about the Old Comedy was what Black translates as its 'sportive' quality, or what Schlegel himself denominates its element of *scherz*. This attitude of jest and playfulness Schlegel saw as applying no less to the form of the drama than to its subject matter in the Old Comedy, for its use of allegory and parabasis often defied the laws of probability and shattered the illusion of dramatic realism. As a dramatic mode, it constantly called attention to what Schlegel's contemporary Schiller called *der Spieltrieb* in art. This instinct for play which Shelley was thus attuned to in the comedy of Aristophanes helped him to break out of the restrictions which hampered him in ironic comedy and to seek a comic mode more congenial to him.

Once again, however, Shelley's growth as an artist was prompted not so much by his encounter with critical theory as by his response as reader to actual literary texts. Having read Schlegel in the spring, Shelley immersed himself in the drama of Aristophanes during June and July of 1818, according to entries in Mary Shelley's *Journal*. He of course began *Prometheus Unbound* in the autumn of the same year, but the reading of Aristophanes is more immediately related in time to Shelley's project of translating Plato's *Symposium* during that same summer. He may have sought in reading his plays to form some idea of Aristophanes' character preparatory to translating his wonderfully playful speech on love in Plato's dialogue, or he may have become interested in his comedy as a result of Socrates' remark that comedy and tragedy are inextricably related. Unfortunately, Shelley left no record of either his motives for reading Aristophanes or his reaction to him. Yet there are sufficient affinities between Aristophanes' plays and Shelley's outlook to form a basis for speculation.

Whether Shelley would have appreciated the satire of Socrates in *The Clouds* is certainly arguable, but the role of women in curbing the excesses of male aggressiveness in *Lysistrata* surely would have struck a sympathetic chord in him. Obviously *The Frogs* exerted a strong appeal for him, and not exclusively for its rude chorus. The affinity between *Plutus* and *Prometheus Unbound*, however, is the most insistent of all. Like Shelley's lyrical drama, the *Plutus* of Aristophanes focuses on the relations between gods and men, and shows how those relations can be altered in a drama that suspends the laws of probability and of everyday circumstance in favour of depicting a 'heart's desire of a world.'

Plutus is a play of allegorical fantasy in which the tables are teasingly turned on the gods; this development comes about when the chthonic god of riches is treated with compassion and incorporated in the social world of men above ground. The instrument of this rehabili-

tation is Chremylus, who treats the god of the underworld with kindness and respect as he assists the blind god in regaining his sight.
Through the allegory, Aristophanes suggests that Plutus is a much
maligned god who in the past has distributed wealth and fortune capri-
ciously only because he lacks the means to discriminate the virtuous
from the vicious. His sight restored, however, he readily falls in with
Chremylus' wish that only the good should reap his rewards. From
being a villian he becomes a sponsor of moral order among men, and
his cult grows so rapidly that it challenges the supremacy of Zeus. This
reversal of the Olympian order so angers the chief of the gods that he
threatens to destroy the world, but discovers that he is now powerless
to do so. The charming fantasy ends with the gods coming down to
earth and joining humanity in the worship of justice and virtue.
Parallels with the agon of the chthonic Demogorgon and the supernal
Jupiter and with the miraculous transformation of the moral universe
in *Prometheus Unbound* naturally suggest themselves.

The use of parabasis in the *Plutus* does not have obvious parallels in
Prometheus Unbound, but its existence in Old Comedy provides at
least a precedent if not a model for some of the effects of Shelley's lyrical drama. Parabasis is a simple form of Brecht's 'alienation effect,'
which simultaneously distances the audience from the dramatic illusion and involves them in the dramatic process. Parabasis prevents the
audience from confusing what is represented on the stage with reality,
jars them out of empathy with plot and character, and establishes a
new relation between the audience and the play in which they become
active participants in the dramatic experience. In *Prometheus Unbound*, Shelley uses different techniques (primarily of musical structure and a discourse in which meaning is deliberately deferred) to
achieve the same end. Parabasis is used repeatedly in *Plutus* to make
collaborators of the audience. At the beginning of the play when Plutus
laments the shortage of honest folk, Chremylus turns to the audience,
scrutinizes them closely, and admits that he doesn't see many among
them who could change Plutus's opinion. This moment in the play
seems designed to make members of the audience re-evaluate themselves in preparation for the great transformation that will shortly
unfold before their eyes. Throughout the play, Chremylus and his servant Carion frequently make asides to the audience admitting selfish
motives for wealth, perhaps in an attempt to defuse feelings of guilt
and to prevent the action on the literal level from being taken too seriously. Finally, at the conclusion of the play, the chorus invites the

audience to join in the ritual celebration of Plutus, an attractive proposition since all the characters in the play, including the gods themselves, have by now given themselves over to his cult. Similarly, in
Prometheus Unbound, the audience is at first challenged by the difficulty of the language, and finally are invited to participate imaginatively in the celebration of the marriage of Prometheus and Asia
through the masque-like ritual of the fourth act.

Allegory and parabasis are also prominent features of *The Frogs*. In
that play, Dionysus descends to the underworld in search of a great
dramatist who can revive Athenian tragedy, of which the god is of
course the patron. After he passes the rude chorus of frogs, he encounters the shades of Euripides and Aeschylus, between whom he is now
forced to choose in order to accomplish his mission. Euripides believes
he merits Dionysus' favour because, he says, 'I taught my audience to
judge.' But Aeschylus lodges what he considers a superior claim on the
basis of a nobler subject matter:

> The poet should hide what is vile and not produce nor represent it on the stage.
> ... We must display only what is good.

Aeschylus forces Euripides to admit that the poet must not just
instruct but also improve his audience, for what is most admirable in a
poet is 'wise counsels, which make the citizens better.' This connection between literature and social good must have appealed to Shelley,
for it is in tune with his poetic aims from his earliest articulation of
them to Godwin to their expression in the *Defence of Poetry*. In Aristophanes, Shelley found a fellow spirit, an artist whose work was dominated by a concern for the welfare of the *polis*. Aristophanes showed
Shelley how drama could incorporate broadly political goals without
degenerating into propaganda, and more specifically pointed the way
out of dramatic realism toward a comic fantasy that did not shun
ethics. But, above all, Aristophanes reminded Shelley that drama must
have a social function.

While the *Defence of Poetry* has much to say about the dialectic be-
tween drama and society, its only comment on comedy is that 'com-
edy should be as in *King Lear* universal, ideal and sublime' (J, VII, 120).
In his *Lectures*, Schlegel commented at length on the function of the
Fool in *Lear*, emphasizing always his wisdom rather than his irony.
Shelley was alive to the function of foolery in other drama besides
Shakespeare's; Medwin recalls (p. 244) that, reading Calderón's *Cisma*

di'Ingalaterra, 'Shelley was much struck with the characteristic Fool, who plays a part in it, and deals in fables.' The wisdom of folly and the seriousness of play are constant values for Shelley, a mental disposition reflected in his taste for works of imaginative fantasy. His preference in comedy was clearly not for the ironic variety, but rather for a comedy that is non-naturalistic, defies ordinary circumstances, and shows adversity ultimately overcome. The probable paradigm in Shelley's mind for this sort of comedy was the *Divine Comedy* of Dante, for Dante comes closer than any other high comic writer to formulating a notion of comedy to which Shelley could subscribe. 'Comedy,' wrote Dante in his dedicatory letter to Can Grande, 'introduces a situation of adversity but ends its matter in prosperity. ... The end of the whole as of the part is to remove those living in this life from the state of misery and to lead them into the state of happiness.'[9] For Dante, comedy is a structure of experience which leads from catastrophe and sorrow to triumph and rejoicing; its order creates a mood in which we as readers or auditors are invited to participate, even while we may suspend our judgment about its content. Shakespeare's finest comedies are of this sort, and there is a suggestive propinquity between Dante's comic vision and what Northrop Frye has taught us to call 'Shakespeare's romantic comedy.'[10]

Shelley's intellectual curiosity was so extraordinarily catholic that his inspiration can never be traced to a single source. Works of literature and philosophy, both ancient and modern, whether dramatic or discursive, whirled in his mind until they coalesced into the unique poetic universe of *Prometheus Unbound*. Shakespeare cannot be seen in isolation as the literary ancestor of Shelley's romantic comedy, but instead must be placed within the staggering context of Shelley's reading. Shelley himself never seems to have read works in isolation; instead, he constantly drew parallels within his literary experience and sought to range himself within the various axes he thus created. Certainly, he came to see himself as running on a divergent line from Byron. Shelley complained that Byron 'will follow the French tragedians and Alfieri, rather than those of England and Spain. ... This seems to me the wrong road' (L, II, 349). Shelley's atavism as far as the drama was concerned filiated him with the greatest dramatists of England and Spain, who Schlegel and Hazlitt together had taught him were Shakespeare and Calderón. 'A kind of Shakespeare is this Calderon,' Shelley confided to Peacock in 1819 (L, II, 115), drawing a correspondence of genius that would climax in *Prometheus Unbound*.

Shelley's interest in Calderón quickly shifted from the Spaniard's tragedies to his mysterious and unworldly *Autos Sacramentales* during the writing of *Prometheus Unbound*. Calderón's *Autos* provided Shelley with an appreciation of how indispensable ritual was to drama, especially to that higher comedy designated by Dante. This awareness is evident in the *Defence*, when Shelley points out how the Autos fulfil 'the high conditions of dramatic representation neglected by Shakespeare, such as the establishing a relation between the drama and religion and the accommodating them to music and dancing' (J, VII, 120). The mythological underpinnings of *Prometheus Unbound* show at least some attempt on Shelley's part to re-establish a relation between drama and religion, and the accommodation of music and the dance was crucial to his development of the form of the lyrical drama, as we shall see. However, Calderón was not an infallible model for Shelleyan comedy. Calderón's ritual drama remains wedded to a doctrine Shelley regarded as superstition, and so its discourse can never free itself from transcendental reference in order to meet the requirements of free play.

Shakespeare presented no such problem. His celebrated self-effacement and 'negative capability' enable the audience to concentrate on the play of signifiers without seeking for reference beyond the dramatic experience itself. His text is a process that 'generates occasions' for meaning and welcomes inconclusiveness and infinite variety. This open-endedness of Shakespeare's text and his decentred dramatic form were models for Shelley. Shelley's admiration for Shakespeare was constant throughout his life: as early as *Queen Mab* Shelley's poetry attempted to draw its authority from Shakespeare's text, and his wish to call his fatal sailboat the *Ariel* shows his continued attachment near the end of his life. Shakespeare's willing acknowledgment of the uses of illusion ('the truest poetry is the most feigning' says Touchstone) and his evolution of a comic drama 'universal, ideal and sublime' ally him to Shelley's practice. If Shakespeare's drama can be seen as an ancestor of *Prometheus Unbound*, that poem ceases to be so strange and singular. In his lyrical drama, Shelley does not create a new type of play so much as attempt to revive a lapsed tradition of idealization and fantasy in literary art that has affinities with the classics of continental literature, ancient and modern, but which finds its native expression in the romantic comedies of Shakespeare, of which *The Tempest* is the supreme example. That work is perhaps the most illuminating literary intertext for *Prometheus Unbound*; the fact that Shelley was rereading

The Tempest during the period of his greatest creative output is therefore not merely coincidental.[11]

Thematically, *The Tempest* and *Prometheus Unbound* have much in common. As with Shelley's lyrical drama, the general movement of Shakespeare's comedy is from chaos to order, in both the natural and the moral world. The opening storm of Shakespeare's play is the elemental counterpart to the political disorder by which Prospero was expelled from his dukedom by a usurping brother, and mirrors also the disorganized aspirations and unfocused resentment of Caliban. It is Prospero's 'project' in the play to discipline these lawless forces and subject them to a moral order governed by reconciliation and love, symbolized by the blossoming affection between Ferdinand and Miranda. This moral order is achieved in the play not by the imposition of arbitrary law or the application of force, but by the exposure of the various characters to Prospero's 'art.' His 'charm so strongly works 'em' that they fall into an ethical order that reflects an aesthetic order. They become what they contemplate in accord with that strategy of Platonic optimism which taught that, the order of goodness and the order of beauty being essentially the same, the *kalon* of art could promote the discipline of the soul which the Greeks called *sophrosyne*.[12]

In the course of the play, all the characters gradually develop a control over their disorganized passions as a result of the influence of Prospero working through the instrumentality of his special magic. Prospero 'generates occasions' for each group of characters in which they may learn and grow. Each group – the infatuated lovers, the scheming court party, and the ruffians – must undergo an ordeal that prepares them to behold a climactic symbolic vision that invites their response, though it does not dictate it. *The Tempest* is thus an allegory of dramatic presentation, in which Prospero is the dramatist and each of the parties form an audience. This allegory of aesthetic effect is made explicit in the case of Ferdinand. Through the ritual task of the log pile, he must learn to distinguish lust from love by gaining control of his passions. In the symbolic vision of the wedding masque, this central theme of self-restraint is illustrated in the ritual denial of the influence of Venus and Cupid over the young lovers:

> Here thought they to have done
> Some wanton charm upon this man and maid,
> Whose vows are, that no bed-right shall be paid
> Till Hymen's torch be lighted; but in vain. ...　　　(IV, i, 94–7)

But the virtue of *sophrosyne* is not learned by the lovers only. Prospero, too, must learn to restrain his desire for vengeance upon those who have wronged him. Like Prometheus, he must win a victory, not over his enemy, but over himself, and do so through an act of forgiveness. Prospero becomes a truly *sophron* man in the play only when he can admit that 'the rarer action is in virtue than in vengeance' (V, i, 27–8). Prospero's forgiveness of his brother, whether accepted or not, is a moral act akin to the forgiveness of Jupiter by Prometheus ('It doth repent me,' etc., J, II, 188). *Prometheus Unbound*, in a sense, begins where *The Tempest* leaves off, showing the consequences in the human world of Promethean *sophrosyne*, the transcendence of selfish desires.

The relation between the two texts is even more compelling at the formal level. *Prometheus Unbound* does not so much import general meanings from Shakespeare's play as reflect a structure and adopt an ethos that is exemplified by *The Tempest* and works of a similar type. Both plays are comedies in a sense that far transcends laughter; each moves from chaos to order and culminates in festivity, each features the emotion of love and an act of forgiveness as harmonizing agents, and each transports us to a level of experience apart from the empirical world.[13] Both are comedies in the sense that Shelley understood the term, 'universal, ideal and sublime.' They are symbolic dramas that project a communal dream of the world as it could be, a world perhaps of illusion, but a world of shared experience that nevertheless can serve as a measure of comparison for the flaws of our everyday world and as a standard or model for their eradication. It was in this hypothetical space of imaginative language that Shelley thought poetry worked its most important effects. Inside the cover to the notebook in which Shelley drafted the *Defence of Poetry*, he jotted the following:

Poetry proposes perfect models to men, to the likeness of which the mind is excited to aspire. Poetry – not moral directly.[14]

This manifesto of subtle poetic pragmatism delineates the method of *Prometheus Unbound*. Its poetry does not use its power to enforce a moral but instead arouses and 'excites' its reader to pursue meanings and to aspire toward the good and the beautiful. The faith that moral order can grow out of aesthetic order is the poetic faith of which *Prometheus Unbound* is an act.

A similar poetic faith is evident in the masque which constitutes the symbolic vision of Ferdinand and Miranda. A self-proclaimedly artificial form of drama, the masque employs verse, music, spectacle, and dance to achieve 'the high conditions of dramatic representation.' The masque is a dramatic 'presencing' as far removed from realism as possible, yet at the same time inviting the participation of the audience in the play of artistic effects. Prospero's 'revels' are in fact a highly organized dramatic representation of *The Tempest*'s central theme of *sophrosyne*, an order which is common to both beauty and goodness. Iris, Ceres, and Juno bless, fortify, and excite to emulation the young couple in a condensed ritual which is delivered in solemn recitation and song. Music, and the order it projects, play a leading role in *The Tempest*, lending the play its aura of strangeness that lifts it far above the plane of ordinary experience while at the same time symbolizing the possibility of such another cosmic order.

This power of music to render drama 'universal, ideal and sublime' is something that Shelley knew at first hand. It would be unforgivably narrow to think that all the intertexts for Shelley's dramatic poetry were exclusively literary. His connoisseurship of the arts exposed him to a wide range of aesthetic orders, among which music figured prominently. And his lifelong disposition to think of poetry on the model of music provides a clue to the decisive factor in our attempt to understand the rules by which we are asked to play the game of the text of *Prometheus Unbound*.

8

The Lyrical Drama

Shelley evaluated his talents most shrewdly when he said, 'My *Prometheus Unbound* is the best thing I ever wrote' (L, II, 164), for the lyrical drama is surely the crowning achievement of his discourse of desire. Since this discourse is dedicated not so much to persuasion as to engagement, it finds itself at home not in conventional rhetorical forms but in a form that is dialectical, a form which unsettles readers' expectations and challenges them with unfamiliar literary experiences. This form allows the author to relinquish his sole responsibility for the text by inviting the reader to share in the production of its meanings, and thus enables Shelley to throw off the relation of dominance and submission imposed by more didactic and authoritarian forms for a relation of sympathy, co-operation, and reciprocity between the text and its audience. Such a text is designed not to convince but to invite participation, not to seduce but to interact. The way its game should be played is better described less in terms of rhetoric, or even abstract poetics, than according to the erotics of poetry, for in his lyrical drama Shelley at last finds the means to touch his audience without violating them.

Especially as a political poet, Shelley had always been driven by an urge to communicate with others. Mary Shelley had ruefully acknowledged (J, II, 158) that 'the master passion of his soul' was 'a desire to diffuse ... those opinions and sentiments with regard to human nature and its destiny' embodied in *Queen Mab* and *The Revolt of Islam*, and once more in *Prometheus Unbound* Shelley would seek to 'influence to good.' But now, however, he had learned how literary form coerces. 'Didactic poetry is my abhorrence,' he declares in the preface to *Prometheus Unbound* (J, II, 174), forswearing all claim to disseminate particular ideas or opinions in his lyrical drama. Instead, he was developing a new form which would allow him to disseminate desire itself by taking a risk on the tendency to the endless deferral and dis-semination of meaning in language itself.[1] Preferring now to scatter the 'unseen seeds' of his vision abroad rather than to target them, he sought a means that would allow the dissemination of delight as opposed to the insemination of ideas.

Not finding an already formed literary vehicle adequate to the needs of dissemination among the central conventions and traditions of literature, Shelley had to invent one by drawing disparate materials from the margins of the arts. As Shelley's creative development seems to have been fostered as much by his own aesthetic experience as by philosophical reflection, his boldness to innovate and freedom to grow as an artist were not always inhibited by theoretical considerations. Both his curiosity and his catholicity of taste exposed him to so great a variety of creative models that he must be excused if he sometimes focused on their fecundity rather than their limitations. This wide-ranging appetite was characteristic of him not only as a reader but also as a theatre-goer, for besides his interest in the productions of the legitimate stage he also became a devotee of the Italian opera. Indeed, it is possible that the musical drama provided a unique heteroglossial thread that wove itself into the text of his lyrical drama.

I

In *Prometheus Unbound* Shelley finally realizes to its fullest extent the implications of the metaphor that likens poetry to music. The musical analogue is precisely what enables Shelley to detach poetry from ordinary functions of reference and allow literary discourse to create its own special conditions. His poetry is like music in that it has its own internal consistency ('a logic of its own,' as Coleridge knew), that it generates a self-sufficient sense as distinct from a reference, and that through its own rhythms and harmonies it creates its own order of time, a tempo beyond clock time. The kinship of *Prometheus Unbound* with music is the proud emblem of that poem's 'artificiality.'

By intertextualizing music and drama, Shelley provided a link between the ancient world and cultural developments in his own century. In ancient Greece, music and poetry were sister arts. One of the constituents of Athenian education, *mousiké*, the art of the muse, included both what we should call music, strictly speaking, and poetry, especially lyric poetry set and sung to music. In classic drama, particularly, this confluence produced our richest articulation of the dynamic human spirit. The more static pictorial and representational hypothesis of the Horatian *ut pictura poesis* bestowed a neoclassic calm on succeeding theory until Romanticism, with its passion for the antique, rediscovered the affinity between music and poetry.[2] What painting had been for the eighteenth century music became for the nineteenth, the model art. When Pater advises us that all art aspires toward the condition of music, he merely fulfils the promise of Romantic aesthetics.

To the Romantic temperament, music became the standard by which poetry was to be judged, and it was by this measure that the art of Shelley has often been prized. Swinburne, in his essay on Shelley (1903), praised *Prometheus Unbound* for its 'perfect music,' and Arnold unwittingly struck the precise note in saying that 'the right sphere for Shelley's genius was the sphere of music,' though in the context of the essay on Maurice de Guérin (1863), which champions natural Romanticism, he meant his remark disparagingly. What they were responding to was Shelley's mastery for expressive purposes of rhythm, melody, and lyrical harmony, his ability to create an ideal poetic universe detached from nature and history – in short, his music, which Leavis and his followers later dismissed as Shelley's 'abstractness.' So long as Romanticism was understood as a single-minded movement originating in a return to nature, the work of Shelley was bound to be misjudged. His inspiration comes not immediately from nature and its temporal processes, but through the mediation of art. The tendency to expression, autonomy, and abstraction that allies his poetry with music marks him as a representative not of natural but of an aesthetic Romanticism.

That is not to say that Shelley was a mere aesthete. Though he abhorred didacticism, he seldom wrote without a purpose and never regarded poetry as an end in itself. Between these two extremes he came to rest in an instrumental view of poetry which he formulates most clearly in the preface to *Prometheus Unbound*: 'My purpose,' he reveals, 'has hitherto been simply to familiarize the highly refined imagination of the more select classes of poetical readers with beautiful idealisms of moral excellence' (J, II, 174). In yoking art and morality Shelley was in tune with both the temper of his times and the pragmatic strain in English poetics from Sidney through Johnson. The old doctrine that art might instruct and delight was bolstered by his instinctive identification of the good with the beautiful – as he puts it in the *Defence*, 'The greatest secret of morals is ... an identification of ourselves with the beautiful' (J, VII, 118). Added to this faith was the growing opinion in revolutionary Europe that awakening a sensitivity to beauty might open an avenue to moral receptivity and so pave the way for political liberty. Schiller, for example, advanced his concept of the aesthetic education of man in the conviction that 'we must indeed, if we are to solve that political problem in practice, follow the path of aesthetics, since it is through Beauty that we arrive at Freedom.'[3] In an indirect way, then, composing *Prometheus Unbound* was a political act for Shelley. His drama proposes a new order and makes its own laws, providing the reader with a unique alternative to customary experience. Autonomous from history, Shelley's play suspends the question of origins to pursue ends and consequences. Its poetry is not mimetic but telic, fusing the arts to create 'beautiful idealisms' that contribute to forming the minds of his audience. Concerned with the world not as it is but as it could be, it stands apart from nature but not from social engagement.

Shelley's social and political commitment bears truly artistic fruit only when he evolves the form of the lyrical drama. The story of how he came to that form is the story of how he fused his manifold interests in classical literature, contemporary politics, and the musical theatre into a highly original poetic venture. Shelley the scholar, Shelley the revolutionary, and Shelley the connoisseur come together in the lyrical drama, whose form derives ultimately from the union of poetry and music in Greek tragedy, but whose closest contemporary representative was the opera, especially the musical comedy of Mozart.

Perhaps because realism is foreign to both, opera came into favour during the Romantic period. It emerged as the foremost Regency entertainment partly as a result of the decline of a theatre top-heavy with the 'sickly and stupid German tragedies' and their pallid gothic imitations banished by Wordsworth, and partly as a result of the resurgence of continental fashion that followed upon the defeat of Napoleon. Italian opera, its home then the King's Theatre, Haymarket, appealed to both the aristocracy and the cosmopolitan segment of the educated middle class. Shelley was swept up in this tide of Regency taste, and this phase of his aesthetic experience was to have profound consequences for his poetry. To spend in those days an evening at the opera was to be immersed in a world of artifice, a town pleasure as opposed to a country pursuit. On the operatic stage, painting, music, and poetry came together along with architecture, sculpture, and the dance in a sublime interfusion of the abstract and the plastic arts. Such evident artistic mediation transfigured the social realism of drama, transporting the play beyond the level of nature. And the effect of this detachment from the everyday world could not help but be enhanced by the long hours occupied by a theatrical evening. The fashionable novelty of all things French meant that a night at the opera was incomplete without several *divertissements* and a performance of the ballet. Though the program might last six hours or more, Shelley absorbed it readily and received a lasting impression. His interest in opera, and, even more, his keen delight in ballet, contributed to the unusual dramatic form of *Prometheus Unbound*, while its content derived from classical sources revived by the operatic mode.[4]

The kinship between music and poetry emerges, as we have seen, in Shelley's earliest writings and remains a persistent theme throughout his career. Indeed, his musical sensibilities were cultivated from earliest boyhood. Shelley always cherished a love of music and was as accomplished at singing and the piano as might be expected of a member of his class. While still at Eton he had attended the opera, though more by way of a debut in the fashionable world than out of any genuine interest. Even so, he eagerly and often invited his friend Edward Fergus Graham to set his earliest poems to music (L, I, 7, 16, 22, 106). Growing into radicalism, however, deprived Shelley of his appetite for theatrical amusements. Impatient with the licentiousness of the audience and the decadent and corrupt society reflected in the contemporary comedy of manners, Shelley sometimes nursed a puritanical hostility toward the theatre. However, his distaste for comic realism, recalling Aristotle's notion that comedy shows men worse than they are, is a natural consequence of his aesthetic idealism. Though he found the conventions of the legitimate stage unattractive, he showed no similar antipathy to opera, where song abstracts the action from the conditions of everyday life, and art (as Schopenhauer said) takes away the mist of contingency.[5] In the ideal space created by Mozart's music, Shelley's taste for a comedy that bordered on romance could flourish.

After Peacock introduced him to *Don Giovanni* in 1817, Shelley became, according to his friend, 'an assiduous frequenter of the Italian opera.' During the following season, Shelley attended the opera intensively, sometimes twice weekly, often in the company of his wife, whose own taste for opera encouraged the development of her husband's. Entries in Mary's journal show that, either with her, Leigh Hunt, or Peacock, Shelley saw *Don Giovanni* three times and *The Marriage of Figaro* at least twice in 1818. He was such a devotee that on the eve of his departure for Italy in March of that year he troubled to attend with Peacock the London première of Rossini's *Barber of Seville*, no doubt pleased to learn more of the story of the wily servant Figaro. Once in Italy, the Shelleys welcomed the opportunity to enjoy the opera at its fountainhead, in April attending five performances at La Scala, as well as taking in various productions at Turin, Rome, Naples, and Pisa as their base changed over the succeeding years. Still, Mozart remained his favourite; Shelley delighted in *Figaro*, and almost certainly shared Peacock's judgment that 'there is nothing perfect in this world except Mozart's music.'

Shelley's enthusiasm for the opera was shared by Byron, although their interests differed considerably, as one might expect. Byron, who as befitted his station maintained a box at La Scala in Milan and La Fenice in Venice during his residence in those cities, found the opera-house attractive primarily because of its function as a social centre. There he could mix with the fashionable world, hear scandal, and form liaisons. He was by no means insensible to what passed on the stage, as his complaints about the Italian habit of incessant talking during the performance make plain, but his musical tastes were less developed than Shelley's. His playful satire of the captive opera company in the fourth canto of *Don Juan* suggests that he saw through the pretensions of singers, as Raucocanti (whose name means noisy singing) deflates each of his colleagues in turn. Byron recorded few specific impressions of the music he heard, but from what he does say it is evident that he preferred the furious Rossini to the range and subtle powers of Mozart. During their residence in Pisa, Hunt recalled that Byron habitually sang snatches from Rossini, although Shelley confided to Medwin that Byron put him in mind of Don Giovanni, and his servant, Fletcher, of Leporello.[6]

Although Dr Johnson dismissed it as an 'exotic and irrational entertainment,' opera found an increasing number of advocates in the later eighteenth century whose continental ties helped them recall the descent of musical drama from the sister arts in antiquity. The painter John Brown, who was fond of inter-art analogies, praised opera in his *Letters upon the Poetry and Music of the Italian Opera* (1789) as 'the most perfect junction of Poetry, Music, and Action (or Dancing, as the ancients called it).' The age of Wincklemann understandably saw authors turn to antiquity in support of their case for opera. Moreover, they found a modern precedent for their views in the stated intention of the Florentine Camarata, who during the Renaissance sought to restore the musical element once vital to Greek tragedy in creating the new form of opera. The second stage of this classical revival flowered in Romantic Hellenism, the offshoots of which are evident in Schiller's letter on opera to Goethe:

I have always trusted that out of opera, as out of the ancient festival of Bacchus, tragedy would liberate itself and develop in a nobler form. In opera, servile imitation of nature is dispensed with, and although this is allowed only as a special concession to operatic needs, here is nevertheless the avenue by which the ideal can steal its way back into the theatre.[7]

The spirit of an age dedicated to the rediscovery of classical models and to their mediation in new forms is given voice in Schiller's comments. The same spirit breathes in *Prometheus Unbound*, where Aeschylean tragedy is likewise liberated into 'a nobler form.'

Representative of a distinct trend in Romanticism, Schiller and Shelley are equally inclined to reject the limits of nature. Schiller's aspirations toward aesthetic autonomy and abstract idealism in the drama are the healthy youth of an impulse that was to age into the decadence of Wagner and the English aesthetes as the nineteenth century wore on. Indeed, Wagner's idea of a total art-work was anticipated by an Italian, Count Francesco Algarotti, as early as 1755. Having received a copy of Algarotti's treatise, *Saggio sopra l'opera in musica*, Thomas Gray replied with courteous skepticism:

I see with great satisfaction your efforts to reunite the congenial arts of Poetry, Musick, and the Dance, which with the assistance of Painting and Architecture, regulated by Taste, and supported by magnificence and power, might form the noblest scene, and bestow the sublimest pleasure, that the imagination can conceive. But who shall realize these delightful visions?[8]

In the next age, Romantics like Shelley who located the ideal in culture rather than in nature would undertake such daring experiments in the arts. Schiller's vision of a 'nobler form' that would lure the ideal back into the theatre begins to take shape in the 'beautiful idealisms' of Shelley's lyrical drama.

Affinities between Shelley's play and Greek tragedy, particularly

Oedipus at Colonus, have been noted before.[9] But in the nineteeth century, Shelley's generic description of *Prometheus Unbound* inevitably associated itself with the operatic stage. *Drame lyrique* was the term applied in 1809 to the French production of *Don Giovanni*, and in 1847, when the Royal Italian Opera was formed at Covent Garden, a prospectus was issued stating that the company was founded 'for the purpose of rendering a more perfect performance of the lyric drama than has hitherto been attained in this country.' The roots of Shelley's art are never single but always multiple and syncretic. In calling *Prometheus Unbound* a 'lyrical drama,' Shelley alluded to this twofold tradition, Greek and Italian, ancient and modern.

Prometheus Unbound was inspired by every aspect of Shelley's aesthetic experience, then, and not by literary models alone. If the plot owes something to Aeschylus and the characterization something to Milton, the unfolding of the action and the revelation of character may equally well be indebted to the spectacle Shelley and his contemporaries enjoyed at the opera house. That British taste was becoming receptive to opera by the late Georgian era is evident from the favourable reviews and packed houses for performances at the King's Theatre after its recovery in 1814 from years of mismanagement. Leigh Hunt was delighted to see the opera so well attended, he wrote in the *Examiner* (no. 482), 'for we like Italian, and music, and dancing, and beautiful mythologies.' This was the golden age of comic opera, dominated by Mozart and the arrival of Rossini, and the Anacreontic ballet, in which classical themes were domesticated and sweetened through the narrative *ballet d'action*.[10]

Shelley's acquaintance with these trends in the performing arts extended beyond Peacock's tutelage. Entering the Hunt circle in 1817, Shelley met not only poets like Keats but influential critics like Hazlitt and accomplished musicians like Vincent Novello. Hazlitt, who (judging by his reviews) had a profound appreciation for the ethereality of Mozart's music, helped form Shelley's musical consciousness; and Novello, who had conducted the orchestra of the Italian Opera and was a founding member of the Philharmonic Society, entertained the Shelleys with airs from Mozart and even made his good offices available to assist Shelley in the purchase of a piano for his home at Marlowe.[11] There, Shelley repaid Hunt's hospitality in kind. Mary's stepsister, Clare, sang to the piano's accompaniment and Hunt contributed his musical powers for the amusement of the company.

It is small wonder, then, that music, especially vocal music, should emerge as a subject for poetry in Shelley's lyrics of 1817. Under the influence of song, Shelley began no fewer than four poems at Marlowe; the finest of these, 'To Constantia Singing,' commemorates the effect on him of Clare's voice, which, according to her instructor, was like a string of pearls. Shelley's opening simile, however, is at once more dynamic and less material:

> Thy voice, slow rising like a Spirit, lingers
> O'ershadowing me with soft and lulling wings   (J, III, 155)

Judith Chernaik has finally extricated this poem from its biographical context by reading its obvious eroticism as a metaphor for aesthetic response; on this assumption she infers the theme of the poem to be that 'reality is mediated, its significance created, through art.'[12] That Shelley conceived of aesthetic mediation as a process of etherealization, moving away from reference to the material world, is suggested by the imagery of ascent in the poem. Clare's voice rises 'in fast ascending numbers ... / Till the world's shadowy walls are past, and disappear' (lines 26, 33). 'Rising like a Spirit,' her song invites the poet to do likewise, becoming what he contemplates in his identification with beauty:

> My heart is quivering like a flame;
> As morning dew, that in the sunbeam dies,
> I am dissolved in these consuming extacies.   (lines 9–11)

Nature is not Shelley's subject matter, but provides analogues for his spiritual states. His inner being follows that of the singer, rising up like fire and water vapour toward a consummation. Music is the medium of this exaltation, for it dissolves the barriers of subjectivity ('I am dissolved') at the same time as it dissipates meaning as reference to the external world. Like music, the kind of poetry Shelley would write in *Prometheus Unbound* must be judged not by what it means but by how it means, and how it operates to evoke a response.

In this melodic atmosphere, one of the finest lyrics of *Prometheus Unbound* began to take shape, the fragment, 'To One Singing':

> My spirit like a charmed bark doth swim
> Upon the liquid waves of thy sweet singing,
> Far away into the regions dim

> Of rapture – as a boat with swift sails winging
>   Its way adown some many-winding river.
> Speeds through dark forests o'er the water swinging. ... (J, III, 157)

As in 'To Constantia Singing,' this early draft explores the aesthetic effect of music. As emotion given form, music produces the effect both of rapture and of discipline. Shelley's poetry benefits particularly from the latter. Within two years, after absorbing the music of Mozart and the Italians, Shelley smartens his cadences, tightens his metrics, and discards the literary terza rima to fashion Asia's beautiful air from Act II:

> My soul is an enchanted boat,
>   Which, like a sleeping swan, doth float
> Upon the silver waves of thy sweet singing;
>
> And thine doth like an angel sit
>   Beside the helm conducting it,
> Whilst all the winds with melody are ringing.   (J, II, 225)

The soul is not only enrapt but guided, while the mediation of music provides the principle of order to the inner and outer world alike. Music transforms wind and breath, giving them direction and purpose. This melodic correspondent breeze provides the imagistic power with which Asia, and indeed the whole action of the drama, sail on (in the words of her song) 'by the instinct of sweet music driven.'

The wind disciplined by music appears, of course, in the *Ode to the West Wind*, written only a few months later and published with *Prometheus Unbound* in 1820. The ode's apocalyptic 'trumpet of a prophecy' is not far removed from the sublime melodies of Constantia – the two coexist because Shelley shares with Dryden ('What Passion cannot Musick raise and quell!') an appreciation of the subtle powers of music. As in 'A Song for St. Cecilia's Day,' music can form a universe, control its creatures, and shape its destruction; music is an analogue of the force that fashions the beginnings and endings of all being, creator and destroyer, displacing God and the poet. So, in 'To Constantia Singing,'

> The cope of Heaven seems rent and cloven
>   By the enchantment of thy strain,
> And o'er my shoulders wings are woven
>   To follow its sublime career. ...   (J, III, 156)

Music supersedes reality with a reality of its own, and offers an experience of order so superior to the flux of mutable everyday life that we willingly follow its lead. Music thus functions in *Prometheus Unbound* as a strategy of engagement; it is the means by which the poem generates an occasion to embrace us, and it is the method by which Shelley surrenders the power of the word to dissemination.

II

Because *Prometheus Unbound*, in the phrase of one commentator, 'abstracts itself into music,' it is a remarkable attempt to give objective form to subjective content.[13] Though dramatic in structure, it is lyrical in its communication of the inward life of the human spirit. Since Shelley's play depicts an inner drama of spiritual transformation, it is best understood as unfolding not by the usual means of legitimate drama but according to the conventions of opera, in which, not action, but the quality of an action, the intensity of the moment, is elaborated musically. Music abstracts and internalizes the social realism of drama, allows the characters to express their motives and passions in song, and shifts the attention of the audience from narrative to essential emotion and thought. Shelley's drama occupies its own imaginative space, beyond the bounds of realism, according to the conventions of a vast psychodrama that gives expression to desire and hope.

As always, more than the expressive urge is involved in Shelley's poetics. The demands must be met, as he says in *A Defence of Poetry*, of 'the highest conditions of dramatic representation. ... such as the establishing a relation between the drama and religion, and the accommodating them to music and dancing' (J, VII, 120). Expressionism, if it is not to degenerate into self-indulgence, requires self-transcendence and the discipline of aesthetic form. Borrowing Shelley's term in a review of operatic memoirs, Peacock described 'what the lyrical drama ought to be':

The business, indeed, of the lyrical dramatist is to present, with the most perfect simplicity, the leading and natural ideas of an impassioned action, divested of all imagery not arising from spontaneous feeling.

(*Works*, IX, 229–30)

'The most perfect simplicity' must exclude the egotistical sublime. Though spontaneous emotion, as Wordsworth claimed, may be the source of poetry, it is not necessarily its end; and Shelley, as we have seen, is less concerned with origins than he is with ends. His goal is 'to quicken a new birth' through his poetry, to reform the world by reforming the human spirit. This reform he hopes to bring about, in the lyrical drama at least, through the aesthetic education of man, through the creation and contemplation of 'beautiful idealisms of moral excellence' that evoke our admiration and emulation. Abhorring didacticism, the poet refines himself out of existence in order to give free play to the self-sufficent image of our best self in a better world; however, the lyrical drama's decentring of the authorial self does not leave the reader with chaos. As with the west wind, wild spontaneity is transformed into aesthetic order and harmony through the music of the verse and the prophetic image of renovated man. Operatic form, combining poetry, music, and the dance, is the most authentic vehicle for this ambitious enterprise because its conventions admit their artifice; the ideals it presents are not superhuman and inaccessible but attainable by human skill, discipline, and effort. In *Prometheus Unbound*, Shelley constructs an alternative universe, 'another nature' as Sidney called it, which although a pure fiction of the imagination offers an experience of order that interacts with the reader's perceptions, potentially transforming them. The 'nobler form' of the lyrical drama represents rather than relates its central action; it mediates the ideal more effectively than epic since it frees the reader from the direction of the narrator and allows for those 'discoveries' that Wolfgang Iser regards as indispensable to an instrumental conception of the text.[14] It rejects satire and historical mimesis in favour of romance, because its aim is not simply to expose vice but to animate virtue.

The instrumentality of Shelley's text, conceived on the analogue of musical drama, is what gives *Prometheus Unbound* its political dimension without allowing it to spill over into didacticism. In times of widespread illiteracy, after all, the stage has been an effective medium of communicating with the people. During the Risorgimento, opera for all its unreality (and perhaps because of it) kept alive the impossible dream of Italian unity. While Austrian censorship stifled creative expression on the legitimate stage, the singing of a patriotic chorus, such as that of the Hebrew slaves in *Nabucco*, could provoke demonstrations and uprisings; Madame Pasta barely escaped imprisonment at Naples for singing Rossini's 'Cara patria,' and was ordered to omit the word *libertà* from every role she played.[15] In 1859, after the opening of *Un Ballo in Maschera*, the name of Verdi became a revolutionary cipher, when 'viva Verdi,' blazoned on walls, became an acrostic for *Victor Emmanuel, Re d'Italia.* This is not to suggest that in writing *Prometheus Unbound* Shelley was producing propaganda for violent revolution. His work had a subtler, but no less social and political, intent. 'The connexion of poetry and social good is more observable in the drama than in whatever other form,' he wrote in the *Defence,*

and it is indisputable that the highest perfection of human society has ever corresponded with the highest dramatic excellence. ... The soul of social life. ... may be preserved and renewed, if men should arise capable of bringing back the drama to its principles. (J, VII, 122–3)

If, in the concluding words of Demogorgon, 'Hope creates / From its own wreck the thing it contemplates,' it is vital for it to behold beautiful idealisms as models for social renewal. Realism selects its material from what is typical of life as we know it and attempts to project the norm; romance projects what is exceptional, reflects, embodies, and stimulates hopes and desires, and can excite human aspiration toward a better world. A renewed drama of desire, then, might be instrumental in regenerating 'the soul of social life.'

Bringing back the drama to its principles meant to the classically minded Shelley the restoration of music and dance to the theatre. In his contemporary experience, only operatic convention, with its ritual components of song and dance, met these criteria. The imagery of music and the agency of song inform the whole *Prometheus Unbound,* while the element of the dance is confined, for very good reasons as we shall see, to the fourth act.

The play opens with Prometheus' three-part declamation, following the large-scale ternary design of the traditional aria. Such sustained monologues are common on the operatic stage, where music encourages and supports the total expression of the inner being. Each of the first three acts of *Prometheus Unbound* begins with a speech of similar extent in which each of the major characters reveals his or her essential self. Act II presents Asia, initially alone, addressing Spring ('This is the season, this the day, the hours'), whose reawakening is a correlative of her own vitalizing influence. Act III introduces Jupiter, who celebrates his omnipotence, until his oration is cut short by the crescendo of Demogorgon 'thundering up Olympus.' Opera has a unique ability to arrest the action at a pivotal emotional or conceptual point in the drama while the music allows a character to explore the self, and like an opera *Prometheus Unbound* is a play of intense moments rather than of gradual development. Indeed, the action of Shelley's lyrical drama seems to take place in a moment, in that immortal hour hymned by Asia in which Prometheus' repentance, Asia's descent to the cave of Demogorgon, Jupiter's fall, and the redemption of humankind coincide.

This ritual elaboration of the significant action or emotion governs the pace at which each of these acts proceeds. The four elemental voices that provide choral responses to Prometheus' first speech give way to a dialogue between Prometheus and the Earth; likewise, the succeeding duet between Ione and Panthea is followed by a recitative exchange between Prometheus and the Phantasm of Jupiter, who then gives a formal declamation of the curse. In Act II, dialogues between Panthea and Asia, and between Asia and Demogorgon, are succeeded by the choral songs of spirits. In Act III, Jupiter's passionate verbalization of his fall yields to the calm exchange between Ocean and Apollo. From its inception, then, and throughout, the drama unfolds in accordance with the alternation of recited dialogue and impassioned utterance characteristic of the terminal-melody opera current in Shelley's day.

Mozart's *Figaro* demonstrates both this convention and the capacity of music to transfer farce to a higher artistic plane. While Beaumarchais' play is a comedy of manners that is at once absurd and a serious critique of society, Mozart's version, to da Ponte's libretto, purifies the intentions of the original by highlighting through song the moments of revolt, love, and triumph. Indeed, Figaro's first solo, 'Si vuol balare, Signor Contino,' communicates precisely the spirit of Beaumarchais' attack on social privilege. Even though translations of the libretto were sold nightly at the King's Theatre, Shelley need not have understood the words to be absorbed as others have by the spirit of the song. Sigmund Freud thought 'Si vuol balare' captured the very essence of rebellion, for he found himself humming it when, slighted by titled or official personages, 'all kinds of bold and revolutionary thoughts ... would fit themselves to the words of Figaro.'[16]

Shelley's own rebelliousness, in any case, predisposed him to enjoy *The Marriage of Figaro*, even if in 1818 he had as yet little knowledge of Italian. That his delight in Mozart's opera was primarily musical does not preclude ideological sympathy, for as Joseph Kerman remarks, 'in opera, the dramatist is the composer.'[17] The best opera conveys the drama in all its complexity through the music, evoking a response and leaving an impression that words alone cannot. The drama that Louis XIV suppressed because, as he stormed, 'it would be necessary to destroy the Bastille before the presentation of this play would not be a dangerous piece of inconsequence' appealed to the same Mozart who had thrown off the patronage of the Archbishop of Salzburg and dared outfox the Austrian Emperor. Despite the disapproval of Joseph II, Mozart refashioned the satire of *Figaro* musically and managed its success, significantly, not in imperial Vienna but in subject Prague.

Music supplies the deficiencies of language just as language ekes out the conceptual inadequacy of music – together they generate an occasion for the fullness of response. Music's unique temporal process emphasizes the articulation of thought and feeling, making words less general as signs for concepts and more immediate as revelations of inner life, turning language into speech, a familiar Shelleyan strategy. As Wagner said, only through the voice can the inner man find direct communication. Figaro's mocking aria, then, is a direct presentation of the will to revolt. Even so, it is not the substance of what he says but the form in which he says it that is of prime importance. In the course of the opera, it is not the revolt of servants against master that brings about the comic resolution, but the very convention of comedy itself that love conquers all. Mozart turns this concept into a collective wish when, in the finale, the ensemble sings that they have lived through a day of madness and discord that only love can bring to an end ('Sole amor puo terminar'). The spirit of musical comedy governs the world of both Beaumarchais' play and Mozart's opera, for the last line of the one and the mode of the other leave us with the thought that 'Tout finit par des chansons.' Because music and love are analogous to one another as harmonizing agents, the operatic convention of sung speech surpasses the merely spoken lines of realistic comedy in arousing human aspiration. Mozart's aesthetic form has this advantage over that of Beaumarchais: Mozart makes social change appear not only desirable but harmonious by disarming his audience with music that penetrates their very being.

It is precisely when aesthetic effect is considered that the operatic analogy most illuminates the dramatic form of *Prometheus Unbound.* Shelley's play is musical not only in its structure, its content, and its autonomy from nature, but also in the mode of its operation. Shelley is wisely very sparing in his use of actual musical effects in the verse, but there are times when the poetry has a music of its own. After the curse has been repeated in the first act, Earth's brief lyric, 'Misery, Oh misery to me,' with its choral repetitions, creates the dramatic tension of misunderstanding:

> THE EARTH
> Misery, Oh misery to me,
> That Jove at length should vanquish thee.
> Wail, howl aloud, Land and Sea,
> The Earth's rent heart shall answer ye.
> Howl, Spirits of the living and the dead,
> Your refuge, your defence lies fallen and vanquishèd.
> FIRST ECHO
> Lies fallen and vanquishèd?
> SECOND ECHO
> Lies fallen and vanquishèd! (J, II, 188)

Cadencing on the artificially stressed final syllable, the naturally rising intonation of the first echo's question is answered by the descending scale of the second's confirmatory statement. There is an urge toward symmetry and completion in these lines reminiscent of the balanced phrases of classical sonata form. Later in the act, the Furies' chorus is balanced by a Chorus of Spirits who enter with a decisive triple rhyme, like an opening chord in Beethoven. At the end of the act when their sweet voices die, their music vibrates in the memory of Panthea:

> Only a sense
> Remains of them, like the omnipotence
> Of music, when the inspired voice and lute
> Languish, ere yet the reponses are mute,
> Which thro' the deep and labyrinthine soul,
> Like echoes thro' long caverns, wind and roll. (J, II, 204)

The dying music of the first act melts away to an echo in the soul of the listener, an unheard melody that pervades our own inner life inviting us to become like itself, beautiful. Shelley's lyrical drama lingers with a similar subtlety, drawing the imagination toward perfection, an instrument of spiritual transformation. The operatic model underlying Shelley's lyrical drama clinches its decentred form, in which the unity of the poet's subjectivity dissolves into the voices of a multitude of other singers who scatter thoughts, moods, and feelings for the audience to gather up.

While Shelley's lyrical drama defies the realistic conventions of the British stage, it has strong affinities with the romantic comedy of Shakespeare. *As You Like It, The Tempest,* and *Twelfth Night,* too, contain 'beautiful idealisms' and considerable music. In each, the significant action take place in its own space, in an ideal world that is a feigned alternative to this one. The forest of Arden, for example, is the heterocosmic counterpart to the court; it is a magical place whose charmed circle representatives of the other world like Oliver and Frederick cannot enter without being affected by it. Like Illyria and Prospero's island it has a logic of its own, a logic that realizes abstractions like love, virtue, and justice by purely poetic means. Music lingers throughout these plays as a reminder of the artistic convention they rely upon. They are not comedies of critical realism but romances of desire in which, after much anguish and misunderstanding, a collective wish is fulfilled. Through these plays, in Mark Van Doren's excellent phrase, 'Shakespeare has built a world out of music and melancholy.'[18]

The triumph of a collective will against tyranny is celebrated in the finale of Mozart's *Don Giovanni,* the other talisman of Shelley's theatrical experience during 1818. Once again, a convention peculiar to opera makes this finale possible: the presentation of multiple points of view, diverse yet harmonized, in an ensemble. The great sextet that completes *Don Giovanni* had its poetic correlative in the concluding scenes of Act III of *Prometheus Unbound,* where the transformation of the world on the fall of Jupiter is described by the quartet of Prometheus, the Earth, the Spirit of the Earth, and the Spirit of the Hour.

Don Giovanni is a work of great dramatic complexity. Like *Prometheus Unbound,* it is neither a tragedy nor a comedy; it is closer to a morality play, a fable of good and evil, or a ritual of purification. Giovanni, for all his intelligence and zest for life, deserves his end. Like Faust, he is a creature of appetite which grotesquely grows by what it feeds upon. Despite its Satanic attractiveness, however, the character did not deceive Shelley. When Peacock asked what he thought of the baritone Giuseppe Ambrogetti in the role, Shelley replied, 'He seems to be the very wretch he personates.' Anticipating Kierkegaard in considering Don Giovanni demonic, Shelley regarded him as no tragic hero worthy of sympathy despite his flaws, but as the villain of the piece, the arch-seducer whose crime is that he tries to force love. In his preface, Shelley explicitly lays aside the Satanic figure as a model for his Prometheus; his hero is no mere rebel, but a sign of the will's need to join forces with love, as Prometheus marries

Asia, before liberation can occur and the revolution complete itself. In *Prometheus Unbound*, Jupiter is the heir of Don Giovanni. The heavenly tyrant of Shelley's lyrical drama is a descendant of the earthly tyrant in comic opera – the noble seducer, the Almavivas or Don Giovanni, and the oppressive guardian, like Dr Bartolo in *The Barber of Seville*, who tries to compel his ward Rosina to be his wife. All of their downfalls are occasions for universal rejoicing.

In Mozart and Rossini, however, the tyrant is not overthrown directly by anyone whom he has wronged. Figaro does not finally outwit the Count or prevent Bartolo from removing the ladder, and Don Giovanni ironically escapes Donna Anna's vengeance. Instead, he is punished in conjunction with the conventional happy ending of the comic form itself. In *Prometheus Unbound*, bringing the play to climax and resolution is the function of Demogorgon. He has no form himself, but gives shape to the desires of Prometheus and Asia and fulfils the consequences of their determinations, whether they be tragic or comic. He is a dweller in the nether regions, like the Demogorgon who occurs as a denizen of Renaissance demonology in Spenser, Marlowe, and Milton. Here he ascends as an instrument of wished-for justice: the way he brings down Jupiter is equivalent to the emergence from beneath the stage of the devils who drag Don Giovanni down to Hell, accompanied by blaring chords of brass. Philosophically, Demogorgon may be what he calls himself, 'Eternity'; but in an age when metaphysics is constantly giving way to aesthetics, he is more properly regarded as the spirit of the lyrical drama's decentred form. Like the basis of desire, he is presented in terms of an absence, of that which is lacking; but like the consequences of desire, he brings the play to its climax. Analogous to the author who has refined himself out of existence, he does not enforce his presence but acts simply to provide an occasion in which the desires of others are aroused and can play themselves out.

In concluding the main action of his play with a four-part celebration of the triumph of hope and desire, Shelley transforms apocalypse from myth into ceremony. The play is no longer a private vision but a shared ritual in which the reader may participate imaginatively. If Erik Erikson is right in saying that a process of ritualization is what disposes us to a particular version of human experience, then *Prometheus Unbound* may be understood as staging an alternative ritual process by means of which we arrive at what Erikson calls a new and revolutionary 'collective vision': 'Individuals live, often more than they know or profess, by collective visions, whether in the form of religious world images or of political ones. ... Any revolutionary method of treatment worthy of its name offers itself as a new world vision.'[19] Shelley's drama allows the audience to play out this new collective vision without its being enforced by a single viewpoint. For Shelley, the virtue of dramatic form is not only that it allows the author to share a dream with his audience, but more importantly that it does not impose a revolutionary testament on its readers. Instead, it invites them to enter imaginatively into its higher world of artifice and pursue its significance for themselves. Whether that world was rooted in illusion or reality mattered not at all to Shelley:

Poetry [he writes in the *Defence*] defeats the curse which binds us to be subjected to the accident of surrounding impressions. And whether it spreads its own figured curtain, or withdraws life's dark veil from before the scene of things, it equally creates for us a being within our being. (J, VII, 137)

All the great works of affirmative culture, from Beethoven's *Ninth Symphony* to Shelley's *Prometheus Unbound*, deliver us from chaos, as Asia's love and Demogorgon's co-operation deliver the Promethean will from bondage, by the order of their forms. They depend for their validity not on metaphysical verification but upon aesthetic response and ethical consequence, without the intrusion of external authority. In music as in poetry, decentred form not only can order content but may promote in the audience an inner harmony and spiritual order, 'a being within our being.'

III

In the post-revolutionary era that Shelley knew so well, deliverance is the climax but not the finale. The fall of Jupiter is no more the end of Shelley's lyrical drama than the descent of Don Giovanni to the infernal regions was the end of Shelley's night at the opera. The inevitable conclusion to such an evening in Shelley's day was the performance of a ballet. It is well to remember Shelley's view that 'the high conditions of dramatic representation' included the dance as well as music. Judging by the evidence of Peacock's *Memoirs*, Shelley seems to have been almost more delighted by the ballet than by the opera.

On the night in 1817 when Peacock took Shelley to see *Don Giovanni* (the bill was given daily in the *Times*), they saw a ballet, *Zulica ou les Peruviens*, that was another instance of the rescue tale so beloved by this age in pursuit of liberation. Zulica, the King of Quito's daughter, is abducted by the lustful High Priest of the Sun; a young Spaniard who had been wrecked on the coast comes to her rescue, frustrates the designs of the High Priest, and marries the maiden. Shelley was captivated by Mlle Milanie, the prima ballerina of the Opera Ballet, in the role of Zulica; 'He had never imagined such grace of motion,' says Peacock, 'and the impression was permanent, for in a letter he afterwards wrote to me from Milan he said: "They have no Mdlle. Milanie here." '

Milanie has always remained an obscure figure in Shelley biography, but in the context of Shelley's aesthetic experience she gains significance as a touchstone of artistic excellence. Shelley's taste for ballet grew concurrently with his attendance at the opera, and he continued to cultivate it in Italy. After an evening at La Scala, he expressed more enthusiasm for the ballet (a rendition of *Othello*) than for the opera, taking pardonable pride that Milan was without a Milanie:

We went to the opera last night – which is the most splendid exhibition. The opera itself was not a favourite, and the singers very inferior to our own. But the Ballet, or rather a kind of melodrama or pantomimic dance, was the most splendid spectacle I ever saw. We have no Miss Milanie here – in every other respect Milan is unquestionably superior. The manner in which language is translated into gesture, the complete and full effect of the whole as illustrating the history in question, the unaffected self possession of each of the actors, even to the children, made this choral drama more impressive than I should have conceived possible. (L, II, 4)

His use of the term 'choral drama' here is striking, for it suggests that the ballet was another of those heteroglot filaments that wove themselves into the fabric of his lyrical drama.

The ballet in Shelley's day was passing through an important period of change. The conventions of masque and stately court dance, whose vestiges may be seen in the *sarabande* of *The Sleeping Beauty* (Act III), were being challenged by counter-conventions and new forms. Peasant dances were being absorbed into the repertory, lending the colours and variety of national characters, and classical subjects were being revived in the Anacreontic mode. Moreover, the reforms of Noverre, the great French ballet-master, codified the form of the *ballet d'action* and established its predominance.[20] *Ballet d'action* is a combination of mime and movement designed to convey a story, but in which the narrative line must be harmonized with expression and technique. Transcending language, it develops its own vocabulary of movement that gives form to feeling and ritualizes human interaction. It translates the text into gesture as does the opera into music, and strives to integrate libretto, music, choreography, and décor into 'the complete and full effect of the whole' that elicited such an eager response in Shelley.

Besides *Zulica*, Shelley enjoyed seeing Milanie in the mythological ballets, *Acis and Galathea*, and *Zéphyr, ou le rétour de printemps*. One of the most famous action ballets of the period was *Flore et Zéphyr*. It was one of the earliest works to employ point work, and, indeed, was so daring as to use a complex system of pulleys and wires to accomplish even more spectacular aerial effects. The London *Zéphyr* was probably based on this ballet, or excerpted from it, since the contemporary notices make no mention of mechanisms to assist flight. The fullest account by far is Leigh Hunt's, who could very easily have seen it in Shelley's company:

We do not know which performs better, – M. Baptiste as Zephyr, or Mademoiselle Milanie as Chloris. ... Nothing can be more elegant, alert, powerful, and full of meaning. The scene in which he endeavours to carry off or to whisk the rose out of Chloris's hand was truly enchanting, and as complete an embodying of the idea of spring air as possible. He went close round her at times, stooping and fawning with his head; then glanced hither and thither; then floated in a circle; then stopped and threw his limbs about, like little shoots of a breeze; then darted at her hand again, and missed the rose, which in the meanwhile she carried about in all sorts of graceful attitudes, sometimes with hands downwards, sometimes holding it up on each side of her in the air and gazing at it. We never saw a lovelier scene on the stage. The masques of Ben Jonson could not suggest anything more beautiful and aerial.

(*Examiner*, 1 March 1818)

The delicate gestures of the dancers, not to mention the subject matter, are reminiscent of nothing so much as the opening of *The Sensitive Plant*, printed with *Prometheus* in 1820:

A Sensitive Plant in a garden grew,
And the young winds fed it with silver dew,
And it opened its fan-like leaves to the light,
And closed them beneath the kisses of night.   (J, II, 275)

Clearly, Shelley's Italian poems were inspired by more than the natural landscape: they are motivated by a need to explore the effects of artistic mediation.

Zéphyr was only one manifestation of the prevalent Anacreontic mode, which toward the end of the eighteenth century returned to fashion in the world of arts and letters for the first time since the Renaissance. Ben Jonson had been fond of Anacreon, and it is only natural that an aesthete like Hunt should think of him in connection with this ballet. Jonsonian masque had also combined poetry, music, and dance to mediate abstract ideals, but of course relied on more primitive models in the case of the latter two. The conclusion of a masque also invited the members of the audience to come forward and join with the actors in celebration. Added to the musical dimensions of *Prometheus Unbound*, this second strategy of engagement implicit in the conventions of the court masque serves as a guide to the reader's activity in playing the game of the text. In the wedding masque of Act IV, the habits of this native literary tradition of masque are woven together with current continental trends in the performing arts to produce the dance of the hours and the courtship dance of Earth and the Moon.[21]

While distinctly an afterpiece, the fourth act of *Prometheus Unbound* is far from an afterthought. The final act of Shelley's lyrical drama bears the same structural relation to the story of Promethean liberation that the ballet bore to the opera. Invariably the last act, the ballet capped an evening at the opera, celebrating the triumph of order over chaos, the restoration of harmony, and the union of the sexes. The frankly erotic element in ballet reaffirmed the theme of love central to the comic opera of the day, and recapitulated through gestures the metaphors of the drama. The balletic last act of *Prometheus Unbound* employs ritual movement to reiterate the values verbally and musically expressed in the first three, symbolically harmonizing the conflicting spiritual forces that have issued in the drama's vision of social change. Act IV thus neither confirms nor gives closure to the play's meanings, but is simply a repetition of the traces of meaning with which we as readers are invited to play.

In this version of Shelley's recurring fantasy of human destiny, humanity and time are reconciled in the opening choruses. First, the Chorus of Hours 'weave the mystic measure / Of music, and dance, and shapes of light'; then, the Chorus of the Spirits of the Human Mind enter the scene to 'join the throng / Of the dance and the song' (J, II, 245–6). This ballet ensemble finally yields the stage to Panthea and Ione, who set the scene for the ensuing *pas de deux* of the Earth and the Moon. Their dance recalls the choreography of *Zéphyr*, the roles reversed:

> THE EARTH
> I spin beneath my pyramid of night. ...
> THE MOON
> I, thy crystal paramour,
> Borne beside thee by a power
> Like the polar Paradise,
> Magnet-like, of lovers' eyes;
> I, a most enamoured maiden,
> Whose weak brain is overladen
> With the pleasure of her love,
> Maniac-like around thee move
> Gazing, an insatiate bride,
> On thy form from every side. ...   (J, II, 257–8)

This hypnotically revolving planetary dance, fraught with erotic implications, resolves sexual conflict, for although the male Earth 'penetrates' the frozen female Moon, she reciprocates warmly with a 'spirit' that 'interpenetrates' his very being. Mutually reflecting one another in their rapt gazes, they achieve a self-sustaining equilibrium that seems to defy climax and closure. The aesthetic (and sexual) satisfaction of completion would be denied were it not for the form-giving role of Demogorgon, who fixes 'the seals of that most firm assurance' on 'the wise heart' (J, II, 261–2), and brings these revels to an end.

Drawing forms and images from music and the dance, Shelley sought to fulfil 'the high conditions' of dramatic art. Like Goethe's *Faust*, *Prometheus Unbound* is an operatic poem, though it would be fatal to misunderstand it as Shelley's attempt to write a libretto. The work is best appreciated in the context of musical analogy, especially since it grows out of Shelley's experience of music and the allied arts, but it remains a poem. Although it adopts strategies and structures from opera and ballet, it is a work of dramatic poetry that defies music even while it creates a music of its own. Read silently, it sets up inevitable reverberations in the reader's imagination. Whether these traces of aesthetic experience are precisely congruent with Shelley's intentions in writing the play or whether they blend imperceptibly with the traces of our desires seems to matter less than the fact that the play can activate and exercise the reader's imagination, which Shelley regarded as the 'organ of the moral nature of man' (J, VII, 118). Whether truth or illusion, whether it unites our subjectivity with that of the author or merely situates our subjectivity within the matrix of a collective dream, the text 'equally creates for us a being within our being.'

As always, it is effects and not causes, ends and not means, with which Shelley as a profoundly pragmatic poet is concerned. In *Prometheus Unbound*, he betrays no anxiety over the dispersal of meaning that musical and gestural dissemination risks, and prefers to trust his readers, or, more precisely, those 'select classes of poetical readers' designated in the preface who are able and willing to suspend their disbelief and play its game. The author as origin gives way to the goals of the reading process as the chief motive of Shelley's text; these goals, however, are always deferred in the reader's active pursuit of them because such a text is endlessly productive of potential meanings and never comes to rest in a determinate signified. Constantly weaving and unweaving possible meanings, the 'subtler language' of this kind of text is not a metalanguage but an activity, a play in which the reader becomes interwoven.[22] This play does not *possess* meaning; instead, it 'generates occasions' for meaning – it does not simply express a desire on Shelley's part, but on a deeper level it provides a site for the free play of desire, both his and ours, a desire and a pleasure which it does not enforce but invites.

One recent commentator who sees *Prometheus Unbound* as an allegory of reading focuses on the role of Asia as 'implied reader' of the text. Through the model of Asia, the reader, it is observed, 'is given the responsibility of animating, recovering, and in some sense co-creating a vision which otherwise would "not speak to us, but remain dead." '[23] Indeed, the lyrical drama's strategies of engagement do invite the reader to participate in the consolidation of the poem's collective dream and collective wish, but the way in which Asia exercises her 'responsibility' as a reader needs closer scrutiny. In the first scene of Act II, Panthea conveys 'the delight of a remembered dream' (J, II, 206) to her sister Asia, who searches her eyes for any remaining traces of the vision of Promethean liberation. 'Lift up thine eyes,' says Asia, 'And let me read thy dream' (J, II, 207), but Asia finds the goals of this reading process more elusive than she anticipated. Panthea repeatedly describes the effects of Prometheus' transformation on her in terms of fleeting music:

> his voice fell
> Like music which makes giddy the dim brain,
> Faint with intoxication of keen joy. ...
> I saw not, heard not, moved not, only felt
> His presence flow and mingle thro' my blood
> Till it became his life, and his grew mine,
> And thus I was absorb'd ... in the deep night
> My being was condensed; and as the rays
> Of thought were slowly gathered, I could hear
> His voice, whose accents lingered ere they died
> Like footsteps of far melody.   (J, II, 207–8)

Panthea's experience of the text of this melodic dream leaves her with no determinate sense of *what* she should seek, but her desire to seek has clearly been aroused:

> I cannot tell thee what I seek;
> I know not; something sweet, since it is sweet
> Even to desire.   (J, II, 208)

Asia listens attentively to her sister's tale, but, perhaps because what she hears is the text of a text, the words of her sister seem to dissipate in the atmosphere, an apt image of meaning's endless deferral:

> ASIA
> Thou speakest, but thy words
> Are as the air: I feel them not: Oh, lift
> Thine eyes, that I may read his written soul!   (J, II, 208)

Once again, Asia implores her sister to yield up the supposed true meaning of the text of her dream, and once more a definite reading is deferred. 'What canst thou see,' replies Panthea, 'But thine own fairest shadow imaged there?' But even if Asia can only read the text of her own desire in Panthea's eyes, her desire to know has nevertheless been aroused and she certainly becomes 'absorb'd' like her sister before her, in the play of meanings set in motion by Prometheus' recantation of the curse which bound him in hatred, scorn and defiance.

There is indeed a model for reading *Prometheus Unbound* suggested in this passage, but it is not one which imposes a burden of responsibility on the reader to 'recover' the author's vision. Any such demanding realism with regard to this text will suffer from what Jonathan Culler describes as 'the illusion of a world in which meaning is already there as something to be recovered instead of an activity to be pursued.'[24] The pursuit of meaning is precisely what Asia, and the reader of the lyrical drama, are invited to participate in. After all, Asia begins to be affected by Panthea's dream only as it recedes and eludes her grasp. The dream does not yield up its meanings to Asia any more readily than Shelley's play does to its readers; rather, all it says is 'Follow! Follow!', and this reiterated 'O, Follow, Follow, Follow Me!' (J, II, 209-10) is the text's only injunction, less a command than an invitation to join in the activity of reading. This invitation to pursue meaning is repeated once again by the Echoes who further decentre and diffuse its authority:

> O follow, follow,
>   As our voice recedeth;
> Thro' the caverns hollow,
>   Where the forest spreadeth;
>
> O follow, follow!
> Through the caverns hollow,
> As the song floats thou pursue,
> Where the wild bee never flew ...
> While our music, wild and sweet,
> Mocks thy gently falling feet.   (J, II, 210-11)

Far from promising any ultimate satisfaction, the music of the verse gently 'mocks' the pursuer of disseminated meaning, but that is not in itself discouraging to the activated reader. 'Shall we pursue the sound?' is Asia's question, as it must be the question of any reader who *willingly* suspends disbelief. At this point, the author's power of words in the text defers to the reader's authority. Like Prospero, Shelley finally abjures rough magic, surrenders his verbal power, and chooses to trust his readers. He now relies on their desire to know, their desire to believe, and their desire to join joyfully in the pursuit of meanings, desires which he has used every technique of his 'subtler language' to arouse. They are free to 'follow' the dream, or not, a possibility which Shelley in his preface to the poem seems to accept. But those who do follow Asia in pursuit of meaning down the stream of life will discover, not Shelley's powers, but the 'precious portents' of their own. Their imaginations, that 'organ of the moral nature of man,' will be stretched, their interpretive faculties will be exercised, and they will with Prometheus at least momentarily throw off the shackles that bind them.

Because this play is play it offers no certainties, it makes no promises, either about the world it projects or about the means by which it is projected; but the process of the text does invite us to partake of the possibilities it makes present through its attenuated language. *Prometheus Unbound* is, paramountly, a poem of communion; without a reader who can enter imaginatively its charmed circle, it collapses into nonsense. 'Bringing back the drama to its principles,' as Shelley wrote in the *Defence*, his lyrical drama daringly seeks to regenerate the soul of social life through projecting an autonomous yet instrumental, but ultimately elusive, image of liberty, love, and harmony. The experience of this image, like the visitations of Intellectual Beauty, is ephemeral and unstable, but nevertheless to 'onward life' can supply a calm, confident, and humane faith in human potential. It is a poem that at once creates and decreates the objects it projects, but in the process it is one which decreates and recreates its reader. *Prometheus Unbound* plays with us and makes us play, for it is a poem which teases us out of thought. Its beauty, like the society and the citizens Shelley hopes it will help to shape, is dynamic.

Writing about Shelley's political poems, Yeats has wisely said that Shelley 'does not believe that the reformation of society can bring this beauty, this divine order, among men without the regeneration of the hearts of men,' and it must be admitted that Shelley makes his appeal as a poet as much to the heart as to the head. Perhaps it would be more accurate to say that, as a poet, Shelley makes his appeal to our total being; indeed, the way in which he incorporates desire in language seems best described by the totality of enjoyment that is suggested by Kristeva's term 'jouissance.' Derived from the erotic lexicon, jouissance is a unique word that conveys the twofold sense of 'enjoyment': first, to 'enjoy' may mean to 'use' or possess – jouissance then implies the mastery of meaning through technique; second, to 'enjoy' may mean to 'take delight or pleasure in' – jouissance now implies the mastery of meaning through play. But jouissance, as Kristeva points out, also liberates from mastery, dominance, and repression by taking us beyond meaning. At least one use of language, she writes, 'obliges the reader not so much to combine significations as to shatter his own judging consciousness in order to grant passage through it to this

196 The Poetry of Life

rhythmic drive constituted by repression and, once filtered by language and its meaning, experienced as jouissance.'[25] The discourse of lyrical drama has this quality of what she calls 'maternal jouissance ... a body rejoicing' (p. 242), a penetration of our whole being by a language experienced on many different levels. On at least one of these, the *jouissants* rhythms of Shelley's poetic ballet convey to us a delight beyond the power of words. Ultimately, Shelley's language in *Prometheus Unbound* detaches itself from signification in favour of an outburst of rejoicing (jouissance) that makes the purely rational faculty 'faint with the intoxication of keen joy.' In the process, Shelley throws off the trammels of convention in the manner imaged by the way Asia rescues Prometheus from his prison-house of language. Their marriage allegorizes the erotic union of text and reader in the process of signification. Offering his reader an occasion to pursue meaning joyfully, Shelley embraces us through pleasure and delight rather than force or power, in the likeness not of an orator, a teacher, or a saint, but of a lover.[26]

Shelley's achievement in *Prometheus Unbound* thus shows the primacy of the poet over the philosopher, and even over the politician, in his character. Properly speaking, Shelley 'the thinker' has neither a metaphysics nor a politics, but a rhetoric. Shelley the poet, however, so refines rhetoric that it ceases to be an artistic strategy and instead becomes an aspect of the erotics of his text. He touches us, hearts, heads, and all, but as a lover of humankind and never as its master.

9

The Dramatic Lyric

It is remarkable how many of Shelley's poems prove exceptions to his fancy of the poet as a solitary nightingale. Reviewing what he himself chose to publish during his lifetime, we have found that he chose to present himself more often in posture of public address than in one of private meditation. This inclination to project his discourse outwards is thoroughly consistent with the prominence he accorded to the social role of art in his poetics. If we are to understand the force Shelley has exerted in our literary and political culture, we must appreciate why it was that the ruling class of nineteenth-century Britain found it necessary to neutralize him by promoting an image of Shelley as the author of fragile and ineffectual lyrics. The major published lyrics of Shelley's great Italian period are by no means art for art's sake. They are poems artfully designed to make things happen. *The Masque of Anarchy, Ode to the West Wind,* and *Adonais* are characteristic utterances of Shelley's public voice; they are lyrics that employ speech to dramatize an unfolding process in the poet's mind and to project that process outward toward an audience. Because they have that 'inner structure' which Irene Chayes has so shrewdly defined as characteristic of the 'dramatic lyric,' they are poems that adopt dramatic form as their model and locate their *telos* in the audience.[1] They are among the supreme achievements of Shelley's rhetorical art.

Nevertheless, it is true that Shelley was capable of self-pity when his actual readers failed to coincide with the fictional audiences his poems project. His depiction in the *Defence* of the poet who sings to cheer his own solitude is only one among many instances of this willingness to indulge disappointment, and shows that Shelley was as ready as Coleridge to pluck the poisons of self-harm. But the image of the solitary nightingale is properly viewed as an emotional aberration, a deviation that should not be allowed to obscure the main lines of Shelley's achievement. Still, Coleridge's self-abasement before Wordsworth is repeated more faintly in Shelley's admiration for Byron, an admiration not untinged by a certain envy of Byron's ability to command a great audience. 'Heaven knows what makes me persevere (after the severe reproof of public neglect) in writing verses,' he complained to Byron; 'where did you learn all these secrets? I should like to go to school there,' was his response to *Don Juan* (L, II, 309, 198). How much Shelley smarted under public neglect is a measure of the extent to which he abhorred solitude and craved an audience such as Byron held in sway.

What remains mysterious in Shelley is neither his skeptical detachment nor his obscure self-involvement, but the means by which he was able to sustain his commitment as a poet, especially as one dedicated to the improvement of human life. Though Shelley was often frustrated in his wish to find a ready audience among his immediate contemporaries, his poems nevertheless seek to create an audience by allotting his reader a specific place in the text. The structure of his dramatic lyrics especially inscribes a reader, granting us a footing on which we are invited to participate in the text. As a result, these poems have a pronounced rhetorical dimension evident both in their assumption of audience and in their use of common literary tropes. They invite and guide their readers' responses by devices such as conative address, dramatic reversal, repetition and difference, and the expectations aroused by the use of conventions. *The Masque of Anarchy, Ode to the West Wind*, and *Adonais* are connected by the common theme of rebirth, variously figured in political, vegetative, and metaphysical terms, but moral and emotional regeneration may also be a consequence of reading them. They are poems that 'generate occasions' for the reader to respond with that willing suspension of disbelief which constitutes poetic faith.

I

When Shelley sent *The Masque of Anarchy* to Leigh Hunt late in 1819, he warned him that it was a poem 'of the exoteric species' (L, II, 152). Clearly he thought of the poem as no mere private musing and was eager that it should reach the public that it was obviously meant for. Noting its 'popular tone,' Mary Shelley openly acknowledges the

Masque's pragmatic character when she states that 'the poem was written for the people' (J, III, 307). Its projected audience was not the cultural élite for which *Prometheus Unbound* was so carefully crafted, that 'select class of poetic readers' whose taste needed to be refined before they could be relied upon to govern wisely. Rather, it reached beyond the literary initiates of Shelley's age toward a mass audience which was just beginning to identify itself as 'the reading public.' Written in the interval between the composition of the third and fourth acts of *Prometheus Unbound*, the *Masque* bears the same relation to its more esoteric partner as the popular *Address to the Irish People* bore to the more decorous and selective *Proposals for an Association*. Where *Prometheus Unbound* appealed to that 'select class' who might be expected to take the lead in shaping informed intellectual opinion over the next few decades, the *Masque* was designed like its precursor, *The Address*, 'to increase, support, and *regulate*' the spirit of liberty that it disseminated among what might otherwise be an unruly mob. The youth who went to Ireland and wrote *Queen Mab* still lived in the mature poet who never abandoned his 'passion for reforming the world'; Shelley's aims as a poet remained unchanged, though as he mastered his art his means became more subtle as they became less direct.

While *The Masque of Anarchy* reaches back to *Queen Mab* in its intentions, it is infinitely more sophisticated in its techniques. Both poems employ direct, second-person address, but where *Queen Mab* relies on the crude device of Ianthe as a stand-in for the reader, the *Masque* inscribes its audience as a part of the fiction of its dramatic form. The 'conative function' (to use Jakobson's term) of Shelley's utterance in the poem is restricted to the speech which makes up roughly the last two-thirds of the poem, in which the audience is addressed in accordance with the conventions of the form of the court masque. The response of the audience is evoked by a structural principle in Shelley's *Masque of Anarchy*, then, rather than rigidly directed by the reactions of a single specific character in the text. Because Shelley's rhetoric in the *Masque* is a function of form and not just of content, it provides a richer aesthetic experience than the manipulative techniques of *Queen Mab* can afford. *The Masque of Anarchy* does not impose itself on the reader; instead, it shapes an ideology, gives it dramatic presence in a lengthy and climactic speech, and invites its potential audience to participate in the vision it projects.

Strictly speaking, vision is the content, not the form, of Shelley's poem, though the way form presents content is crucial to Shelley's management of means and ends.[2] Failure to distinguish between form and content has often been the bane of criticism, and, especially in the case of Shelley, emphasis on a content which is often obscure and apparently 'metaphysical' has overshadowed formal considerations which are in fact the prior conditions of his discourse. It is worth reiterating that Shelley was more of a poet than he was either a philosopher or a politician, and while political and philosophical issues are often the material from which he makes poetry, there are formal and final causes in his work that define him more precisely as a poet. Shelley himself calls attention to this possibility in his ultimate choice of title, *The Masque of Anarchy*. Recent commentary has begun to recognize that the masque is as essential to the poem as the anarchy.[3]

Shelley seems to have given considerable thought to his choice of title, quite rightly as a title is and always must be the initial means of orienting a reader to a work of literary art. Manuscript versions of the poem support the usage of 'mask,' but when Shelley sent the poem to Hunt in 1819 he pointedly referred to it in his letter as 'the "Masque of Anarchy" ' (L, II, 152). Hunt followed Shelley's lead when he eventually published the poem under this second version of the title. Nevertheless, 'mask' and 'masque' stand as suggestive alternatives, although it should be noted that they by no means exclude one another. It is possible that in the play between these two signifiers Shelley was seeking the best way to exploit an ambiguity on 'mask' as a means of deception and 'masque' as a dramatic entertainment, in order to generate the play between truth and illusion that is essential to his art.

Certainly, in the 'ghastly masquerade' that unfolds in the first third of the poem, the evils of the old order shelter behind the masks of powerful officials:

> I met a Murder on the way –
> He had a mask like Castlereagh. (J, III, 235)

Shelley's use of the mask, then, performs a dual function, for it at once disguises and reveals. Because evil (like the other 'absolutes' which have been cleansed by Shelley's skepticism) can enter the stream of life only in the actions of people, murder disguised as policy reveals itself as the exercise of personal power. Ironically, the mask presents a real person who cloaks an abstraction, instead of being the representation of an idea that conceals a human face.

Irony is the mode of this poem, for it obviously contains satiric elements, but it is a mark of Shelley's poetic maturity that he generates his profoundest irony through the subversion of a poetic form rather than through the ridicule of determinate contents, such as the most prominent statesmen of the day. In 'the Pageant' of the first part of his poem he clearly reveals that the foremost proponents of law and order in his society wear masks that conceal anarchy.[4] However, he ironically projects this criticism through the medium of a traditional courtly entertainment that had always been used to confirm the value of 'God, and King, and Law.' By calling into play the conventions of the court masque in order to condemn the values of the corrupt and anarchic court party, the dramatic ritual that would ordinarily confirm the monarch's power is turned against him. So complete is this ironic reversal of convention that Shelley's masque turns abruptly from condemnation of power politics to an invocation of the will of the people. When this transition occurs about a third of the way through the poem, the value of 'masque' with a 'q-u-e' comes to the fore.

Reading the *whole* poem as an utterance in the dramatic form of the court masque suggests that the ironic tension of the poem lies not between chaos and order but between misrule and self-rule. *The Masque of Anarchy* unfolds a dramatic process that depicts two kinds of order, the first cruel and repressive, a social order that uses violence and intimidation to constrain the turbulent passions of the people, succeeded by a second kind of civil order that is benevolent and springs from those internal sources of harmony and self-discipline that the Greeks called *sophrosyne*. Whether intuitively or knowingly, Shelley found the conventions of court masque perfectly suited to convey his vision of social regeneration. Court masque gives presence to the development of a central idea through an action governed by ritual and realized in music and dance, those aesthetic vehicles of harmony and engagement that we have already seen at work in Shelley's art. As a literary form, masque has little to do with such efficient causes as plot and character but is shaped through the devices of ritual, music, and dance toward final effect. In its juxtaposition of antimasque and masque proper, it depicts the defeat of the forces of repressive order by the forces of humane order and calls forth from its audience admiration for and approval of the latter.[5] This state of mind is a step toward emu-

202 The Poetry of Life

lation, for the conventional invitation to the masque audience to join in the revels allows the spectators to participate in the virtues fostered by the forms of measured language and movement. In the masque form, Shelley found a rhetorical vehicle that transcends satire, for in *The Masque of Anarchy* Shelley seeks not merely to pillory vice but to animate virtue.

That masque was traditionally a royal entertainment posed no impediment to Shelley; rather he encounters the form in an attitude of resistance that allows him to reshape it to his own purposes. As Stephen Orgel has taught us, in the Renaissance masque 'a deep truth about the monarchy was realized and embodied in action,' but the seriousness of this aim was inseparable from the element of play which was the means by which the monarchy expressed its self-image.[6] Shelley adopts the means, but he radically alters the ends. In a monarchical age the masque may well have served the purpose of elevating monarchy's self-esteem; in an age of revolution, however, Shelley adapts the playful elements of masque to serve the people. His masque harnesses the free play of decentred form to promote the self-esteem of the masses, so that where traditional masque honoured the material magnificence of monarchy his appropriation of its structure sanctifies the ethical magnificence of self-government. Shelley's poem does not stop at satire, for he seeks beyond ridicule of the established order to kindle in his audience a faith in themselves which is indispensable to the building of a new order, a state of civil society in which man is 'king over himself,' as prophesied in *Prometheus Unbound* (J, II, 242).

'Self-esteem' had long been one of the cardinal virtues in the Shelleyan creed when he wrote in 1820 to Leigh Hunt about the need for a secular faith:

If faith is a virtue in any case it is so in politics rather than religion; as having a power of producing that a belief in which is at once a prophecy and a cause.

(L, II, 191)

The model for this political faith was poetic faith. The habits formed in the 'willing suspension of disbelief' of one might carry over into the active life of the other, where the notion of the self-fulfilling prophecy is not unknown. Just as beyond the detachment of irony Shelley always pursues his commitment to poetic faith, so beyond the collapse of the old order humankind must be able to envision new political forms before they can pursue and accomplish them. Once the skeptical deconstruction of traditional values is achieved, Shelley remains eager to play at new language games that construct alternative orders. And he invites his reader to join in this exuberant play of signifiers. Carlyle could never have accused Shelley, as he accused Voltaire, of having 'only a torch for burning, no hammer for building' – Shelley's romanticism expresses itself most fully in his dedication to a language that is 'at once a prophecy and a cause.'

First, however, the old order must be swept away. Stuart Curran has admirably demonstrated the role of antimasque convention in the first part of Shelley's poem.[7] The processional 'triumph of Anarchy' rolls through these lines with inexorable motion, 'trampling to a mire of blood' the multitude naively gathered to wonder at this panoply of established authority. All the vices of state repression that wrought the shocking Peterloo massacre – murder, fraud, and hypocrisy – take part in this 'ghastly masquerade'; this 'glorious triumph' of the state moves 'with a pace stately and fast,' as if the participants are hastening out of step with the customary measure observed by men, an apt symbol of the violence they have inflicted on the social order. As if in parody of the masque convention of audience participation, lawyers and priests join in this ghastly dance of death led by the lords of misrule. Thus reeling together, they rush on, 'tearing up and trampling down' until 'a maniac-maid' called Hope flings herself, suffragette-like, before their horses' trampling feet. Ironically, an act of unreason seems the only possible intervention when the forces of apparent reason and order have chosen to act in an irrational and disorderly way.

Significantly, however, it is not Hope alone who halts the antimasque. Instead, in Shelley's highly theatrical vision, from the steaming mire of trodden bodies 'a shape' arises 'like a vapour of a vale,' and with it comes a voice from the earth. It appears that within the psychological allegory of Shelley's poem an inner dynamic is at work, Demogorgon-like, arising from deep within human experience, an eruption of psychic energy that is capable of transforming our circumstances if only we will let it.[8] On the historical level, this sudden reversal recalls the moment when Hegelian spirit passes through one of its dialectical metamorphoses. Whether it springs from revulsion at institutionalized crime or an affinity for justice or liberty, it equally produces the peripeteia which is an essential feature of dramatic structure. It matters less what this 'Shape' represents, however, than what is does; as a signifier it advances the narrative not because of its referent but because of its effect on the audience. After all, it is in what this half-formed 'Shape' says, rather than in what it is, that the transition from antimasque to masque proper is accomplished.

The most prominent characteristic of the 'Shape' is its voice. Although it at first appears 'arrayed in mail,' it moves so swiftly that its presence is less seen than felt:

> With step as soft as wind it passed
> O'er the heads of men – so fast
> That they knew the presence there,
> And looked, – but all was empty air.   (J, III, 240)

Like the pentecostal breeze which blows on the Ancient Mariner, the presence of the 'Shape' is known not by its causes but by its effects, which are to purge, to renew, to inspire. The romantic fondness for drawing a likeness among wind, breath, and spirit is well known,[9] but in this case there are important differences that distinguish Shelley's from Wordsworth's and Coleridge's use of the same trope. The vivifying wind does not descend from on high but instead rises from within; it is not merely a metaphor of the human spirit but a metonymy in which breath is shaped to voice, a voice signifying as it has before in Shelley 'the presence' of a spirit distinctly human; and the correspondent breeze it awakens is not merely in the poet but is also in the consciousness of the audience. As another one of those voices in Shelley's poetry that summon belief, however, this one represents a distinct advance. The voice of the 'Shape' is not a voice supposed to emanate from the natural sublime, as it does in *Mont Blanc*, nor is it a voice privileged by retrospect and lofty station, as is Laon's in *The Revolt of Islam*; instead, by virtue of its immediate dramatic presence it derives its authority from the reader's participation in the text of dramatic action in which it plays a part. True to the conventions of masque, the second part of the poem is a purely verbal evocation of an ordered and harmonious state of being in which the hearers are invited to participate, and which, by the supplement of their reading activity, they are invited to authorize.

It is an essential feature of Shelley's poetic discourse that this state is evoked, not described. Perfectly adequate readings of this speech have elucidated Shelley's political and economic views,[10] but sufficient attention has yet to be given to this speech as speech, and therefore to the poem as an act of utterance. It cannot be denied that these lines are conveyed as spoken, and therefore they create a context which is at once historical and dramatic. Spoken lines invoke a sense of occasion, recreating and commemorating the ghastly events of 16 August 1819 at the same time as dramatizing an attitude toward them. The rhetorical structure of the speech is hard to ignore: it employs commendatory direct address ('Men of England, heirs of Glory'), it poses provocative questions ('What is freedom?') that receive their answer in due course ('Thou art Wisdom ... Peace ... Love'), and finally it assumes an imperative stance.

Shelley's variations on the imperative mood, however, qualify the authority of the the poem's discourse in a crucial way. The imperative verbs of the peroration, which represent an indisputably direct appeal to the audience to transform the vision into action, are of two types. The famous rallying cry, 'Rise like Lions after slumber,' is a common jussive, but more interesting are the hortative variations on 'Let.' Nine of the final twenty-seven stanzas begin with this form of the imperative, and its repeated iteration has a profound effect:

> Let a great Assembly be. ...
>
> Let the blue sky overhead
> ... Witness the solemnity.
>
> Let the tyrants pour around. ...
>
> Let the charged artillery drive. ...
>
> Let the fixed bayonet. ...
>
> Let the horsemen's scimitars. ...
>
> Let the laws of your own land,
> Good or ill, between ye stand. ...   (J, III, 246–8)

Quite beyond the obvious emotional consequences of rhetorically charged repetition, though, is the subtler rhetoric of difference. Suddenly, the significant differences in Shelley's recurrent use of 'let' here endow the poem with the dimensions of a symbolic act. In some instances, such as 'Let the tyrants pour around,' where 'let' means 'allow,' we have a straightforward exhortation to courage, discipline, and good conduct in the face of violent assault. In others, meanwhile, such as 'Let a great Assembly be,' the verb carries the force of a wish or desire that requests co-operation. 'Let' here has a peculiar idiomatic force akin to its imperative use in the first person plural, such as in Eliot's 'Let us go then, you and I,' where the wish approaches a command. A closer parallel (though a usage which seems confined to poetical or at least rhetorical contexts) is found in Auden's elegy on Yeats:

> In the deserts of the heart
> Let the healing fountain start.

Such a use of the auxiliary 'let' is not so much imperative as optative, where a wish trembles of a verge of realization. Because of the tentativeness of his imperatives, Shelley's discourse permits the willingness to fulfil that wish to rest with the audience. In this poem, Shelley's language calls across the gulf between consciousnesses in the hope of evoking an active response from his hearers. Those who can *willingly* suspend their disbelief in the prospects for radical reform retain their autonomy in the reading process. The play of this tentative imperative transfers authority to the audience and marks Shelley's rhetoric as radical rather than revolutionary, in that, instead of authorizing and imposing a rival ideology, it allows his discourse to penetrate to root conditions of meaning that can generate new potentials.

'Let' in the optative mood is also a conventional feature of the court masque's poetic discourse. The Master of the Revels commonly gives commands to the masquers which are phrased as wishes inviting corresponding actions. In 'Pleasure Reconciled to Virtue,' Jonson's Daedalus calls upon the dancers to 'put themselves in form':

> Then, as all actions of mankind
> Are but a labyrinth or maze,
> So let your dances be entwined
> Yet not perplex men unto gaze.

In this context, where 'let' is the idiomatic equivalent of 'make,' it is appropriate that this song is sung by a supreme maker, Daedalus. Indeed, the role of the dramatic voice which calls all things to order both in the masque and in Shelley's poem is a metaphor of *poesis* itself. This voice assumes what Angus Fletcher calls 'a Daedalian stance' in bringing the revels to a seemly end in the manifestation of a presence.[11] For Shelley, of course, the final cause of his poem is not to show forth the grandeur of the king but to make manifest what Stevens has called 'the precious portents of our own powers.'

Human creativity reveals itself most persistently in our actual use of language, as Noam Chomsky has reminded us.[12] What he calls 'the creative aspect' of language is the capacity it affords us for innovation, not merely to utter sentences never heard before but also to frame alternative ways of thinking and acting. Given the constraints of everyday experience, language is often the only means of projecting other ways of being. Shelley certainly knew this dimension of language, and his poetry is a testament to it. Shelley is neither a mystic groping his way to truth nor a skeptic disengaged from human conflict, but a poet whose discourse defines the objects of the heart's desire and invites us to embrace them.

Because Shelley knows that discourse is an origin, he repeatedly employs the act of speech as a metaphor for human renovation. Thus, when his persona gives voice to the Daedalian imperative in *The Masque of Anarchy*, it is no accident that the people are called to an act of words:

> 'Let a vast assembly be,
> And with great solemnity
> *Declare with measured words* that ye
> Are, as God has made ye, free –
>
> 'Be your strong and simple words
> Keen to wound as sharpened swords,
> And wide as targes let them be,
> With their shade to cover ye.'
>
> (J, III, 247; italics added)

Liberty commences with a declaration of independence, an uttered (and perhaps eventually written) form of words, which declares an intention and in so doing realizes it. The political act Shelley urges to his auditors in this poem is a mimesis of the poetic act, in which words construct a reality. To declare that you are free is the indispensable first step toward being free – such a statement is a clear instance of what J.L. Austin meant by a 'performative utterance,' in which words do things as distinct from merely describing or referring to things.[13] In this poem, Shelley generates an occasion for a speech act that will begin the process of human liberation, an occasion in which the reader is invited to participate through the 'willing suspension of disbelief' in the potentials which that act puts in play. Shelley finally legitimates his language of desire through the decentred discourse of dramatic form.

Nevertheless, Shelley understands that language is a two-edged sword. It can be the instrument of human liberation, but it can as easily be the means of bondage, as Prometheus and Laon before him discovered. Words used as weapons may indeed 'wound,' and not only the enemy but also the self that wields them. What Shelley must constantly struggle against in his poetry is the temptation to lapse into mere rhetoric when the will to weave the 'subtler language' of poetic discourse begins to flag. This problem is at its most acute in his openly political poetry; it is after all what makes *Queen Mab* an artistic failure. Touching his audience without violating them is more difficult when undertaken on a mass scale; the erotic intimacy of the lyrical drama is harder to sustain in the lyric of public display. For Shelley, the problem in art is similar to the problem in society: the need to balance liberty and order at a time of political crisis is congruent with the artistic necessity of balancing practical aims and aesthetic values. *The Masque of Anarchy* is a paradigm of how the mature Shelley could maintain this perilous equilibrium through an act of mimesis. The poem he wrote is not in itself a call to rebellion, but it does contain the mimesis of such a call in the speech of the 'Shape.' By confining practical aims within artistic forms, however, Shelley is able to disseminate an ideology without imposing it on his audience, who must after all *willingly* suspend their disbelief if they are to participate in an act of poetic faith. The audience are free to refuse the text, but if they willingly play its language game they must abide by its rules, chief among which is the rule of order which Plato taught Shelley was essential to the idea of beauty. Those who heed the call of the 'Shape' must declare their freedom 'with measured words,' that is, in words that reflect the measured language of poetry and observe its 'order which approximates more or less closely to ... the beautiful,' as Shelley says in the *Defence* (J, VII, 111).

Poetry, for Shelley, is akin to those political institutions that foster those habits of mind necessary for real freedom. Just as a great poem should 'familiarize the ... imagination ... with beautiful idealisms of moral excellence,' so Shelley thought in his *Proposals for Putting Reform to the Vote* that the annual convening of a reformed parliament 'would familiarize men with liberty by disciplining them to an habitual acquaintance with its forms' (J, VI, 67). An habitual acquaintance with forms of poetry is what Shelley hopes to provide for his readers. He would use the order and beauty of 'measured words' to discipline his readers' passions and marshal their imaginative energy so as to make effective their resistance to tyranny. Just how shrewd a political judgment this was of the temper of Shelley's time is shown by E.P. Thompson, who thus analyses the motives of the Peterloo massacre: 'It was not the flags so much as the *discipline* of the sixty or a hundred thousand who assembled on St. Peter's Fields which aroused such alarm. ... We must understand the profounder fear evoked by the evidence of the translation of the rabble into a disciplined *class.*'[14] Far from being a disorderly mob, the common working men and women who gathered in St Peter's Field, Manchester, were noteworthy for their peaceableness and order. It was the authorities who rioted, not they; and the legacy of order and organization they left to succeeding generations helped turn Britain into a democracy without revolutionary upheaval. Shelley saw that poetry had a role to play in this process. By weaving dramatic illusion, it could provide an experience of order, but an order so radical that it could offer an alternative to the violent and represssive 'order' of the old regime. In Shelley's verse, the new order finds its paradigm in poetic order, an order that could familiarize the people with the personal virtue of self-control and the social virtue of organization. Shelley practised the discipline of beauty, as if he believed that the order of measured language and the order of beauty could communicate themselves to and discipline the mob that had run wild in the French Revolution into a peaceful force for constructive social change.

Shelley's success as as poet should be measured by artistic criteria, but his success as a political poet depends to some extent on whether his poems ever reached his intended audience. When he finally published the *Masque* in 1832, Leigh Hunt commented that the poem 'advises what has since taken place ... the success he anticipates has actually occurred, and after his own fashion' (J, III, 227). Obviously, the poem could have had very little impact on the passage of the first Reform Bill, but 1832 did not see the end of reform agitation in Britain and the poem played some role in succeeding events, especially in the later development of the Chartist movement. Bernard Shaw had reason to believe 'that Shelley had inspired a good deal of that huge but badly managed popular effort called the Chartist movement' and recalled an old Chartist's reminiscence of how the reading of Shelley led him to join the movement.[15] Indeed, the *Chartist Circular* in 1839 hailed Shelley as one of the foremost 'Poets of the People,' and in 1850 another Chartist journal, the *Democratic Review*, praised the poet for his 'soul-inspiring invocations to Liberty.' Though a direct causal link between Shelley's poem and the Chartist movement certainly remains debatable, it can at least be said that *The Masque of Anarchy* was remarkably successful in giving a determinate form to the ideology that motivated Chartism. It formulated a set of desires, beliefs, and attitudes, and disseminated them in such a way that they became very much a part of the shared political reality of Shelley's countrymen.

II

In the *Ode to the West Wind*, Shelley shapes a dramatic voice that first gives form to an ideology of social renewal and then mimes the process of its dissemination. Despite its apparent concentration on the self, the poem dramatizes the speaker in such a way that his discourse is projected outward, first toward the mighty forces of nature which he engages in verbal agon, but finally toward an implicit audience for whom his struggle provides a powerful focus of emotion. The *Ode*, then, unfolds a dramatic process of development from one stage to another in which the voice of the poet moves from the solitude of creative subjectivity to a social discourse that finds its *telos* in its audience.

Once we admit that lyric poems embody a speaking subject, we must leave the world of objectivity and truth for the realm of dream, ideology, and play. Dramatization of this lyric impulse, however, lends a degree of ambiguity to self-expression. The dramatic lyric does not express emotion; rather it is a public representation of emotion and of the self, a mimesis in which what would otherwise be absent is given presence, a presence, however, whose ontological status must remain uncertain. We cannot say of this represented subjectivity that it is true or false, real or illusory. It is simply 'there,' located in the play of signifiers. The question is not whether this subjectivity is correct; instead, the question becomes how this subjectivity comes to be shared, that is, how it is transformed into intersubjectivity. The knowledge such a poem provides is not so much objective as it is that knowledge based on acknowledgment of which Wittgenstein speaks.[16] It is a knowledge that results from the special language game that poets and readers agree to play.

Ideology is very much a part of the language game that political
poetry plays, and that game is one of the chief ways by which ideology
enters our lives. Far from being 'false consciousness' or what our
enemy believes in, ideology (as Louis Althusser writes) is as necessary
to all humankind as the air they breathe, and, we may add, no more
substantial.[17] Its value resides not in its claim to metaphysical or
scientific truth but in its capacity to sustain life and to form the basis
of social activity. Every society requires a system of mass representation by which its citizens are formed, transformed, and equipped to
endure the conditions of life. That sytem is an atmosphere of myths,
beliefs, conventions, and values which animates human activity and
gives buoyancy to human aspiration. It is a product of the human historical and social imagination, and as such it is in a constant process of
development. To say that art is merely a product of ideology is naive,
for when art gives a determinate form to ideology it thrusts ideology
into the dialectic of history by revealing the limitations of a particular
set of values and projecting possible alternatives that transcend them.
Art is an active partner in the process by which idealogy evolves.

Shelley seems to have caught a glimpse of this dialectic when he
wrote his peroration to the *Defence of Poetry*. Poets may be 'the unacknowledged legislators of the world' if their poems embody beliefs
and attitudes that can guide the ethical (and sometimes even the metaphysical) life of humanity. As we are becoming increasingly aware, literature at least since Arnold and Carlyle has been asked to shoulder the
burden of belief, even though its ambiguous fictional status gives it a
tenuous claim to satisfy our profoundest psychological needs. Literary
art has for some time been required to provide the metaphysical solace
religion once did, on the assumption that the objects of literary imagination were signs of some higher level of being. If, on the other hand,
literary works signify only themselves, something of Shelley's dilemma as a public poet becomes apparent. A man of sufficient skepticism to accept the inaccessibility of ultimate truth, he nevertheless
knew that humanity was in profound need of faith. For life to be possible, as Tennyson found, we must believe where we cannot prove.
Taking up the Aristotelian dictum that the end of life is not a thought
but an action, Shelley devoted his poetry to the furtherance of life and
human social activity by directing poetic faith toward ethical progress
rather than metaphysical definition. Poetry might never know the
truth, but it might engage us in acts that work 'the moral improvement of man.'

As a dramatic utterance, then, Shelley's *Ode to the West Wind* may be read as an act of faith in the form of a sustained prayer. The faith it seeks to generate, however, has less to do with religious ideology than an emerging political one. A belief in the necessity of social renewal was indispensable to an age of revolution, and if this renewal could be seen as somehow akin to a 'natural' process the ideology of political change might come to be regarded as less radical and impractical than many might think. The faith evoked in the *Ode*, therefore, is neither a faith in Providence nor even in some immanent teleology at work in nature, but rather a variety of poetic faith in which the reader will accept the parallel between natural regeneration and social renewal through the convention of tropic substitution. What happens in nature, we are asked to believe, will happen in politics – all change is a form of renewal. Or perhaps it is more accurate to say that Shelley the skeptic, as always in the creative act, for the moment of this poem willingly suspends his disbelief in this parallel and invites his audience to share in this act of poetic faith.

As we have seen, Shelley regarded faith as very much a political virtue because he considered 'belief ... at once a prophecy and a cause.' Belief has 'a power of producing' the effects that it envisions when the act of faith becomes a shared experience. Just as ritual makes private myth into public dream, so poetic language, when it assumes dramatic form, removes the process of sign-making from the solitude of the poet's subjectivity into the community of the reading process. Those who are poets 'in the most universal sense of the word,' writes Shelley in the *Defence*, are those in whose work

the pleasure resulting from the manner in which they express the influence of society or nature upon their own minds communicates itself to others and gathers a sort of reduplication from that community. (J, VII, 111)

The *Ode to the West Wind* is no mere private meditation but the public invocation of a myth which provides a focus for that community of worshippers Shelley hopes will transform the world. The poem begins by presenting a self in communion with nature, but as it develops, this self is dramatized in a context of repeated action and in accordance with a conventional decorum and structure.[18] As a dramatic utterance, the poem inscribes an audience even while it avoids addressing them directly. Although the poem is addressed to the wind, its conative function does not exclude auditors any more than the liturgy excludes the congregation. Shelley's *Ode* has a powerful ritual dimension which sweeps up its hearers into the myth it dramatizes, inviting them to participate in this act of poetic faith in which the speaker plays the role of high priest.

The role of the ritual celebrant in this poem is played out in speech. Once again, Shelley adopts the strategy of deploying a dramatic voice in order to focus the experience of the poem. This voice derives its authority from no other source than the fact that it speaks, although the peculiar mode of its speech generates effects characteristic of rhetorical trope. Simple and complex instances of repetition, from the reiterated 'oh, hear!' to the evolving structure of metaphorical respondents to the wind, induce a trance-like effect attributable to what Shelley himself calls 'the incantation of this verse.' This incantatory power of Shelley's poetic language is vitally linked to the ritual and dramatic dimensions of the poem as public dream. Jacques Lacan, in the process of offering his own version of the theoretical topos that discourse is itself an origin, writes provocatively of the psychic energies stirred by the power of this kind of represented speech: 'Hypnotic recollection is, no doubt, a reproduction of the past, but it is above all a spoken representation – and as such implies all sorts of presences. It stands in the same relation to the waking recollection of what is curiously called in analysis ''the material'', as the drama in which the original myths of the City State are produced before its assembled citizens stands in relation to a history that may well be made up of materials, but in which a nation today learns to read the symbols of a destiny on the march.' [19] In Shelley's dramatic lyrics, the drama of the myth-making speaker evokes a corresponding psychodrama in the audience in which the speaker's improvisations become the prototypes of a new mythus. Some such shadowy recognition of how the production of myth comes to be read as 'symbols of destiny on the march' may be asserting itself in Shelley's fascination with the Italian improvisatore, Sgricci (L, II, 266n). By similarly embodying a private urge to self-expression in a public performance, Shelley has learned to transform those 'delineations of human passion' so admired by his wife into tales of 'human nature and its destiny, a desire to diffuse which was the master passion of his soul' (J, II, 158).

In the *Ode to the West Wind* (J, II, 294–7), the ritual action is provided by the repetition and modification of metaphorical presences that illustrate the influence of the wind. Because the wind itself is like Intellectual Beauty an 'unseen presence,' it can be known only by its effects. In the first stanza, it is manifest when it drives the dead leaves of autumn into their 'wintry bed.' Among the leaves are seeds which do not die but merely lie dormant until 'Thine azure sister of the Spring' reanimates them. The mythopoeia of regeneration thus asserts itself early in the poem through a structure of repetition and difference. The old life goes and a new life returns with the seasonal cycle, a cycle marked by the trace of the autumnal west wind in its springtime counterpart. It is the same west wind, but different, just as the newly germinating seeds bear a trace of the same life force that departed in the fall. 'Destroyer and preserver,' the wind plays a double but continuous role in a myth of cyclical renewal, the pattern of which is established in the play of repetition among the signifiers of the first stanza.

The second and third stanzas extend and modify this developing pattern of cyclical regularity. The wind's effects on the land are repeated, first in the sky, then in the sea. The clouds, likened to leaves, are also swept across the sky until finally their pent-up energy is released in the storm that is the climax of the second stanza. Intimations of the water cycle lead through poetic logic to the third stanza, where the Mediterranean waves also answer to the wind's force, creating an endless round of motion. The water itself now provides an instance of repetition, reflecting the 'old palaces and towers' of the shore 'within the wave's intenser day' and revealing a curious marine 'foliage' that again repeats the seasonal cycle of the land. Having by now shown how cyclical regularity pervades the whole natural world, the poem requires only one step in its own logic to discover a similar pattern repeated in the world of social and political life.

This step requires the inclusion of the poet's voice in the structures of repetition and difference that help generate the poem's meanings. The poet's response to the wind initially repeats the response of nature. Because the wind is a mysterious cause whose existence is evident only in its effects, it makes an apt symbol for the unknown 'power' that animates all life. The wind is more suitable than a mountain in this respect, though, because its trace may be found in both nature and the poet – it may denote both the 'breath of Autumn's being' and the breath which gives voice to the speaker of these lines. 'Wind,' therefore, is invoked in the poem not just as a natural force but also as a symbol for inspiration. Where the human world is concerned, however, passive response to external forces is not enough to renew the conditions of existence. Nature may provide a stimulus, but it is the poetic consciousness itself that must give voice to nature and articulate its meanings. In that act of 'giving voice,' the poet shapes the voiceless wind into articulate speech, absorbs brute nature into the human world of signs and meanings, and in this verbal transformation of the natural world asserts his creative subjectivity. In this poem, we are constantly aware of hearing the voice of the poet, not the displaced fictional voices of nature. The *Ode* completes the promise of *Mont Blanc* to reveal 'the precious portents of our own powers' by showing how the aesthetic subject interprets and makes felt the promptings of nature.

The poet's role in this action (as James Reiger suggests) is that of the shaman, whose incantations shape a new language and weave a tribal myth.[20] His vocal display generates an occasion for shared homage in which a private agon is transformed into a collective myth. In his supplication of nature, the speaker has invoked the wind as the energy which drives the cycle of natural renewal. With the interests of the tribe in mind, the incantatory voice of the poem seeks the trace of that energy in human affairs. In human life there also must be a cycle of renewal, akin to the seasonal cycle in nature, on which an ideology of social renovation can be based. In his attempt to generate a new social mythus, however, Shelley finds himself once again speaking the language of desire:

> If I were a dead leaf thou mightest bear;
> If I were a swift cloud to fly with thee;
> A wave to pant beneath thy power, and share
>
> The impulse of thy strength, only less free
> Than thou, O uncontrollable!

The conditional verbs of these lines show how futile this wish is: the human speaker is fundamentally different from a wave, a leaf, or a cloud, by virtue of the very fact that he is conscious and can express that consciousness in speech. This irreconcilable difference between man and nature brings the poem to a crisis, works its peripeteia, and discovers a new meaning in the function of the wind. The myth of natural force is destroyed and preserved (Hegel's term is 'sublated') in the myth of dissemination.

This process of dialectical transformation is initiated by the poetic logic of irony. It is ironic that if the speaker's wishes were granted he would find himself 'only less free' than the force that drives him. The 'only' seems less a minimization than a reservation – it suggests 'but' and 'unfortunately.' If the speaker could be as a wave, a leaf, or a cloud, he must accept a diminution of his freedom. If he could sustain childhood's unconscious, unreflecting, unspeaking (*infans* after all means 'unable to speak') relation to nature, he would not have to make this impassioned prayer in the first place:

> If even
> I were as in my boyhood, and could be
>
> The comrade of thy wanderings over heaven,
> As then, when to outstrip thy skiey speed
> Scarce seemed a vision, I would ne'er have striven
>
> As thus with thee in prayer in my sore need.

The mature poet is no longer one with nature but must contend with it. He must strive with nature to satisfy his 'sore need' for reassurance and faith in the future. The struggle to wrest meaning from life and the world is not easy, however, and the poet must fall back on the conventions of language and myth in his strife with the forces of an indifferent universe. He cannot do otherwise than to admit his frailty, for the task of human redemption customarily consumes the saviour:

> O lift me as a wave, a leaf, a cloud!
> I fall upon the thorns of life! I bleed!

The priestly intermediary must be ready to surrender to the pains of ritual sacrifice. Being human and not divine, Shelley often thus sank under the burden of verbalizing desire. His poetry would be less authentic if it did not occasionally dread the inadequacy of language to his needs, the poet less admirable if he did not from time to time doubt his own adequacy to the task he has assumed. What is important is not so much the tone of this passage as the fact that this forthright admission of mythopoeic impotency does not allow the poem to collapse. Even from within the prison-house of language, the speaking voice reasserts its equivalency with the wind:

> A heavy weight of hours has chained and bowed
> One too like thee: tameless, swift, and proud.

Ironically, time can still the voice of the poet no more than it can tame the wind. Words defy time with their semantic persistence, vibrating in the memory and continuing their play of meaning long after the voice that uttered them is stilled. And that commitment to shaping a language, that dynamic verbal energy which delights in the play of signifiers, drives the poem forward to its conclusion.

The fifth and final stanza of the poem recapitulates the agon of man and nature developed in the first four. The stages of this dramatic process are recapitulated by the rival musical metaphors which balance the beginning and ending of this concluding passage. The first depicts the poet as a natural and dying being in passive response to the wind:

> Make my thy lyre, even as the forest is:
> What if my leaves are falling like its own!
> The tumult of the thy mighty harmonies
>
> Will take from both a deep, autumnal tone,
> Sweet though in sadness.

This elegiac tone is one possibility for any poet who chooses to rely on natural structures alone. To be born is to begin dying, and the leaves measure the passing of time. But the 'mighty harmonies' of nature are challenged in the next few lines by 'the incantation of this verse.' Commitment to the poetic act, with its man-made structures and its own temporal measure, achieves the dramatic peripeteia of Shelley's *Ode*. The verbal formula 'Be thou me' reverses the relation of instrument to agent in the next lines. The speaker does not simply identify himself with the wind; instead he swallows it, absorbing nature into his own being so that he might use it instead of being used by it:

> Be thou, spirit fierce,
> My spirit! Be thou me, impetuous one!
>
> Drive my dead thoughts over the universe
> Like withered leaves to quicken a new birth!
> And, by the incantation of this verse,
>
> Scatter, as from an unextinguished hearth,
> Ashes and sparks, my words among mankind!
> Be through my lips to unawakened earth
>
> The trumpet of a prophecy!

The winds of inspiration, now internalized as 'spirit fierce / My spirit,' are shaped by the poet's lips into articulate speech likened not to a passive aeolian lyre but to an active trumpet that heralds 'destiny on the march.' The imperative verbs here demand of the wind that it serve the poet, that it become the medium to disseminate his thoughts. They may 'scatter' as he utters them, but if they can reach their destination in the audience they may 'quicken a new birth.' The thoughts themselves are withered leaves, but in the act of speech his words are not just ashes but also sparks to ignite other human consciousnesses with a repetition and reduplication of his vision.

As Donald Reiman has noted, the imagery of this climactic passage recurs in two other perorations among Shelley's works.[21] At the conclusion of the first chapter of *A Philosophical View of Reform*, Shelley writes:

It is impossible to read the productions of our most celebrated writers, whatever may be their system relating to thought or expression, without being startled by the electric life which there is in their words. ... They are the priests of an unapprehended inspiration. ... the trumpet which sings to battle and feels not what it inspires; the influence which is moved not but moves. Poets and philosophers are the unacknowledged legislators of the world. (J, VII, 20)

As always, origins are less important to Shelley than ends. The poet may be passive and lyre-like in relation to inspiration, which comes from 'unapprehended' and mysterious sources. But in relation to his audience he is a trumpet, a sufficient origin in itself that inspires and moves its auditors. The inspiration that matters most to Shelley is not that which originates his poems but the influence they will exert when they are scattered throughout the world.

When almost two years later Shelley adapted this passage to close his *Defence of Poetry*, the only substantial change he made was to alter 'priests' to 'hierophants.' The change introduces an ambiguity that must not be overlooked: the priest reveals the divine, but the hierophant is literally a 'shower forth,' one who engages in the act of expounding, one who sets forth some sacred mystery. This shift in terms to describe the poetic act may be read as an admission on Shelley's part of the element of mystification in poetic language. After all, repetition is a rhetorical device that lends significance to discrete events. It links the wind of autumn with the wind of spring and asserts their identity despite their difference. This identification depends on a trope of analogy which substitutes one for the other merely verbally, and which is reinforced by further analogies drawn from the sky and the sea. But a contradictory conclusion could just as easily be drawn: if each leaf, cloud, and wave is unique, so may the winds be distinct from another, and so may be the events they represent. The rhetoric of the poem, however, has chosen to emphasize their affinities to the exclusion of their differences, and so has made them into signs for recurrence. We read a myth of cyclical renewal into nature because the rhetoric of the poem instructs us to do so, but this notion of repetition is a strictly semiotic phenomenon that depends on the poem's deployment of substitutable signs. The authority of this particular arrangement of signs derives not from the objective structure of nature but from our experience of the order of the poem's language.

Nevertheless, poetry bears a relation to human historical and social activity because its language encourages the exercise of belief. The dialectic between belief and political change is explored in the *Philosophical View*, written in the months immediately following the composition of the *Ode*. Here Shelley articulates in prose his mature understanding of the relationship between poetry and practical life. Political change, he writes, depends as much on the sentiment that change is inevitable and desirable as on actual social conditions (J, VII, 21). He shows his awareness that expectation can influence circumstances as much as circumstances affect expectation; and he knows that when poetry gives determinate form to ideology it raises expectations. Ideology, after all, does not describe reality so much as express a will or a hope that operates, says Althusser, in the realm of imagination.[22] Shelley's *Ode to the West Wind*, by expounding the orderliness of natural change, seeks to generate just such expectations of order and necessity with regard to political change. The poem is less description of objective conditions in nature and society than an attempt to evoke in its auditors that belief 'which is at once a prophecy and a cause' of future events.

For Shelley, the measure of a poem's worth resided not in its value as truth but in its effects upon an audience. Shelley knew that the analogy between the seasonal cycle and political renovation was rhetorical and not logical; therefore he refrains from enforcing a moral at the end of the poem. Instead of a flatly declarative conclusion that compels the reader, he uses a rhetorical question in order to defer meaning to the reader:

O, wind
If Winter comes, can Spring be far behind?

As Paul de Man has written of such questions, 'rhetoric radically suspends logic' and opens the way to endless possibilities.[23] The question that the *Ode* finally poses is the question implicit in the analogical rhetoric of the first three stanzas: is winter a sign of spring, or not; that is, is there a necessary connection between signifier and signified, such that the appearance of the former involves the expectation of the latter? The poem has worked mightily to rouse such an expectation of meaningful relations in the natural and the political worlds, but its final lines defer those meanings from the text to the reading process itself. Readers who can detach themselves from the poem's rhetoric might easily pose the counter-question: if Autumn comes, can Winter be far behind?

The rhetoric of Shelley's poetic language in this poem thus reflects the by now familiar distinction between insemination and dissemination. Because the poem's rhetoric can be so readily deconstructed, it cannot inflict its code on the reader. The poem cannot impregnate its reader either genetically or ideologically, but can only give itself up to be read just as Shelley surrenders his voice to the wind:

> Drive my dead thoughts over the universe
> Like withered leaves to quicken a new birth!
> And, by the incantation of this verse,
>
> Scatter, as from an unextinguished hearth
> Ashes and sparks, my words among mankind!

The poem cannot 'quicken' its readers without first allowing itself to be 'scattered.' Shelley finally surrenders his words to the wind because he trusts the reading process enough to prefer dissemination to insemination. He has become enough of an artist not to force his meaning on his auditors but to yield them their autonomy. His discourse does not transmit meaning but instead now truly 'generates occasions' for meanings. He no longer wields words as weapons, though he persists in playing the language game of poetry. He is confident that his readers will freely join in that game, and pursue the relations between signifiers and signifieds in the process of playing it. In a lyric which dramatizes desire, Shelley willingly surrenders his authority as poet to the reader, who can if he chooses cancel the deconstruction of the text and recover the authority of the sign in the pursuit of meaning. Such willing suspensions on both sides are essential to the erotics of Shelley's poetry.

III

In *Adonais*, Shelley explores the limits of desire in language. In contrast to the rolling energy of the *Ode* and the calm resolve of the *Masque*, *Adonais* is a poem fraught with anxiety. Like its fellow public lyrics, *Adonais* evolves a discourse that serves to focus the desires of the community of auditors, but unlike them it strives to project that communal energy beyond the very stream of life that generated its discourse in the first place. It is a poem that tries to look beyond death, beyond the limits of human thought and action; and yet, though it strains at transcendent desire, it has nevertheless succeeded in persuading generations of readers, in Earl Wasserman's words, of our 'destiny in the "world divine" beyond the grave.'[24] Certainly, convictions about immortality and divine realms are not the stock in trade of skepticism. Some form of poetic faith is surely operating in such metaphysical readings of this poem.

If the poem succeeds in achieving what Wasserman says it does, it is because *Adonais* is a triumph of Shelley's rhetorical art. Shelley's proud announcement of the poem to the Gisbornes as 'a highly wrought *piece of art*' (L, II, 294; Shelley's italics) might equally well be read as an ironic warning to more critical readers. The art of *Adonais* is an art that conceals art, a traditional art at least as old as the Greeks, wrought from the conventions of public discourse. The poem is less a sincere lyrical expression of grief than a dramatization of grief that relies on a powerful marshalling of literary conventions to constitute the conditions of its discourse.

To say that the highly wrought *Adonais* is a rhetorical poem is not so much to disparage it as to describe accurately the kind of utterance it is. It is above all not a philosophical or a religious poem. It is neither a logical nor an emotional discourse directed toward certainty; directed instead toward its audience, it is an accomplished example of epideictic speech, a discourse of display whose temporal province is the present occasion – in this case, the death of John Keats. The poem is a strictly conventional funeral oration, a formal speech whose structure provides orderly opportunities for the expression of grief, for praise and blame, and for consolation. Its conventions govern not only the decorum of its speaker but also the response of its hearers. *Adonais* draws heavily on the tradition of the pastoral elegy to instruct its audience in their responses and to govern their expectations. Shelley was pleased when at least one contemporary reader penetrated the poem's strategy: 'I am glad you like ''Adonais,'' ' he wrote to Horace Smith, 'and, particularly, that you do not think it metaphysical' (L, II, 349). The poem, then, was not intended (like philosophical or religious discourse) to signify anything beyond itself. It was simply a verbal structure erected, Shelley adds in the same letter, because 'I was resolved to pay some tribute of sympathy to the unhonoured dead.'

This 'tribute of sympathy' was to be no mere private and inward meditation but a public manifestation of grief in which the reader, as so often in Shelley's public verse, is invited to participate. From the poem's very opening, the epideictic speaker quickly turns outward from his own grief to supplicate the grief of a fictional audience who are invited to join in mourning the death of Adonais:

> I weep for Adonais – he is dead!
> Oh, weep for Adonais! though our tears
> Thaw not the frost which binds so dear a head!
>
> (J, II, 389, 1–3)

Immediately, the poem inscribes its readers, passing with lightning speed from first person declarative to second person imperative to a first person plural possessive, from self to other to community. In his eagerness to motivate the sympathetic imagination of his auditors, the speaker momentarily sets aside the question of the real efficacy of 'our tears' in the face of death. The discourse of the epideictic speaker aspires only to 'display,' in its root sense of 'to set forth' or 'to unfold'; and his role recalls the function of the hierophant who is indifferent whether he 'withdraws life's dark veil' or 'spreads [poetry's] own figured curtain' before us. Making no claims to metaphysical truth, this speaker is satisfied with the play of signifiers. What matters to him is not whether his claims are true or false, but 'the being within our being' fostered by his discourse. Working as it does pragmatically, his discourse should be measured by its effects, that is, by what it does for its audience, and not by the reliability of its reference.

But *Adonais* has a more ambitious aim than simply to help us mourn the passing of Keats. It seeks to weave a mythic fabric of consolation that transcends earthly and temporal life, and robs death of its sting. The very act of naming Keats 'Adonais,' as Wasserman has so exhaustively shown, associates the dead Keats with divinities from diverse traditions and lends him attributes that transcend the human and temporal world.[25] Now that Shelley's mythological syncretism has been so amply demonstrated, it is worth considering to what extent Shelley's use of myth authorizes his discourse. This poem certainly asserts some kind of transcendent immortality, even though Shelley in his more skeptical moods knew that we could have no real knowledge of such a state. Belief in immortality, Shelley wrote in his *Essay on a Future State*, could be founded only on the 'desire to be for ever as we are,' and arguments in its favour were likely to persuade 'only those who desire to be persuaded' (J, VI, 209). *Adonais*, then, is written in the language of desire, a language authorized by myths and other institutionalized beliefs that the audience has already absorbed from other sources and which they have previously found adequate to their psychological needs. The speaker of the poem knows how to exploit these predispositions of his audience and appeals quite consciously to their 'desire to be persuaded.' He knows the extent to which metaphysical solace feeds on emotional need.

Shelley's deployment of Greek epigraphs at the beginning of the published text of the poem establishes the context in which the poem is to be read. The epigraph from Moschus invokes the classical tradition most fundamental to the poem, that of the pastoral elegy. Since the conventions of the pastoral elegy grow out of the fertility rites of the ancients, there is implicit in the genre an impetus to rebirth that counteracts the grief over the loss of the loved one. The connection between death and revival is therefore authorized by the mythic code the text invokes from its very outset. As Bion wrote a lament for the dying and reviving Adonis, so Moschus wrote of his mortal friend Bion, and so the elegist of *Adonais* speaks of Keats. To reinforce this pattern of expectation, death and revival are also invoked by the speaker's reliance on the myth of Venus and Adonis to provide a narrative structure for his discourse. The reassurance that death is but a prelude to rebirth is derived not only from the code of seasonal myth but also from myths of transformation represented by allusions to the fate of Hyacinthus and the presence on the title page of the epigraph from Plato. Plato simultaneously mourned and consoled himself for the death of his favourite, Aster, in an epigram that plays on the significance of his name:

> Thou wert the morning star among the living,
>   Ere thy fair light had fled; –
> Now, having died, thou art as Hesperus, giving
>   New splendour to the dead. (J, IV, 283)

Transformation of the dead into a thing of beauty is also the theme of the myth of Hyacinthus, alluded to in Moschus' elegy on the death of Bion:

> Ye Dorian woods and waves, lament aloud, –
> Augment your tide, O streams, with fruitless tears,
> For the beloved Bion is no more.
> ... and thou, O hyacinth,
> Utter thy legend now – yet more, dumb flower,
> Than 'Ah! alas!' – thine is no common grief.   (J, IV, 286)

Shelley's own translations of these works show how deeply he was immersed in the structures and codes of Greek elegy when he came to write *Adonais*.

Shelley need not have sought outside this tradition for literary authority to transform the dead Keats into the immortal Adonais. For example, the title of the poem is perfectly explicable on the basis of Shelley's syncretization of Greek myths alone. According to Ovid, when Phoebus Apollo unintentionally kills his favourite, Hyacinthus, he transforms the bloody remains into a beautiful purple flower on which appears to have been written the Greek exclamation of sorrow and desire, 'ai.' A faint reminder of this myth is found too in Bion's elegy on the death of Adonis, once again in Shelley's translation:

> For Venus whilst Adonis lived was fair –
> Alas! her loveliness is dead with him.
> The oaks and mountains cry, Ai! ai! Adonis!   (J, IV, 285)

The fictional name 'Adonais,' then, may arise from a fusion of the Hyacinthus and Adonis legends – indeed, it may be a result of no more than the arbitrary collocation of signifiers in the line from Bion. The interposition of the cry 'ai' in the last syllable of the name 'Adonis' is nevertheless productive of significance to the attentive reader. 'Adon-Ai-s' suggests first of all a primordial grief for one who is lost, but the Homeric usage of the cry 'ai' also carries with it overtones of strong desire. The 'ai' in Adonais, perhaps, suggests at once sorrow and the wish to alleviate that sorrow, the desire to entertain possibilities that compensate for loss. That poetry can be an expression of that desire is indicated by the allegory of the Hyancinthus myth. Apollo, god of poetry, cannot bring the dead back to life, but he can transform the beloved victim into a thing of beauty that commemorates his loss and evokes a 'tribute of sympathy.'

The notion of poetry as a verbal supplement indispensable to transform brute fact into a meaningful cosmos had been with Shelley at least since the writing of *Mont Blanc* in 1816. In *Adonais*, he puts that notion to the test. The epideictic speaker he creates exploits every aspect of the mythological and literary tradition in a desperate effort to transform the death of Keats into a triumph of the human spirit. The speaker of *Adonais* does not simply express emotion: he uses poetic form, mythological codes, and literary convention to order his emotion in the service of controlling the emotions of his audience. That he largely succeeds in the latter is a credit to his rhetoric, but it is a success for which he must pay a price.

Adonais is a poem that relies very heavily on convention to achieve its effects. Of no other poem by Shelley could Northrop Frye's remark that poems are made out of other poems be more apt.[26] *Adonais* marshals a body of poetic precedent, from the Greeks to Milton, to lend authority to its discourse. It draws not only on the codes of mythology but also on the genre of the pastoral elegy of which it claims to be the inheritor. It luxuriates in the pre-established symbolic order of myth, ritual, and language that makes its discourse not just possible but authoritative. Its long ancestry in the genre of the pastoral elegy is evident in the chief feature of its rhetorical structure, the ordering of its materials. The poem opens with the traditional invocation to both the auditors and the muse, begging co-operation in the undertaking of mourning for the lost one. With the ninth stanza, the poem describes the procession of those who mourn, a conventional element firmly established in Milton's *Lycidas*. This procession includes the dead poet's personified emotions, such as 'Desires and Adorations,' 'Splendours and Glooms,' but a rhetorical conception of poetry transcending mere emotional expressionism is indicated by the presence of 'Winged Persuasions' among the train. In stanzas 17 to 29, the sympathy of nature is invoked, as it had been from Bion down to Milton, though here it is futile and unavailing. The living poets join in the lament in stanzas 30 to 35, which includes Shelley's personal digression, an intrusion which is that much less startling for the precedent set by Milton's reflections on fame in his own poem. Shortly thereafter, the poem reaches a nadir of gloom which suddenly in stanza 38 gives way to the peripeteia that motivates the last movement of the poem. We are informed that the poet is not lost; instead, 'He wakes or sleeps with the enduring dead' (J, II, 400). Such a sudden reversal of mood is of course perfectly consistent with the conventions of this genre – indeed, it is the essence of the type. Edward King was similarly resurrected into a divine fellowship:

> Weep no more, woeful shepherds, weep no more,
> For Lycidas, your sorrow, is not dead, ...
> There entertain him all the Saints above,
> In solemn troops, and sweet societies. ...

Both poems seek their consolation in an assertion of immortality. Like Adonais, Lycidas has 'sunk low, but mounted high'; the chief difference is that where Lycidas is exalted 'through the dear might of him that walked the waves,' Adonais must be resurrected through a complex verbal fabric of Platonic symbolism, ranging from 'the burning fountain,' through 'the one Spirit's plastic stress,' to the 'white radiance of Eternity.'

Where Milton could be confident of a response to a strictly Christian faith in immortality, Shelley tends to be less so about poetic faith. His speaker invokes images of great energy and purity with words like 'burning' and 'white,' but they remain only images unless they somehow link up with the reader's inclination to view life in terms of religious transcendence. For those who already believe in the immortality of the soul, Adonais has considerable power, but then it must be admitted that it can persuade 'only those who desire to be persuaded.' The poem is truly effective only for those who have already assimilated the conventions necessary for reading it. To others, more skeptical and detached, the poem imposes a way of reading which they resist. One recent commentator, for example, sees the poem primarily as a rhetorical exercise whose use of the conventions of pastoral elegy 'instructs the reader to anticipate a glowing conclusion' and whose energy stems 'not from any conviction of Keats's apotheosis but from contrary resources of indignation ... [at] the horrors of present existence in this "dull dense world."' [27]

Adonais, then, presupposes familiarity with mythic codes and conventions of reading that are very much part of the institution of literary tradition. And it is the weight of these codes and conventions themselves that lends authority to the voice that utters the poem. [28] The poetic persona of Adonais is less a free, creative subjectivity than a construct of the poem's highly deterministic discourse, as if the institutions of myth and genre had usurped the role of the poet. The rhetoric of *Adonais* assumes a demonic function, seizing control of him who should be in control of it. Language seems to write itself in this poem, victimizing the speaker who has invoked it and threatening to overwhelm the reader who seeks critically to struggle with it.

This peril of Shelley's rhetorical art had been foreshadowed, at least metaphorically, by Mary Shelley as early as *Frankenstein*, in which the risks of creating a creature that might turn on its creator are projected. Judging by her remarks on *The Cenci*, Mary often played the role of devil's advocate with regard to her husband's creative enterprise, calling him to account when she felt he had pursued fantasy at the expense of human feeling and warning him of the pitfalls that loomed in a too-exclusive trust in verbal means. *Frankenstein*, as James Reiger has subtly suggested, can be read as just such an admonition to her husband.[29] It is as if she sensed well before he did that all creations necessarily assume a degree of autonomy once they are created, and that therefore their end results could not be reliably predicted. As a poet deeply interested in ends and means, Shelley had to encounter this problem eventually. That he did so several years after his wife formulated it is a tribute to her perceptiveness and a comment on his immersion in his own habits of discourse. But finally in *Adonais*, he does face squarely the problems of persuasion. Like Victor Frankenstein, the speaker of *Adonais* has called into being a monster which threatens to rise up and destroy him. Swept up in his own rhetoric, he comes dangerously close to rejecting the stream of life in which alone his discourse can have any meaning.

The demonic rhetoric of *Adonais* reaches its climax in the mounting lyric intensity of its consolation. This last phase of the poem (beginning with stanza 38) is dictated by the conventions of its genre, but it takes on a life of its own in its ecstatic affirmation of immortality. The vitality of these lines in praise of death depends on the ability of their flat declaratives to appeal to some residual religious emotion in the largely secular and this-worldly audience whom Shelley normally addressed. 'He has awakened from the dream of life,' 'He has outsoared the shadow of our night,' 'He lives, he wakes – 'tis Death is dead, not he; / Mourn not for Adonais' (J, II, 400–1) are all statements of wishes rather than facts, but statements whose grammar and rhetoric brook no dissent. As utterances of compelling desire they would be sufficiently authentic expressions of an inner need for emotional reassurance did they not shade so readily into the imperative mood. Even the poem's most powerful figurative expression of transcendence is marred by this impulse to compel the reader:

The One remains, the many change and pass;
Heaven's light forever shines, Earth's shadows fly;
Life, like a dome of many-coloured glass,
Stains the white radiance of Eternity,
Until Death tramples it to fragments. – Die,
If thou wouldst be with that which thou dost seek!   (J, II, 404)

Of course, the climactic imperative, 'Die ... !' cannot be taken literally as a counsel to suicide. Were it understood so, it would ironically undermine the rhetorical thrust of a poem which seeks to generate a faith to live by. Nevertheless, the naked ferocity of its utterance discloses a genuine conflict in the mind of the speaker. Beginning with an invitation to lament the death of a fellow mortal, he concludes by demanding that his hearers embrace death, not as something lamentable but as something desirable. What begins as a lyric expression of living emotions swells into a dramatized repression of the will to live.

The intense lyrical impulse toward death in the poem is restrained only by the poem's dramatic form. After all, Shelley has created a character in the elegist of Adonais who, like the speaker of one of Browning's monologues, explores his innermost thoughts and reveals his essential psychological nature by means of his own discourse. And just as with a dramatic monologue, irony is the chief device used by the poet to distance himself from his creation. That a poem which ultimately attempts to challenge the fact of death should come into existence in the first place is the leading irony of the first part of the poem. Even as the speaker sets out to establish the mythic and generic context of his utterance, he repeatedly admits the inadequacy of language in the face of death. From the outset, we are invited to mourn for Adonais, even 'though our tears / Thaw not the frost which binds so dear a head!' The futility of lyric expression to counteract death is openly acknowledged – expression of grief is of value to us only in so far as it helps to relieve the burden of anxiety we feel when confronted with death.

Early in the poem, images of the void and of desperate sinking into an abyss express this anxiety with as much urgency and authenticity as the imagery of Platonic idealism expresses the desire to transcend death in the latter part of the poem. Both forms of imagery wonderfully poise the poem between desire and anxiety. Where Adonais rises like a star to 'outsoar the shadow of our night' in stanzas 38 to 40, here he is swallowed up by the jealous depths:

He is gone, where all things wise and fair
Descend: – oh, dream not that the amorous Deep
Will yet restore him to the vital air;
Death feeds on his mute voice, and laughs at our despair. (J, II, 389)

Death is depicted as a predatory lover who hungers for the departed and defies our emotional needs. Thus motivating our rivalry with death, the speaker rouses an expectation in his auditors of struggle and possible triumph that is fed by the rhetorical structure of a dramatic plot that rises through peripeteia to climax. Such a conventional plot structure tends to place the emphasis on the second, triumphant species of images and so long as we remain captivated by this rhetorical strategy we naturally assume the superiority of the burning fountain over the amorous Deep. However, this strategy only works if we experience the poem in a linear fashion, as a unique oration on a single occasion. Regarding the poem as a linear progression clearly privileges the climax over the opening situation, but viewing the poem as a whole on subsequent rereadings reveals the artfulness of such a strategy. If we can detach ourselves from the poem's language game and view it critically, it must be acknowledged that the anxious despair of the opening is just as genuine an emotion as the aspiring desire of its climax. And it will be recognized that the source of those emotions is the same in both instances, the poet himself.

Ironically, Shelley's elegiac speaker emphasizes the poet as origin of rhetorical mystification very early in the poem. Here, his anxiety is roused most forcibly by the extinction of the dead poet's voice, as if the passing of the poet signalled the death of poetry:

The quick Dreams,
The passion-winged Ministers of thought,
Who were his flocks, whom near the living streams
Of his young spirit he fed, and whom he taught
The love which was its music, wander not, –
Wander no more, from kindling brain to brain,
But droop there, whence they sprung; and mourn their lot
Round the cold heart, where, after their sweet pain,
They ne'er will gather strength, or find a home again   (J, II, 391)

This passage reveals the fatal imperfection of the whole of *Adonais*, that is, its total blindness to the autonomy of literary language and the autonomy of the reader. The elegiac speaker assumes that the affective potential of poetry depends exclusively on the presence of the poet; he discounts the presence of an autonomous reader, preferring to absorb his audience into his manipulative strategy. Without the poet, poetry falls mute, because the assumption seems to be that poetry is no more than the projection of a single consciousness. The notion that poetry might depend on the co-operation of numerous consciousnesses in a willing suspension of disbelief is not even canvassed by this speaker.

Even as he develops one of the poem's leading myths, this speaker betrays his narcissistic emphasis on the self. Among the procession of mourners, Apollo and Narcissus stand significantly side by side:

> To Phoebus was not Hyacinth so dear,
> Nor to himself Narcissus, as to both
> Thou, Adonais; wan they stand and sere
> Amid the faint companions of their youth,
> With dew all turned to tears; odour, to sighing ruth.   (J, II, 393)

It is either very daring or very foolish tactically thus to associate the god of poetry with the classic representative of self-deception. This collocation of poetry and narcissism ironically raises questions about the validity of poetical transformations of sorrowful experiences at the very time when the speaker is trying to get just such a transformation under way. Does Apollo transform the stricken Hyacinth into a flower only to assuage his own guilt? Are the transformations of the myth-making poet evasions, is mythopoeia a species of self-delusion for the purpose of alleviating our anxieties and expressing our desires? It is ironic that even while the epideictic speaker is intent on shaping his transcendent myth of Adonais, he unconsciously reveals motives that are essentially self-serving.

As that myth is developed in the poem, it involves itself in further aporias. Though the affective potential of poetry is seen at an early stage to depend on the presence of the poet in this life, as the poem continues that potential somehow becomes shifted to the world of death. By the twenty-first stanza, death, rather than life, comes to be hailed as an origin:

> Whence are we, and why are we? of what scene
> The actors or spectators? Great and mean
> Meet massed in death, who lends what life must borrow. (J, II, 395)

Instead of shaping meanings in the stream of life, the poet must seek for meanings in death. Death is seen as lending to life a borrowed meaning already formed in an eternal realm from which we as living human beings are excluded. If this assumption is correct, answering the questions posed here ('Whence are we, and why? ... ') would seem to entail a fellowship with death and the rejection of the very life that made it possible to pose the question in the first place. Indeed, that is the logic which the poem expresses in its imagery. Death becomes the origin of spiritual vitality and the locus of its return:

> the pure spirit shall flow
> Back to the burning fountain whence it came,
> A portion of the Eternal   (J, II, 400)

Meanwhile, life is characterized by images of delusion and repugnance: 'stormy visions' make up 'the dream of life,' we subsist in 'the shadow of our night,' we are consigned by 'the contagion of the world's slow stain' to 'decay / Like corpses in a charnel' (J, II, 400). So complete is the rejection of life at this point in the poem that the speaker himself comes to locate the only true source of vitality in the brute natural world which previously in stanzas 18 to 22 had failed to revive the corpse:

> He is made one with Nature ...
> He is a presence to be felt and known
> In darkness and in light, from herb and stone,
> Spreading itself where'er that Power may move
> Which has withdrawn his being to its own   (J, II, 401)

The speaker neglects the hard-won lesson of *Mont Blanc* that the 'Power' which seems resident in nature is no more than a construct of our own powers of verbal imagination. Instead, he readily abandons both himself and Adonais to some transcendent 'Power' beyond themselves. In doing so, the speaker alienates himself from the power that informs his own discourse and surrenders his ability to shape meanings in the stream of life to the authority of some determinate signified deemed to reside outside himself. Ironically, he seeks to validate his own discourse by surrendering it to the Other.

Having thus become thoroughly alienated from his own consciousness, the speaker now begins to express doubts about his whole mythopoeic undertaking. Readers swept away by the language of desire in the latter part of the poem are understandably unlikely to notice those moments when the transcendent impulse is called into question, but those moments are nevertheless available. At the moment of decision, images of trepidation ironically undermine the speaker's own testament to transcendence. On the brink of death, the speaker agonizingly hesitates:

> Why linger, why turn back, why shrink, my Heart? ...
> 'Tis Adonais calls! oh, hasten thither,
> No more let life divide what Death can join together.   (J, II, 404)

The hortatory injunction of the final line of this passage sounds more like a plea for courage in the face of the unknown than a command. The shrill imperative of the preceding stanza – 'Die, / If thou wouldst be with that which thou dost seek!' – seems to settle into a quietly hysterical confusion, so that in the final stanza of the poem the speaker finds himself desperately trying to resist the fatal attraction of the myth he has been creating:

> The breath whose might I have invoked in song
> Descends on me; my spirit's bark is driven,
> Far from the shore, far from the trembling throng
> Whose sails were never to the tempest given;
> The massy earth and sphered skies are riven!
> I am borne darkly, fearfully, afar;
> Whilst burning through the inmost veil of Heaven,
> The soul of Adonais, like a star,
> Beacons from the abode where the Eternal are.   (J, II, 405)

Anxiety clearly reasserts itself in these concluding lines. Adonais is ineluctably 'Beyond,' but joining him requires the transit of terrifying and unknown territory. The emotions of the poem have now been whipped to 'tempest' force, and images of earthquake and storm ('The massy earth and sphered skies are riven') indicate the extent of the personal cataclysm this discourse has wrought in the speaker. Not only does he voyage on tempest-tossed seas that threaten to destroy him, but he does so in vain isolation, 'far from the trembling throng' whom he began by addressing. In his single-minded pursuit of his own rhetoric, he has cut himself off from human community and now must pay the tragic price for his hubris. Like the young Visionary poet in *Alastor*, he has overreached himself imaginatively, and now finds himself ironically the victim of his own powers.

The final irony of *Adonais* is therefore a romantic irony, in which the speaker of the poem calls his own discourse into question. 'The breath whose might I have invoked in song' vexes itself and descends vengefully on the poet himself. His rhetorical art has after all been art that attempts to conceal art, but evidences of that repression of creative responsibility have stubbornly asserted themselves in the poem's recurrent self-contestations. The conclusion of the poem shows the inevitable return of the repressed, now in a dark and fearful form, threatening to bear the speaker away. The rhetorical poet has tried to control language and compel his reader's assent, but he instead finds that language has seized control of him and forces him to undertake a quest he now would prefer to resist. The poem has turned itself demonically on him. His only hope is to confess his responsibility for what he has created and, like Dr Frankenstein, try to destroy it. He flees from the lyric sincerity of the emotions he has aroused and takes shelter in the authenticity of self-revelation and self-consciousness. Instead of continuing to conceal art, the artist reveals his artistry; instead of projecting the poem as an objective work of art, the speaker reveals himself as the subject who constituted it in order to fulfil his own psychological needs. The poet must call back 'the breath whose might I have invoked in song' to the breast from which it first issued.

As a purely lyric utterance, *Adonais* finally acknowledges its own contradictions. It seems that Shelley's lyrics frequently prefer such authenticity to perpetuating the illusion of emotional sincerity. Judith Chernaik observes that what she calls 'the irresistible pull of Eros or Thanatos' in Shelley's lyrics is usually resisted by a certain rootedness in the dilemmas of life in this world: 'The common reader has usually cherished the love poems for their humanity as well as their charm. They are not simply love complaints; they express rather a sophisticated awareness of social complexities, and the recognition that human passions operate in a framework of limited possibilities.'[30] This recognition of the limitation imposed on human desire by life in this world is evident not only in the love lyrics but also in Shelley's great death lyric, *Adonais*. In an attempt to express the common human desire for immortality, the poem fails to take into account the inadequacy of language to fix meanings outside the stream of life. To achieve its end, the poem must attempt to dominate the reader's critical sense. It adopts the techniques of authoritarian discourse in order to establish a relation of dominance and subserviance between itself and its audience. Eschewing the 'subtler language' evolved in Shelley's lyrical drama, it fails to sustain that equality and reciprocity between text and reader on which poetic jouissance depends. In terms of the erotics of poetry, *Adonais* tries to seduce the reader, while *Prometheus Unbound* offers an open embrace.

As a dramatic utterance, however, *Adonais* rescues itself from lyric collapse. That Shelley chose to end his poem by calling its discourse into question is at least a sign of his own growing self-awareness as a poet. If the speaker of *Adonais* can be seen as another *Alastor*-like instance of Shelley's self-projections in his poetry, then the poem can be read as an ironic meditation on the dilemma of the rhetorical poet. In dramatizing the emotions of his elegist, Shelley is testing the limits of his language of desire. The success with which he locates those limits in *Adonais* makes the poem a key example of the way Shelley uses dramatic form to contain the failings of lyrical rhetoric.

10

'Last' Poems

Let us conclude at least this much, that poetry is not a thing but an activity. The writer and the reader both have a part to play in the poetic process, the one constructing orders of discourse and the other entering, experiencing, and interpreting the poem's verbal cosmos. Not containing its meaning in itself, the poem 'generates occasions' for meaning that require the active participation of the audience to fulfil the poetic act. Poetic meanings (need we go farther?) are not fixed, then, but are formulated and reformulated in an unending reading process wherein poems are put to the only use for which they can properly be intended, that is, to be read. 'Let the use teach you the meaning' is Wittgenstein's most direct statement of the functional theory of meaning which holds that discourse has meaning only in the stream of life.[1] A similar kind of semantic pragmatism informs both Shelley's poetry and his poetics. The meaning of any of his poems is not a function of what would have to be the case if the poem were true in itself, but a function of the difference that the poem makes to the lives of those who read it.

Because the poem's potential for meaning is not fulfilled until it is incorporated into the lives of its audience, the reader must be allowed to be at least an equal partner in the poetic process. The notion that poetry, like love, must be a co-operative venture rather than the imposition of one ego upon another was, as we have seen, essential to both Shelley's theory and his practice and was rooted in his political ideology. As early as the Irish pamphlets, he sought to form partnerships with others by verbal means. The *Proposals for an Association of Philanthropists* stressed the need to reclaim presence from absence and to exercise the sympathetic imagination before the world can be reformed:

A recollection of the absent and a taking into consideration the interests of those unconnected with ourselves is a principal source of the feeling which generates occasions wherein a love for humankind may become eminently useful and active. (J, V, 253)

Believing that a change in sensibility and outlook was a necessary prerequisite to social and political change, Shelley undertook to work the revolution at a psychological rather than an institutional level. Poetry was his chosen vehicle for this radical reform because he regarded the pleasure arising out of the play of literary language as a vital means of access to the psyche. 'Poetry is ever accompanied with pleasure,' he would write in the *Defence*: 'All spirits upon which it falls open themselves to receive the wisdom which is mingled with its delight' (J, VII, 116). Poetry, for him, was therefore a living instrument, not so much of communication as of arousal and dissemination. A poet and not a politician, he eschewed mere rhetoric because he wanted less to convince than to excite us with a view of the world and our place in it. He strove not merely to express what Yeats called his 'heart's desire of a world' but universalize that wish into a rule of life. Hence he defied Godwin's *laissez-faire* atomism in Ireland to call for an 'association of philanthropists' who pursued ends beyond personal rectitude. He found that he could transcend the self by seizing upon those occasions

that generalize and expand private into public feelings, and make the hearts of individuals vibrate not merely for themselves, their families, and their friends, but for posterity, for a people, till their country becomes the world and their family the sensitive creation. (J, V, 253)

This principle of co-operation he extended from the political to the poetic sphere. In doing so, he found in poetry a power far subtler than persuasion. Because his reader could respond with delight rather than merely with agreement or disagreement, he made poetry an harmonious occasion for fellowship.

To achieve this communion with the reader, Shelley had practically to reinvent the notion of rhetoric. Traditional rhetoric has a somewhat masculine and authoritarian bias, for in it a speaker seeks to subdue his auditors. If he would convince them of something, he must engage in a discourse that overcomes objection and conquers the minds of his hearers. Indeed, the verb 'to convince' is rooted in the Latin verb *vincere*, which means to conquer or overcome completely. Shelley, as we have seen, constantly struggled with this tendency to dominance in his literary discourse, a tendency which he was astute enough to realize was at odds with his most cherished political beliefs. The challenge for him was how to urge the desirability of liberty in a discourse that did not infringe the reader's own freedom.

Because he was a skeptic, an atheist, and a republican, the central problem for Shelley was the problem of authority. Having set aside as false and oppressive all the guarantees of the established order, he was faced with the question of where to locate authority. He could locate authority in nature, but to surrender the autonomy of consciousness to a world of objects betrayed his intuition of his own creativity. Though he flirted with it, Shelley did not long remain a proponent of materialism. In the process of the poem *Mont Blanc*, he threw off the shackles of objective reality by uncovering in his language the rules for the production of metaphysical notions. The 'Power' was not authorized by its existence prior to the linguistic act that brought it into our consciousness, but instead was authorized by the very act of naming it. Authority then could not be located in language's references to objects, because Shelley could find no valid criterion for distinguishing thoughts from things. Alternatively, he could locate authority in the self, but to rely exclusively on his own subjectivity would isolate him, as it did the young poet in *Alastor*, from humankind. Shelley's imagination (like his ideology) was essentially social, and no matter how often it would explore the dark passages of mere personal and private concerns it would always reassert its fundamentally outward dynamic, flowing toward the reader like the recurrent symbolic river of his poetry. Authority could be located in this dynamic, but to find in the power of language directed to an audience the justification of his discourse implicated his poetry in the very compulsion Shelley most abhorred. He did not wish to master his audience any more than he cared to be mastered by the objective world of nature or of social relations, for he suspected the tyranny of rhetoric as much as he resisted the tyranny of circumstances.

Living in an age of revolution, though, he was alive to new and experimental modes of relationship. Thomas Paine's revolutionary concept that the monarch governs by the consent of the governed provided a valuable new model for social relations upon which Shelley built his theory of verbal interaction. Shelley could locate authority in the community of his readers. By developing a poetic discourse that consciously defers meaning to the reading process, Shelley could allow the author's influence to depend on the consent of his readers. Rather than persuading his readers to accept any specific beliefs, he invites them to willingly suspend their disbelief and to join him in playing the language game of his verse. His poetry thus becomes a communal venture, stepping ouside of patriarchal structures and generating occasions for meanings that are neither specifically masculine nor feminine. Rejecting the old orders and distinctions, he creates in his poetry a new order of words subject to its own special rules and conditions.

Hence, his poetic problem was to find a means to disseminate his 'heart's desire' without forcing it on others. He learned from Coleridge, if he did not know already, that poetry is distinguished from other forms of discourse 'by proposing for its *immediate* object pleasure, not truth,' and this obligation to provide pleasure lifted from poetry itself the burden of meaning. It could content itself with providing an experience of joy and beauty quite apart from reference to the actual world. Its goal was not knowledge, but the creation of circumstances in which author and reader could meet to pursue possible meanings. The pleasure taken in playing this language game breaks down our resistance to new modes of thought, so that our habits of disbelief are subtly undermined. Shelley's poetry does not so much provide us with new beliefs as give us the opportunity to entertain possibilities we might not otherwise have considered, but may now find congenial. If in the end we embrace those possibilities, we do so of our own volition. To share Shelley's vision for the moment of the poem is not to be possessed by it, but only to be exposed to it. It does not authorize itself but waits upon the reader to acknowledge it.

The solution to the problem of authority, then, lay in the poet's exploration of non-authoritarian rhetorical forms. While the narrative structure of the epic imposed a specific point of view on the audience, the drama offered no such difficulty. The drama always invites the audience to suspend its disbelief, it allows for the play of differing points of view, and it depicts an immediate and present action which depends on the consent of the audience rather than on the authority of events fixed in the past. Drama is a model of those occasions 'that generalize and expand private into public feelings' and is therefore an apt vehicle for the dissemination of lyrical desire. In the form of the lyrical drama, this desire is validated not by its intensity, its sincerity, or by any other subjective criterion, but is authorized by its reception by the audience. In the words of *Hellas*:

> Nought we see or dream,
> Possess, or lose, or grasp at, can be worth
> More than it gives or teaches. (J, III, 48)

It is the essence of Shelley's poetic pragmatism that the value of his art is always thus to be measured by its results.

The writing of *Hellas* during the last year of his life shows once again how Shelley was less concerned with origins than he was with ends. *Hellas* is not an historical but a lyrical drama in that it depicts events drawn not from the actual world but from the world of the heart's desire. It is not a reflection of the past or a prophecy of the future, but a work that mimes the possibility of what could be.

Returning to the lyrical drama late in 1821, Shelley shows his satisfaction with this rhetorical form as a vehicle adequate to his public voice. By framing his vision of a better world in dramatic form, he can overcome the authoritarian tendencies of epic and the subjective dominance of lyric in an openly artificial aesthetic experience that invites the participation of the audience. *Hellas* in no way practises the arts of deception. 'A mere improvise,' as Shelley describes it in his preface, it enlists the delights of art to open our spirits to 'the cause he [the poet] would celebrate.' Shelley no longer attempts to instruct his audience; instead he contents himself

with exhibiting a series of lyric pictures, and with having wrought upon the curtain of futurity, which falls upon the unfinished scene, such figures of indistinct and visionary delineation as suggest the final triumph of the Greek cause as a portion of the cause of civilization and social improvement. (J, III, 7)

Openly admitting the motives of lyrical desire, the poet seeks to disseminate it through dramatic form where the 'pictures' of character and action play across the 'figured curtain' of poetic representation. These signifiers playfully 'suggest' a possibility to the audience rather than enforcing a moral in an authoritative voice. Transfusing lyric desire through dramatic form, Shelley enlarges private wishes into public concerns. After years of restless experimentation with literary form, Shelley finally found in the lyrical drama a means to touch his audience without violating them.

In *Hellas*, Shelley in no way wishes to dogmatize about the revolt of the Greeks. Instead, he prefers using language to cast 'upon the curtain of futurity' images of a potential course of events which will exercise the imaginations of his readers. Only a few months before, in March of 1821, Shelley in his *Defence of Poetry* had come to understand clearly the relation between poetry, imagination, and 'the moral improvement of man':

A man, to be greatly good, must imagine intensely and comprehensively; he must put himself in the place of another and of many others; the pains and pleasures of his species must become his own. The great instrument of moral good is the imagination; and poetry administers to the effect by acting upon the cause. Poetry enlarges the circumference of the imagination by replenishing it with thoughts of ever new delight. ... Poetry strengthens that faculty which is the organ of the moral nature of man in the same manner as exercise strengthens a limb. (J, VII, 118)

Poetry need not convey determinate messages to its audience because, in Shelley's view, poetry works our good not through the communication of specific ideas but through encouraging habits of mental activity. Of these mental habits, the most important is the exercise of the sympathetic imagination, that is, one's ability 'to put oneself in the place of another.' That 'other' need not necessarily be the poet; the object of our sympathy may be no more than the fictional beings that dance across the figured curtain of the text. Such a text can 'generate occasions' without authorial presence, for the consequence of decentring is to open the way for free play.[2] To experience, as we do through poetry, thoughts and feelings not our own is an important step toward that self-transcendence which Shelley sees as essential to making a better world. Poetry cannot solve metaphysical problems, but it can provide opportunities for imaginative play that strengthen our moral beings.

   Hellas differs from *Prometheus Unbound* only in so far as the later lyrical drama puts consciously into operation a theory that developed out of the creative practice of the earlier work. Shelley's remarks on the choruses of his second lyrical drama indicate how much his poetics had matured and the extent to which he could absorb his metaphysical skepticism into a moral and an aesthetic faith:

Let it not be supposed that I mean to dogmatize upon a subject concerning which all men are equally ignorant, or that I think the Gordian knot of the origin of evil can be disentangled by that or any similar assertions. ... That there is a true solution of the riddle, and that in our present state the solution is unattainable by us, are propositions which may be regarded as equally certain; meanwhile, as it is the province of the poet to attach himself to those ideas which exalt and ennoble humanity, let him be permitted to have conjectured the condition of that futurity towards which we are all impelled by an inextinguishable thirst for immortality. (J, III, 56)

Shelley wishes to harness the energies of human desire and direct them toward ends in this life. He does not seek for a justification of those desires or for an assurance that they will ever be satisfied, but only to activate them through the openness of his text.

We must not demand more of Shelley than, as a poet, he can possibly give. He can excite the mind and awaken desire, but its fulfilment rests with us. Nor should we expect that every desire *can* be satisfied, for desire is not boundless and at its edge awaits anxiety. There are, of course, discourses that seek to master anxiety, but Shelley's discourse does not aspire to religious or philosophical certainty; instead, he explicitly restricts 'the province of the poet' to conjecture and the discourse of uncertainty, governed only by the ethical criterion that the poet's work must 'exalt and ennoble humanity.' Shelley's choice of ideal fantasy over the imitation of life is as much moral as it is aesthetic. He writes in accord with an ethical imperative, to project models and standards 'to the likeness of which the mind is excited to aspire,' as he once noted to himself. He does not strive for truth. Even at the risk of anxiety, he hopes to make humankind superior to present circumstances by encouraging us to have a faith in ourselves and in our future. Such faith is a habit of mind built up by the exercise of a poetic faith called into play by Shelley's discourse of uncertainty.

Hellas, as Timothy Webb has observed, is a poem that invites us 'to make an act of faith in man.'[3] As an attempt to provide his reader with images of a better world, it is one of the more successful manifestations of his public poetry, a project reaching back through the triumph of *Prometheus Unbound* to the crude *Queen Mab* and the failure of *The Revolt of Islam*. The more immediate genesis of the poem, however, may well be found in a plan which Shelley mentioned to Hunt in 1820 'to publish a little volume of *popular songs* wholly political, & destined to awaken and direct the imagination of the reformers' (L, II, 191). Though maintaining this popular orientation, *Hellas* avoids the deterministic implications of the intention 'to awaken and direct' by allowing its readers to play a part in authorizing the public dream of dramatic representation. As a dream, the lyrical drama is less a piece of wish-fulfilment than an act of wish-formation and definition. It employs fantasy to lend shape to the aspirations of the Greeks and instil confidence in the inevitability of their eventual triumph. The poem is therefore less a prophecy or a call to arms than an attempt to bring the benefits of a communal dream to bear on life. *Hellas* generates an occasion for the exercise of poetic faith in which the audience is invited to suspend its disbelief in the vulnerability of Turkish rule. Its success may be measured not by the accuracy of its depiction of actual conditions but by its use of aesthetic means to generate a faith in the future that animates political courage. As Shelley wrote to Hunt, 'If faith is a virtue in any case it is so in politics rather than religion; as having a power of producing that a belief in which is at once a prophecy and a cause' (L, II, 191). Thus belief is both an end and an origin for Shelley – poetic faith is what Shelley seeks to generate in his readers in the hope that this faith will generate further consequences for the improvement of our lives. It is by such means that the dreams of the poet become the standards of our life.

Bachelard writes that 'the great poets teach us to dream – they nourish us with images.'[4] The state of dreaming is very much the subject of *Hellas* and provides its central action. What plot there is revolves about the dream of Mahmud, the Ottoman Emperor. The burden of this dream is the yearning for freedom, expressed in lyrical form by the chorus of captive Greek women at the opening of the play. Their desire for liberty is projected not only according to the rituals of Greek drama but also in metrical forms that recall the operatic choruses Shelley was so familiar with. Parallel structures, repetitions, and complex patterns of rhythm and rhyme suggest music and song:

> Breathe low, low
> The spell of the mighty mistress now!
> When Conscience lulls her sated snake,
> And Tyrants sleep, let Freedom wake.
> Breathe low – low
> The words which, like secret fire, shall flow
> Through the veins of the frozen earth – low, low!   (J, III, 20)

So disturbed is the slumbering tyrant by the 'secret fire' that burns within the words of the chorus that he suddenly starts from his sleep, half-expecting that this dream of threatened revolt induced by the singing of his slaves will carry over into waking existence. Finally coming fully awake, he is most relieved to find that 'the truth of day lightens upon my dream / And I am Mahmud still' (J, III, 23). Nevertheless, he remains more deeply affected by the fantasies of night than by 'the truth of day.' He cannot rest until he learns the meaning of his dream. He sends for Ahasuerus, a Jew (whom Shelley had cast as the Wandering Jew in his earliest work), because ''tis said his tribe / Dream, and are wise interpreters of dreams' (J, III 23–4). Hoping to master his restless thoughts by finding a clear and distinct interpretation of them, he seeks not nourishment from his dream but to repress its power by reducing it to 'the truth of day.'

The second chorus of *Hellas* is a comment on the folly of thus trying to fix meanings. The captive women do not flinch from the Heraclitan flux of human experience:

> Worlds on worlds are rolling ever
>> From creation to decay,
> Like the bubbles on a river
>> Sparkling, bursting, borne away.
> But they are still immortal
> Who, through birth's orient portal
> And death's dark chasm hurrying to and fro,
>> Clothe their unceasing flight
>> In the brief dust and light
> Gather'd round their chariots as they go;
>> New shapes they still may weave,
>> New Gods, new laws receive,
> Bright or dim are they, as the robes they last
>> On Death's bare ribs had cast.   (J, III, 25–6)

They accept the stream of life with lyric joy, and seek to shape meanings within it, even though these meanings may be no more lasting or substantial than 'bubbles on a river.' These meanings are constantly shifting configurations glimpsed in 'the brief dust and light' thrown up by the relentless progress of the 'chariot' of life. The imagery that these lines have in common with *The Triumph of Life* suggests a way in which the last poems of Shelley can be seen to comment on one another. Like the leading characters in Shelley's final vision, Mahmud tries to master his anxiety by trying to locate a meaning beyond the rolling stream of life.

Unlike Mahmud, the women are not disturbed by this fluidity of meanings; instead, they seize upon the free play of signifiers as an opportunity for liberation, in which they are permitted to 'weave' new meanings and new authorities. These women, like Cythna in *The Revolt of Islam*, have laid aside the patriarchal dominance of fixed referential meanings in favour of a 'subtler language' that constantly weaves and reweaves new meanings out of the material that experience endlessly provides. Their success is measured not by standards of fixed and eternal 'truth' but by the effectiveness with which they clothe Death at any one moment in 'the robes' verbally woven out of their faith in life.

Lacking such a faith, Mahmud yearns for certainty. He wants above all to fix the meaning of his dream outside of life in some determinate 'fate' or destiny that must surely be his. His strategic error is his insistence on trying to extract some 'truth' from an experience that can offer only uncertainty, and his tactical mistake is the surrender of his own autonomy as an imaginative being to the authority of the Jew. Taking at face value the popular notion that Ahasuerus and 'his tribe ... are wise interpreters of dreams,' Mahmud is defeated on the psychological battlefield even while his troops score victories in the actual war. Abandoning the task of interpretation to another, he re-enacts the downfall of Nebuchadnezzar, another oppressor who demanded to know the 'meaning' of his dream. Ahasuerus is another Daniel, who it will be remembered was called upon to 'explain' the dreams of his Babylonian overlord. Like Mahmud, Nebuchadnezzar awakens from restless visions to find his spirit 'troubled to know the dream' and calls upon the prophet to provide him with 'the interpretation thereof' (Daniel 2:3–6). When Daniel offers his interpretion, he presents it as 'the decree of the most High' (Daniel 4:24), and Nebuchadnezzar has no alternative but to accept such a centre of authority. Having surrendered his mind to another, the king becomes a victim of his own imaginative fecklessness and ends up acting out the 'fate' Daniel has assigned to him. That the Babylonian monarch was 'driven from men, and did eat grass as oxen' is less a sign that his dream has been fulfilled than a symbol of his bestial abasement before the interpretive power of another. He thus 'becomes what he contemplates' not only in the empirical sense that he lives out the imputed meaning of his dream but also in the psychological sense that he succumbs to the contemplated powers of another rather than trusting 'the precious portents of his own powers.' Like Nebuchadnezzar, Mahmud presents an allegory of the type of reading Shelley had put behind him in *Mont Blanc*, but which reasserts itself in the Rousseau figure of *The Triumph of Life*. The 'Power' and the authority vested in it reside not beyond the stream of life but in our own imaginings about the transient phenomena that arise like bubbles on its surface.

The character of Ahasuerus, as Shelley imagines it, is not, however, exhaustively explained by the analogue with his Biblical counterpart. Unlike Daniel, Shelley's Jew forswears the authority of the supernatural and the exercise of psychological dominance through the power of words. Ahasuerus does not claim to be delivering the verdict of 'the most High' upon Mahmud. Instead, Shelley explains Mahmud's demoralization strictly in terms of his own reactive psychology:

I have preferred to represent the Jew as disclaiming all pretension, or even belief, in supernatural agency, and as tempting Mahmud to that state of mind in which ideas may be supposed to assume the force of sensation, through the confusion of thought with the objects of thought, and excess of passion animating the creations of the imagination. It is a sort of natural magic. ...

(J, III, 57)

Mahmud is not persuaded, convinced, or deceived by Ahasuerus; rather, the latter merely encourages in the tyrant 'that state of mind' in which he deceives himself. The phantasmal vision Mahmud beholds and in which he reads signs of his defeat is no more than the workings of his own mind, though because he is so alienated from himself he confuses his own mental activity with the 'truth' of reality. Mahmud is changed not by rhetoric but by his reactions to his own experiences, much like the characters in *The Tempest*, a play that was much on Shelley's mind during his most creative years. Like Prospero, Ahasuerus works his 'natural magic' indirectly upon his antagonist, until Mahmud convinces himself, all unawares, of a potential reality. Ahasuerus seems to be recalling Prospero's famous speech ending the revels (which was a special favourite of Shelley's) when he tries to explain to Mahmud the primacy of thought amid the flux of sensation:

> ... this Whole
> Of suns, and worlds, and men, and beasts, and flowers,
> With all the silent or tempestuous workings
> By which they have been, are, or cease to be,
> Is but a vision; – all that it inherits

Are motes of a sick eye, bubbles and dreams;
Thought its cradle and its grave, nor less
The Future and the Past are idle shadows
Of thought's eternal flight – they have no being;
Nought is but that which feels itself to be.   (J, III, 43–4)

Likewise, Prospero dismisses the revels by revealing 'the baseless fabric of this vision' and by acknowledging that the world of experience he has conjured up and 'all which it inherit' (compare 'all that it inherits' above) are no more than an 'insubstantial pageant' (IV, i, 148–58). No more than Prospero does Ahasuerus resist the decreation of his 'visions'; both are willing to call their respective discourses into question, for they are confident that the value of their creations lies not in their 'truth' but in what each 'gives or teaches.'

For both these fictional natural magicians, as for Shelley, poetic discourse has a value for the moral lives of human beings even though it may be readily deconstructed to reveal the rules of its production. Indeed, this authenticity with respect to the conditions of its being may be its greatest strength. An artifice which admits its insubstantiality, it cannot be said to deceive; rather, it creates circumstances in which thought is invited to exercise itself. Instead of using the power of his words to conquer Mahmud, Ahasuerus merely generates an occasion in which Mahmud convinces himself of the inevitability of his own defeat. Mahmud reads on 'the curtain of futurity' signs of his own downfall just as the Greek women read there signs of their victory, neither recognizing in these 'bubbles and dreams' the shadows cast on life by their own imaginings. Reading the same signs, they each make an interpretation appropriate to themselves. They each find a meaning in their experiences, never realizing that these meanings are partial and complementary. But in all cases, that partial meaning is sufficient to influence their lives, their hopes, and their state of mind.

In the bubbles that rise on the stream of life, the captive Greeks read a message that sustains their dreams of freedom. As Mahmud's partial understanding of the desire for liberation leads to his own demoralization, so their partial understanding of its meaning leads to their gathering strength. In a lyric outburst of hope and desire, they project the inevitability of their triumph;

> The world's great age begins anew,
> The golden years return,

The earth doth like a snake renew
Her winter weeds outworn:
Heaven smiles, and faith and empires gleam,
Like wrecks of a dissolving dream.

A brighter Hellas rears its mountains
From waves serener far. ...   (J, III, 52)

The vibrant musical choruses of *Hellas* contrast sharply with the tormented and relatively prosaic dialogue of the Turks. It is appropriate
that musical effects are confined to the speeches of the chorus, for they
alone project the communal dream of a renovated and liberated world.
But in pursuing their partial vision of the future, the chorus lends a
dimension to dreaming activity that was wholly lacking in the case of
Mahmud. The orderly, harmonious, and formal elements of their discourse that contribute to its musical quality produce effects that transcend meaning. A verbal projection of their desire, the music of their
verse so delights the reader as to suspend the quest for meaning, partial
or otherwise. In the play of this subtler language, we are preoccupied
less by the possible references of words than by the pleasure their pat-
terned arrangement gives rise to in the experience of reading. This
delight in the order of discourse issues in a climactic and exuberant joy
that diverts us from meaning to jouissance. It does not satisfy our will
to know, but nevertheless releases a puissant psychic energy that has
consequences for the way we live our lives. This subtler order of poetic
language arouses us to an act of faith in the vision the chorus projects:

Another Athens shall arise,
    And to remoter time
Bequeath, like sunset to the skies,
    The splendour of its prime.   (J, III, 53)

Shelley's lyrical drama, then, stops short of the serious business of
meaning and asks us to be content with the orderly play of signs. It
offers possibilities for formulating partial meanings in our own acts of
interpretation, but it never promises to deliver a total meaning that
can be fixed and determined. Indeed, the final chorus of *Hellas* warns
us against forcing the drama's fragile prophetic vision toward ultimate
conclusions:

> O cease! must hate and death return?
> Cease! must men kill and die?
> Cease! drain not to its dregs the urn
> Of bitter prophecy.   (J, III, 53)

The poem is finally only a poem and does not claim to put a stop to time, change, and the evils of this world. It simply invites us to join in imaginative play, in the hope that by engaging in this particular language game our spirits might be exercised and renewed, so that we can return refreshed to the struggles of existence. Those struggles are not abolished by the poem, nor is the anxiety which they entail, but a text like *Hellas* can at least rekindle our desire to engage them.

Just as Mahmud's anxiety to wrest from his dream a clear meaning leads to frustration and demoralization, so in the last poem Shelley was to write the figure of Rousseau can read in life only signs of his own defeat. *The Triumph of Life*, which was left unfinished at the time of Shelley's unfortunate death, is sometimes regarded as the poet's recantation, an admission of poetic defeat, and 'an approach to silence.'[5] Yet the poem's very incompleteness is itself suggestive, and ought to serve as a warning against drawing overly definite conclusions from fragmentary evidence.

The tendency to regard *The Triumph of Life* as the terminus of Shelley's career reflects a need in many critical readers to impose the sort of final narrative closure on his life that Shelley always resisted in his art. Implicit in this approach to the poet is the unstated and wholly unwarranted assumption that his death was not an accident, or, at least, that his death happened at an opportune moment, that is, at the very time that he lost his faith in poetry. Even though *Hellas* was the last poem Shelley published during his lifetime, it has become a commonplace of Shelley criticism to read *The Triumph* as if it were more than in the purely chronological sense Shelley's 'last' poem, but was in some way Shelley's farewell to his art. Yet there is no evidence to show that the sudden storm in which Shelley went down and the writing of *The Triumph* were more than merely coincidental. Shelley's career 'ended' only because he drowned, and not because he was overwhelmed with despair over the inadequacy of language or the falsity of his vision. *The Triumph of Life* is not the palinode to Shelley's career, nor is it the herald of a new stage in his work; instead, it is a detour from the main line of his successful work in the public voice, a regression to an earlier stage of perplexity, and ultimately a dead end, poetically speaking.

The Triumph of Life is a poem of the private voice, a personal meditation on the complexities of existence in a far from perfect world that recalls *Alastor*. Both poems bring to the surface that fundamental skepticism that was a constant option for him but which his greatest poems overcome. Poems such as *Prometheus Unbound* and *Hellas* project desire outward so that it can be shared, employing the form of the lyrical drama in which the play of illusion authorizes itself in the activity of the audience. A failure to suspend disbelief, however, is often characteristic of those poems that project desire inward. The wish to trace back to its origins the stream of life is evident in both *Alastor* and *The Triumph*, and in both the quest for truth and total meaning ends in futility.

The processional spectacle offered in *The Triumph of Life* presents itself as a vast scene of reading. Both Rousseau and the speaker of the poem contemplate what Shelley once described as 'that mixture of energy and error which is called a Triumph' (L, II, 86), and seek to interpret its significance:

> 'And what is this?
> Whose shape is that within the car? And why – '
>
> I would have added – 'is all here amiss?' –
> But a voice answered – 'Life!' (J, IV, 173)

The voice, we soon learn, belongs to Rousseau. He too interrogates an indefinite 'shape' in the poem, though he imputes more authority to the beautiful 'Shape all light' than the poem's speaker does to the shape of the charioteer:

> If as does seem,
> Thou comest from the realm without a name
>
> Into this valley of perpetual dream
> Show whence I came, and where I am, and why –
> Pass not away upon the passing stream. (J, IV, 180)

Even as he seeks to plumb the meaning of his existence, the shape eludes Rousseau. It recedes along life's 'passing stream,' miming the process of endless deferral. Rousseau, however, yearns for a stable and ultimate 'realm without a name' beyond life's processes, a fixed origin which will explain the mystery of his being. Similarly, the speaker locates a realm of absolute being beyond the passing show of this life to which certain favoured spirits have won access:

> the sacred few who could not tame
> Their spirits to the conquerors ...
>
> Fled back like eagles to their native noon.   (J, IV, 171)

Both Rousseau and his interlocutor posit a realm that transcends life, even as the triumphal procession rolls on before them indifferent to their wishes. Repeatedly, the images of the poem call into question the existence of this fixed centre beyond life.

Though the image of Life's chariot leading the procession of human history dominates the poem, it should not be allowed to obscure the poem's insistent analogies between life and a river. Before the figure of the chariot comes into focus, the poet sees 'a great stream / Of people ... hurrying to and fro,' and notes that in this stream 'old age and youth, manhood and infancy, / Mixed in one mighty torrent did appear' (J, IV, 168–9). Later, we learn how 'Imperial Rome poured forth her living sea' (J, IV, 171), even after this 'great stream' of life has resolved itself into the image of the rolling chariot. What the poem's two alternative metaphors for life have in common is their sense of inexorable, unidirectional motion, a flow and a progress that cannot be resisted and in which all are immersed. Those 'sacred few' who escape life's traumas do so by rejecting life and embracing death. For the rest, ordinary mortals like Shelley and ourselves who must live within the stream of life if we are to live at all, it is in life's brief passage alone that we seek for meaning. 'Borne onward ... like bubbles on an eddying flood' (J, IV, 182), humankind is immersed in a series of experiences not unlike those similarly described in *Hellas*:

> Worlds on worlds are rolling ever
> From creation to decay;
> Like the bubbles on a river
> Sparkling, bursting, borne away.   (J, III, 25)

So long as we remain alive and refrain from joining the 'sacred few,' we must make a choice. We can either content ourselves with the 'bubbles and dreams' of experience as the Hellenic chorus does, or we can, as Mahmud does, attempt to burst those bubbles and interpret those

dreams in search of their essential and determinate inner content. It is
on just such a quest for unconditional meaning that the chief speakers
of *The Triumph of Life* have embarked, just as the youth in *Alastor*
pursued the visionary maid. Indeed, the inquiring spirits of both poems
express themselves in hauntingly similar forms. Confronted with the
mystery of life, the speaker in *The Triumph* gropes toward the meaning of what he sees:

> Struck to the heart by this sad pageantry,
> Half to myself I said – 'And what is this?
> Whose shape is that within the car? And why?'   (J, IV, 173)

Likewise, the young poet in *Alastor* embarks on his journey upriver
filled with 'obstinate questionings':

> O stream!
> Whose source is inaccessibly profound,
> Whither do thy mysterious waters tend?
> Thou imagest my life.   (J, I, 191)

It is no doubt the recognition of parallels like these, that has led some
recent deconstructive readers of the poem to believe that '*The Triumph of Life* is a revision rather than a reversal of *Alastor*.'[6] Far from
being a climactic effort, Shelley's 'last' poem is a retreat from the confidence of his public poetry toward the doubts and fears he so frequently expresses during times of stress throughout his career.

As he had when he wrote *Alastor*, Shelley felt isolated and neglected
when he began to compose *The Triumph of Life*. Writing on the 25th
of January, 1822, he confided to Leigh Hunt the anxiety he felt over the
reception of his recent publications:

Pray tell me if Ollier has published *Hellas* and what effect was produced by
Adonais. My faculties are shaken to atoms & torpid. I can write nothing, & if
Adonais had no success & excited no interest what incentive can I have to
write? (L, II, 382)

Shelley's concern for the 'effect' of his poems underscores his pragmatic motivations as a writer. If so calculated and conventional a work
of art as *Adonais* failed to find an audience, what hope could Shelley
have for his more subtle and unorthodox lyrical dramas? His 'incen-

tive' for writing was so bound up in winning over an audience that his immediate failure to do so called into question his whole poetic enterprise. Had Shelley lived beyond thirty, though, this depression of spirits would undoubtedly have passed as his appreciative readership grew to embrace not just the educated middle classes but also the working men's societies who were inspired by his political poems. *The Triumph of Life* is the product of a time of temporary setback, and represents a phase in his career that he could easily have put behind him had he lived. There is no reason to believe that he could not recapture the mood of his lyrical dramas, as he had done before, and once again recover his poetic faith.

Nevertheless, *The Triumph* is still symptomatic of one deep-seated and persistent strain in Shelley's temperament, the tendency to skeptical doubt. An uncertainty about the ultimate nature of life and the world is characteristic of his thought whenever, as he puts it in the *Essay on Life*, we 'look down the dark abyss of how little we know.' However, skepticism dominates his poetry only when he indulges his self-analytical and introspective private voice. When he turns desire inward, its energy is invariably stymied, because it is a desire that demands to be satisfied. So long as desire is given free play in the disseminative activity of his public voice it remains unfocused, but when even in his public poems desire fixes on a determinate object it leads to an impasse. Such is the case with *Adonais*, in which (as we have seen) the desire for immortality becomes of overriding concern. This focusing of desire toward realization gives rise to a quest for ultimate meaning in *Adonais* that is phrased in questions very similar to the demand for origins in *Alastor* and *The Triumph of Life*:

> Whence are we, and why are we? of what scene
> The actors of spectators?
>
> (*Adonais*; J, II, 395)

In the sort of discourse Shelley is pursuing, such ultimate questions are undecidable. Whenever he invites his reader to put aside delight in the play of signifiers for the sake of pursuing a final and total meaning in some field of metaphysical reference beyond poetic language, Shelley is least satisfactory as a poet.

Shelley indicated his own awareness of this fault when he wrote to John Gisborne only three weeks before his death, once again expressing his concern for the way in which his most recent publications were

faring. Using the terminology of mortality and eternity in which the
religious metaphysics of his age habitually expressed itself, he admits
his increasing distrust of trying to recover some ultimately signified
truth from the flux of experience:

I think one is always in love with something or other; the error and I confess it
is not easy for spirits encased in flesh and blood to avoid it, consists in seeking
in a mortal image the likeness of what is perhaps eternal. (L, II, 434)

This common human failing is what poisons the life of Rousseau in
The Triumph. Aroused to love by the form of the 'Shape all light,' he is
not content to enjoy the effects of the Shape's beauty. Instead, he
allows his desire for the beautiful to be transformed into the will to
know:

> ... like day she came,
> Making the night a dream; and ere she ceased
>
> To move, as one between desire and shame
> Suspended, I said – If, as it doth seem,
> Thou comest from the realm without a name
>
> Into this valley of perpetual dream,
> Show whence I came, and where I am, and why –
> Pass not away upon the passing stream.   (J, IV, 180)

Rousseau's desire is tinged with shame when he asks more of a purely
aesthetic experience than it can possibly give. He is unwilling simply
to enjoy the stimulus the Shape offers, demanding instead that it give
him a solution to the ultimate mystery of his existence. This is the
'particular seduction' of Rousseau by the quest for total meaning of
which de Man writes, when he says that *The Triumph of Life* is
marked by 'the transition from pleasure to signification, from the
aesthetic to the semiological dimension.'[7] Rousseau insists on trying
to name 'the realm without a name' in order to valorize the 'perpetual
dream' of life, never understanding that signification is an activity that
can only be conducted while immersed in 'the passing stream' of life.
The Shape itself means him no harm; instead, the way he insists on
reading it is what works to deprive him of his happiness.
    As readers, both the speaker and Rousseau are dismayed when they

can find no more than traces of meaning rather than meaning itself. The speaker is troubled by the inevitable loss that results when individuals are swept away in the progress of life's course:

> the chariot hath
> Passed over them – no other trace I find
> But as of foam after the ocean's wrath
>
> Is spent upon the desert shore   (J, IV, 172)

This evanescence seems totally debilitating to a consciousness that cannot accept change and uncertainty. Rousseau, too, is shattered when the traces of a meaning he clings to are similarly washed away by the tides of life:

> And suddenly my brain became as sand
>
> Where the first wave had more than half erased
> The track of deer on desert Labrador;
> Whilst the wolf, from which they fled amazed,
>
> Leaves his stamp visibly upon the shore,
> Until the second bursts; – so on my sight
> Burst a new vision, never seen before   (J, IV, 180–1)

This constant ebb and flow of signs is imaged again in terms of moving water, when Rousseau describes how he was caught up in life's stream:

> all like bubbles on an eddying flood
> Fell into the same track at last, and were
>
> Borne onward – I among the multitude
> Was swept.   (J, IV, 182)

Waves, bubbles, and foam image the constant movement and insubstantiality of life's meanings in the poem, meanings that recede as soon as they appear on the surface, leaving only slight traces behind at the same time as new meanings are formed. Because meanings are borne away like bubbles on the stream of life, Rousseau finds Life unreadable. As he complains, Life is a text which reflects only our hopes and fears, but not one which surrenders meaning:

> Figures ever new
> Rise on the bubble, paint them as you may;
> We have but thrown, as those before us threw,
>
> Our shadows on it as it passed away.   (J, IV, 175)

He does not value the shifting and partial meanings that float like 'bubbles' upon life's stream, nor can he take any delight in playing with their airy insubstantiality. He wishes only to burst them in order to retrieve some supposed essence he thinks they must enclose. Because he has none of the mental agility of the chorus in *Hellas*, Rousseau sees all of the error and none of the energy in life's triumphal procession.

Similarly, the troubled poet who with Rousseau observes life's progress seeks to stem its flow in order to wrest from it some final meaning. So baffled is he by what he has seen that, despite Rousseau's exhaustive attempt to explain what has passed before them, he persists in asking the very question which all along has defied an answer:

> 'Then, what is life?' I cried. –   (J, IV, 185)

Despite ingenious attempts to explain the fragmentary few lines following that have been rescued from the manuscript, this question properly marks the end of the poem.[8] The poet, like the reader, reaches a dead end when he demands that some determinate signified must arise from his experience. The text of life, like the text of poems, is a rich web of implication that cannot be reduced to a single meaning. At best, we must content ourselves with partial meanings that arise in the experience of both living and reading. As Derrida remarks of *The Triumph of Life*, its 'essential unfinishedness cannot be reduced to inadequacy or incompleteness,' and that is primarily because the poem reflects the 'essential unfinishedness' of living.[9] *The Triumph of Life* ends where it does because Shelley cannot and never could answer the question posed there; yet this ending does generate a sort of conclusion. The fragmentary form of the poem is one of its meanings. Because life's 'triumph' is a procession that highlights process, its final meaning must always remain incomplete and uncertain; attempting out of anxiety to arrest its flow in order to fix meanings and achieve certainty is to risk the triumph of life over one's vain desires.

Though the poem concludes with the suggestion that the quest for final meaning is doomed to failure, it does not therefore discourage us from pursuing meaning as an activity. The play of potential meanings generated in the unending process of reading is a paradigm for the unfinishedness of our own lives. So long as we can enjoy the pursuit of these possibilities for their own sake without yearning for ultimate satisfaction, we can take delight in the continuing process of our own lives. The language game of poetry does not generate fixed meanings; rather it 'generates occasions' in which we the readers are stimulated to play the game of interpretation. It is we and not the poet who must supply a pattern of meanings satisfactory for the moment to ourselves. This fundamental conviction of the reader's autonomy and activity is illustrated by the elaborate allegory of reading that is the Cave of Demogorgon in *Prometheus Unbound*. There, Asia learns that 'truth' is not to be retrieved from the depths but is a construct authorized by the activity of each reader's interpretive consciousness:

> ASIA
> Who is the master of the slave?
> DEMOGORGON
> If the abysm
> Could vomit forth its secrets. ... But a voice
> Is wanting, the deep truth is imageless. ...
> ASIA
> So much I asked before, and my heart gave
> The response thou hast given; and of such truths
> Each to itself must be the oracle.   (J, II, 221)

No more than a bubble does the poem contain the 'deep truth' within itself; but gazing on the play of signifiers about its surface, we may see reflected there some truths about ourselves.

I have argued that the essence of Shelley's poetics lies less in his view of what poetry is than what poetry does. In his *Defence of Poetry*, he praises a discourse that

arrests the vanishing apparitions which haunt the interlunations of life and, veiling them, or in language or in form, sends them forth among mankind, bearing sweet news of kindred joy to those with whom their sisters abide.

(J, VII, 137)

We must learn to read the figures that 'rise on the bubble' even as they burst, and take joy in their continual creation, decreation, and recreation. As inhabitants of a verbal universe, we cannot escape situations in which our desire to know is met by anxiety or uncertainty. *The Triumph of Life* enacts this dialectic of desire and anxiety that is at the heart of Shelley's poetry, for it expresses what Derrida calls a 'desire for the center,' a desire for a reassuring certitude with which anxiety can be mastered. [10] However, the poem deconstructs this desire by failing to find any centre of authority outside the stream of life. Because the interpretation of any chain of signifiers is only another chain of signifiers, we must acknowledge that meaning is endlessly borne away from us each time that we reach for it. But that in itself is a useful lesson, for even in an age of deconstruction poetry may still teach us how to live. The deferrals and indeterminacies encountered in the reading process prepare us to cope with the uncertainties of our lives, and experiencing the limits of the language of desire helps us to accept the limitations of life in this world.

Notes

CHAPTER ONE

1 *The Complete Works of Percy Bysshe Shelley*, ed. Roger Ingpen and
  Walter E. Peck (the Julian edition in 10 volumes; London: Ernest Benn,
  1926-30), III, 182. All references to Shelley's poetry and prose, excluding
  his letters, are to this edition, which will be cited in the text and notes
  as J.
2 *The Letters of Percy Bysshe Shelley*, ed. Frederick L. Jones (2 vols.;
  Oxford: Clarendon Press, 1964), I, 335. All references to Shelley's letters
  are to this edition, which will be cited in the text and notes as L. Note
  that Shelley originally wrote 'infidel' rather than 'skeptic'; see *Shelley
  and His Circle: 1773-1822*, ed. K.N. Cameron and Donald H. Reiman (6
  vols.; Cambridge: Harvard University Press, 1961-73), III, 109.
3 Chief among them have been C.E. Pulos, in *The Deep Truth: A Study of
  Shelley's Skepticism* (Lincoln: University of Nebraska Press, 1971); Earl
  Wasserman, in his *Shelley: A Critical Reading* (Baultimore: Johns Hopkins University Press, 1971), writes that 'it is from Pulos' analysis ...
  that any study of Shelley's thought must begin' (p. 136n.). Stuart Curran,
  in *Shelley's Annus Mirabilis: The Maturing of an Epic Vision* (San
  Marino: Huntington Library, 1975), shifted the ground slightly when he
  observed of Shelley's Italian period that 'a brave and unostentatious skepticism informs every major poem' (p. 82). This trend of critical thinking
  reaches its logical conclusion in Lloyd Abbey's *Destroyer and Preserver:
  Shelley's Poetic Skepticism* (Lincoln: University of Nebraska Press,
  1979), a study intended 'to show that skepticism is both the central
  theme of Shelley's poetry and the primary cause of its artistic excellence'
  (p. ix).

4 Sir Philip Sidney, *A Defence of Poesy*, ed. Dorothy M. Macardle (London: Macmillan, 1963), p. 33. Walter R. Davis, in *Idea and Act in Elizabethan Fiction* (Princeton: Princeton University Press, 1969), writes that in his *Defence* Sidney 'squarely faces the problem of imaginative fiction' (p. 28).

5 Edmund Husserl, in *Logical Investigations*, trans. J.N. Finlay (2 vols.; London: Routledge and Kegan Paul, 1970), says, for example, that 'the function of a word is to awaken a sense-conferring act in ourselves, to point to what is intended ... in this act, and to guide our interest exclusively in this direction' (I, 282). Maurice Merleau-Ponty, in *Phenomenology of Perception*, trans. Colin Smith (New York: Humanities Press, 1962), maintains that 'the hidden art of the imagination ... forms the basis of the unity of consciousness' and adds that our 'inner life is an inner language ... alive with words' (pp. xvii, 183).

6 Ludwig Wittgenstein, in *On Certainty* (Oxford: Blackwell's, 1969), pp. 52, 59, 66, and 74, ponders the relation of what he calls 'language-games' to our experience of reality. Northrop Frye, in *Anatomy of Criticism* (Princeton: Princeton University Press, 1957), defines the language game of literature as follows: 'Literary meaning may best be described, perhaps, as hypothetical. ... In literature, questions of fact or truth are subordinated to the primary literary aim of producing a structure of words for its own sake' (p. 74). John Dewey, in *The Quest for Certainty* (New York: Minton, Balch, 1929), thinks that 'judgment or belief regarding actions to be performed can never attain more than a precarious probability' (p. 6). Dewey replaces truth with the idea of probability because he is forced to admit that 'every proposition concerning truth is really in the last analysis hypothetical and provisional'; see *Philosophy and Civilization* (New York: G.P. Putnam's Sons, 1931), p. 24.

7 See Fredric Jameson, *The Prison-House of Language: A Critical Account of Structuralism and Russian Formalism* (Princeton: Princeton University Press, 1972), especially p. 140: 'Our possession by language, which "writes" us even as we imagine ourselves to be writing it, is not so much some ultimate release from bourgeois subjectivism, but rather a limiting situation against which we must struggle at every instant.'

8 Jacques Derrida, *Dissemination*, trans. Barbara Johnson (Chicago: University of Chicago Press, 1981), p. 63, where he also urges (p. 64) that 'the reading and writing supplement must be rigorously prescribed, but by the necessities of a game, by the logic of play.' On the extent to which deconstruction is defined by disclosing the rules governing the text, see Jameson, *The Prison-House of Language*, p. 136, and Frank Lentricchia,

After the New Criticism (Chicago: University of Chicago Press, 1980), p. 176.

9 For the Romantics, 'the chaos of the universe was fertile rather than destructive. ... Life, and the ironic artistic process that actively partici- pates in life, is play,' writes Anne Mellor in *English Romantic Irony* (Cambridge: Harvard University Press, 1980), p. 24. She suggests (p. 73) that the authenticity of the Romantic ironist depends on the fact that he 'is constantly moving, creating and decreating his fictive world.'

10 Mikhail Bakhtin, *The Dialogical Imagination*, trans. Caryl Emerson and Michael Holmquist (Austin: University of Texas Press, 1981), p. 284.

11 Discussing the part played by the functions of 'competence,' 'convention,' and 'naturalization' in the reader's relationship to the insti- tution of literature, Jonathan Culler, in *Structuralist Poetics* (Ithaca: Cor- nell University Press, 1975), remarks (p. 107). that 'meaning is ... an activity to be pursued' rather than something 'already there ... to be recovered.' Wittgenstein likewise sees meaning as arising in the context of human activity, when he notes in his *Philosophical Investigations*, trans. G.E.M. Anscombe (Oxford: Blackwell's, 1963), p. 43, 'the meaning of a word is its use in language,' and again, p. 212e, when he says, 'To interpret is to think, to do something. ... Let the use teach you the mean- ing.'

12 Ludwig Wittgenstein, *On Certainty*, p. 49. Roman Ingarden, in *The Liter- ary Work of Art*, trans. George G. Grabowicz (Evanston: Northwestern University Press, 1973), p. 126, shows how shared word meanings enable literary works to become intersubjective intentional objects. Jacques Bar- zun, in *Classic, Romantic, and Modern*, (Boston: Little, Brown, 1961), p.68, relates intersubjectivity ('experiences that are shared') to Romanti- cism.

13 See John Dewey, *Philosophy and Civilization*, pp. 17–22; Dewey here and elsewhere reformulates William James's 'humanistic' pragmatism as 'instrumentalism,' which he describes (p. 35) as 'a faith in intelligence as the one and indispensable belief necessary to moral and social life.' Ken- neth Burke, who in *The Philosophy of Literary Form* (2nd ed.; Baton Rouge: Louisiana State University Press, 1967) calls his critical mode 'pragmatic' (p. 89), describes poetry as 'equipment for living' (p. 61). M.H. Abrams provides an historical survey of pragmatic critical theory in *The Mirror and the Lamp* (New York: Oxford University Press, 1953), pp. 14–21. William James formulated pragmatism as a philosophy reconciling the conflicting demands of fact and faith, of empiricism and idealism, which are the very traditions Abrams found 'imperfectly assimilated' in

Shelley's aesthetics (p. 126). James's dialectical resolution of these traditions in *Pragmatism* (New York: Longman, Green, 1907), pp. 9–33, seems more appropriate to Shelley, as Donald Reiman acknowledges in *Percy Bysshe Shelley* (New Tork: Twayne Publishers, 1969) when he writes that, for Shelley, 'systems are at best pragmatic constructs that come to terms with the most troublesome data of experience' (p. 113).

14 Jacques Derrida, in discussion following 'Structure, Sign, and Play in the Discourse of the Human Sciences,' in *The Languages of Criticism and the Sciences of Man*, ed. Richard Macksey and Eugenio Donato (Baltimore: Johns Hopkins University Press, 1970), p. 271.

15 Mikhail Bakhtin, *The Dialogical Imagination*, pp. 270–2.

16 T.S. Eliot, *The Three Voices of Poetry* (London: Cambridge University Press, 1953), pp. 19–20. His discussion of the lyric, epic, and dramatic voices (pp. 4–12) may owe something to the distinctions Hegel drew among epic, lyric, and dramatic poetry in his *Aesthetics: Lectures on Fine Art*, trans. T.M. Knox (2 vols.: Oxford: Clarendon Press, 1975), II, 1037–9.

17 James Joyce, *The Portrait of the Artist as Young Man* (London: Jonathan Cape, 1968), p. 218. Joyce's distinctions parallel Hegel's, although they have their roots in scholasticism; see Maurice Beebe, 'Joyce and Aquinas: The Theory of Aethetics,' *Philological Quarterly*, 36 (1957), 22n., and H.M. McLuhan, 'Joyce, Aquinas, and the Poetic Process,' *Renascence*, 4 (1951), 3–11.

18 Kenneth Burke writes in *The Philosophy of Literary Form* that observations about form are most meaningful when they take into account 'the *functioning* of a structure' as what he calls 'tactics for the attainment of the game's purpose' (p. 74). His approach might seem less 'idiosyncratic' when it is remembered that it was a fundamental assumption of the Prague Circle that the study of literature is the study of the functional structure of the text; see, for example, 'Thèses presentées au Premier Congrès des Philologues Slaves,' in *Travaux du Cercle Linguistique du Prague*, 1 (1929), 7: 'La langue est un système de moyens d'expressions appropriées à un but.' Burke's view that 'a poem's structure is to be described most accurately by thinking always of the poem's function' (p. 89) is the basis of pragmatic (or rhetorical) criticism.

CHAPTER TWO

1 Cf. Paul de Man's discussion of the functional implications of intentional objects in *Blindness and Insight* (New York: Oxford University Press, 1971), p. 25.

2 M.H. Abrams, *The Mirror and the Lamp*, p. 48.
3 Jacques Derrida, *La voix et le phenomène* (Paris: Presses Universitaires de France, 1967), p. 34.
4 Walter J. Ong, in 'The Writer's Audience Is Always a Fiction,' *PMLA*, 90 (1975), 9–21, examines 'the practice of orienting a work, and thereby its readers, by writing it at least purportedly for a specific person or persons' (p. 18).
5 K.N. Cameron, *The Young Shelley: Genesis of a Radical* (New York: Macmillan, 1950), p. 28.
6 A.M.D. Hughes, in *The Nascent Mind of Shelley* (Oxford: Clarendon Press, 1947), p. 36, comments on 'the titanic philosophy' of the novels.
7 Richard Holmes, in *Shelley: The Pursuit* (New York: E.P. Dutton, 1975), p. 124, observes that 'Shelley's Irish expedition lay within the context of what was, by 1812, almost a venerable tradition of co-operation between Irish Freedom fighters, English Whig aristocrats of the liberal wing and radical and revolutionary intellectuals of the nineties.'
8 Earl Wasserman, in *Shelley: A Critical Reading*, firmly interprets Shelley's tentative remarks on 'the one mind' (J, VI, 196) in strictly metaphysical rather than social or linguistic terms when he states that Shelley's 'monistic idealism ... identifies the One Mind with Existence' (p. 147). His resolve to use capitalized terminology without the authority of Shelley's text is symptomatic of his determination to reify Shelley's concepts and give them a transcendental reference; see, for example, his claim (p. 179) that Shelley is 'inclined to deny the ultimate reality of individual identity and to consider the individual a factor or passive agent of some transcendent One.'
9 Lucien Goldman's concept of 'genetic structuralism' introduces language as the means by which intersubjective cultural structures come into being; see his 'Structure: Human Reality and Methodological Concept,' in *The Languages of Criticism and the Sciences of Man*, pp. 99–101.
10 For a discussion of Shelley's disagreement with Godwin on this important point, see Richard Holmes, *Shelley*, pp. 129–30.
11 Holmes, *Shelley*, p. 125.
12 'In the order of spoken or written discourse,' says Derrida, in *Positions*, trans. Alan Bass (Chicago: University of Chicago Press, 1981), p. 26, 'nothing ... is anywhere ever simply present or absent. There are only, everywhere, differences and traces of traces.'
13 Noting that '*Queen Mab* is a rhetorical poem,' Donald Reiman, in *Percy Bysshe Shelley* (pp. 29–30), thoroughly describes the narrative development of the poem. For the distinction between symbolic acts and practical acts, see Kenneth Burke, *The Philosophy of Literary Form*, pp. 8–9.

14 In *The Rhetoric of Fiction* (Chicago: University of Chicago Press, 1961),
Wayne Booth (speaking of D.H. Lawrence) describes a similar difficulty
arising from the reader's 'inability or refusal to take on the characteristics
he requires of his "mock reader" ' (p. 138).
15 Newman Ivey White, in *Shelley* (2 vols.; New York: Alfred A. Knopf,
1940), I, 624–6, speculates on the extent of Ensor's influence on Shelley.
16 Terry Eagleton, in *Marxism and Literary Criticism* (London: Methuen,
1976), states that 'the true bearer of ideology in art are the very forms,
rather than the abstractable content, of the work itself' (p. 24); cf. the
comments of Georg Lukács on the relation between social change and literary form in *Studies in European Realism*, trans, Edith Bone (London:
Hillway Publishing, 1950), p. 189.
17 K.N. Cameron, *The Young Shelley*, p. 113.
18 See Derrida's essay on 'Plato's Pharmacy' in *Dissemination*, esp. pp.
115–16, where the sophist Gorgias is cited.

CHAPTER THREE

1 'It is consciousness, ultimately, which alienates them from life' is an apt
summary of Geoffrey Hartman's discussion of 'Romanticism and "Anti-
Self-Consciousness," ' in *Romanticism and Consciousness*, ed. Harold
Bloom (New York: Norton, 1970), pp. 45–56.
2 Earl Wasserman thought that the poem is a 'skeptical representation of
the human dilemma' and 'displays Shelley's division between the inadequacy of the temporal world and the possible illusory, certainly torment-
ingly solipsistic, aspirations of the mind,' but felt that the 'identification
of the addressee as Coleridge ... contributes nothing to the meaning of
the poem (*Shelley: A Critical Reading*, p. 8). Judith Chernaik, in *The
Lyrics of Shelley* (Cleveland: Case Western Reserve University Press,
1972), remarks that 'the figure of the failing poet appears repeatedly in
Shelley's poetry' (p. 9).
3 White describes the attack on Shelley as 'imaginary' in *Shelley*, I, 283.
For a more recent re-examination of this episode, see Holmes, *Shelley*,
pp. 163–98, who comments that one result of his experience was that
'his trust and confidence in the larger democratic community was
shaken' (p. 198).
4 Earl Wasserman, *Shelley: A Critical Reading*, p. 5.
5 In *The Lyrics of Shelley*, p. 49, Chernaik compares the poem to 'Tintern
Abbey' and 'Dejection: An Ode,' remarking that in these works 'the poet
moves naturally from the physical scene to the reflection it suggests.'
6 For a discussion of the poem and its date of composition, see *The Esdaile*

Notebook, ed. K.N. Cameron (London: Faber and Faber, 1964), pp.209-11.

7 See Earl Wasserman, *Shelley: A Critical Reading*, p. 34, on the need 'to take into account the function of the Narrator.'

8 A.C. Bradley, *Oxford Lectures on Poetry* (London: Macmillan, 1909), p. 240. See also H.L. Hoffman, *An Odyssey of the Soul: Shelley's Alastor* (New York: Columbia University Press, 1933), pp. 51-2; Carlos Baker, *Shelley's Major Poetry* (Princeton: Princeton University Press, 1948), p. 46; Harold Bloom, *The Visionary Company* (New York: Doubleday, 1961), p. 285; and Earl Wasserman, *Shelley: A Critical Reading*, p. 20.

9 On Wednesday, 14 September 1814, *Mary Shelley's Journal*, ed. F.L. Jones (Norman: University of Oklahoma Press, 1947), p. 15, records that Shelley 'brings home Wordsworth's "Excursion", of which we read a part, much disappointed. He is a slave.'

10 See *The Journals of Clare Clairmont*, ed. Marion Kingston Stocking (Cambridge: Harvard University Press, 1968), p. 61; White, *Shelley*, I, 702; and Lorraine Robertson, 'Unpublished Verses by Shelley,' *MLR*, 48 (1953), 181-4.

11 Donald Reiman, in *Percy Bysshe Shelley*, pp. 36-7, follows the Visionary's 'allegorical journey ... backwards through the history of human civilizations.'

12 Luther L. Scales, in 'The Poet as Miltonic Adam in *Alastor*,' *Keats-Shelley Journal*, 21-2 (1972-3), 136-7, traces the symbolic journey upriver of the Visionary and concludes that 'Shelley symbolizes the Poet's solitary attempt to clear the boundary between the Paradisal world of visionary perfection and the world of physical existence as a search for the physical location of the origin of human life, vision, and love.' Scales thinks the Visionary's quest carries him towards a Biblical origin, the Garden of Eden (p. 139).

13 Quoted in Edward Dowden's *Life of Percy Bysshe Shelley* (London: 2 vols.; Kegan Paul, 1886), I, 529.

14 Jacques Derrida, *Of Grammatology*, trans. G.C. Spivak (Baltimore: Johns Hopkins University Press, 1974), p. 61.

15 Shelley probably knew this extract from *The Prelude* (XI, 142-4) through its publication in Wordsworth's *Poems in Two Volumes* (1815), where it appears as the concluding lines of a poem titled 'The French Revolution, as it appeared to Enthusiasts at its Commencement.' 'Wordsworth's *Poems*' appears as an entry in Mary Shelley's journal-list of Shelley's reading for 1815 (p. 47).

16 Maurice Merleau Ponty, *Phenomenology of Perception*, p. 294.

17 Sigmund Freud made the psychological distinction between illusion and delusion in *Civilization and Its Discontents* (London: Hogarth Press,

1972), pp. 17–18. Illusion, he says, is the province of art, while delusion he consigns to religion. The logical distinction between sense and reference was made by Gottlob Frege in his essay 'On Sense and Reference,' trans. Max Black, in *Translations from the Philosophical Writings of Gottlob Frege*, ed. Peter Geach and Max Black (Oxford: Basil Blackwell, 1952), pp. 56–78.

18 See Schlegel's aphorism #69 in the *Athenaeum*: 'Irony is clear consciousness of an eternal agility, of the infinitely abundant chaos.' Anne Mellor, in *English Romantic Irony*, p. 12, comments that for Schlegel 'philosophical irony ... is the ability to hold two opposed ideas in the mind at the same time, while still retaining the ability to function.'

19 Harold Bloom, *The Visionary Company*, p. 305.

20 Anne Mellor writes most eloquently of the humane effects of romantic irony in her conclusion to *English Romantic Irony*: 'Romantic irony demands just such exuberant playing with the possibilities of an ever-changing world and life, such expanding participation in a variety of selves and modes of consciousness, such openness to new ideas and experiences. In so doing, it embraces a mental habit of tolerance and a discourse of ambiguity' (p. 188).

CHAPTER FOUR

1 See White, *Shelley*, I, 405–6, for the state of Shelley's health; Holmes, in *Shelley: The Pursuit*, states that 'the death of Harriet presented Shelley with one of the most severe emotional crises of his life' (p. 352).

2 J.H. Van den Berg, in 'The Subject and His Landscape,' in *Romanticism and Consciousness*, writes (p. 62): 'In the *Nouvelle Héloïse* (1761), the emotion felt upon observing nature was completely described. Like an epidemic the new sensation spread through Europe. Everyone wished to see what Rousseau had seen to experience the same ecstasy.' Marjorie Hope Nicholson, in *Mountain Gloom and Mountain Glory* (Ithaca: Cornell University Press, 1959), traces this momentous change in aesthetic attitudes back through theological debate to Sir Thomas Burnet's *Sacred Theory of the Earth* (1681). She notes how literature shaped sensibility in this regard when she concludes (pp. 372–3) that 'as the century went on, the traveller, armed with his "guides" and with the poems of Wordsworth, Byron, and Shelley, gazed at the Alps or the lesser sublimities of the Lake District and felt, or thought he felt – or pretended to feel – as Burnet or Dennis or Wordsworth actually had felt.'

3 See Norman Fruman, *Coleridge, the Damaged Archangel* (New York: George Braziller, 1971), pp. 26–30, 450 nn. 13–14.

4 Charles E. Robinson, in 'The Shelley Circle and Coleridge's *The Friend*,' *ELN*, 8 (1971), 269–74, presents the case for Shelley's reading of Coleridge's periodical. He thinks (p. 273) that Shelley may have brought a copy of *The Friend* to Geneva and discussed it with Byron. If he is right, Shelley would have had access to the text of Coleridge's *Hymn* while he was composing *Mont Blanc*, and Bloom's contention in *Shelley's Mythmaking* (p. 12) that 'Coleridge and his "Hymn" were in Shelley's thoughts when he stood in the vale of Chamouni' would receive additional support. For the text of the poem, see *The Friend*, ed. Barbara E. Rooke (2 vols.; Princeton: Princeton University Press, 1969), II, 156–8.

5 I.J. Kapstein, 'The Meaning of Shelley's "Mont Blanc," ' *PMLA*, 62 (1947), 1046. Earl Wasserman, in his chapter on *Mont Blanc* in *Shelley: A Critical Reading*, pp. 222–38, has developed the definitive metaphysical reading of the poem, while Harold Bloom, in *Shelley's Mythmaking*, pp. 19–35, reads it as an 'assertion of the Shelleyan variety of religion.' In addition to Kapstein, Peter Butter, in *Shelley's Idols of the Cave* (Edinburgh: Edinburgh University Press, 1954), pp. 18–26, has found the poem obscure and contradictory.

6 Lloyd Abbey, in *Destroyer and Preserver*, pp. 11–30, has ably demonstrated the community of imagery and theme in the two poems.

7 Shelley's knowledge of the water cycle was probably derived from his reading of Erasmus Darwin, as Carl Grabo indicates in *A Newton among Poets: Shelley's Use of Science in Prometheus Unbound* (Chapel Hill: University of North Carolina Press, 1930), p. 55.

8 Leavis remarks of the opening lines of *Mont Blanc* that 'the metaphorical and the actual, the real and the imagined, the inner and the outer, could hardly be more unsortably and indistinguishably confused,' in *Revaluation: Tradition and Development in English Poetry* (London: Chatto and Windus, 1949), p. 212.

9 Earl Wasserman describes the opening lines of the poem as 'a metaphorical definition of the universe in terms of the "intellectual philosophy" ' (*Shelley: A Critical Reading*, p. 222).

10 Norman Malcolm, in *Ludwig Wittgenstein: A Memoir* (London: Oxford University Press, 1958), p. 93, records this statement, made during the philosopher's stay at Cornell, as 'summing up a good deal of his philosophy.'

11 A generation ago, Walter J. Ong, in his essay 'Voice as Summons for Belief,' in *Literature and Belief* (New York: Columbia University Press, 1958), pp. 80–105, taught us how poets use the metaphor of voice to evoke faith in a spiritual presence (pp. 88, 95); today, Jacques Derrida

reminds us that 'la voix simule la garde de la presence' ('Voice feigns the vigilance of presence') – cf. *Speech and Phenomena*, p. 15.

12 Thomas Weiskel, *The Romantic Sublime: Studies in the Structure and Psychology of Transcendence* (Baltimore: Johns Hopkins University Press, 1976), pp. 28–9.

13 See M.H. Abrams, 'Structure and Style in the Greater Romantic Lyric,' in *From Sensibility to Romanticism*, ed. F.W. Hilles and Harold Bloom (New York: Oxford University Press, 1965), esp. pp. 527–8, where he concludes: 'Often the poem rounds upon itself to end where it began, at the outer scene, but with an altered mood and deepened understanding which is the result of the intervening meditation.'

14 See Gaston Bachelard, *l'air et les songes: Essai sur l'imagination du mouvement* (Paris: Jose Corti, 1943), p. 18, where he interprets the vertical as the axis of value: 'Toute valorisation est verticalisation.' Weiskel, in *The Romantic Sublime*, pp. 24–5, writes that 'the sublime moment establishes depth because the presentation of unattainability is phenomenologically a negation, a falling away from what might be seized, perceived, known. As an image, it is an abyss. When the intervention of the transcendent becomes specific, however, the image is converted into a symbol, and height takes over as the valorizing perspective.'

15 Anne Mellor, in *English Romantic Irony*, writes (p. 5) that the Romantic ironist 'is as filled with enthusiasm as with skepticism. ... Having ironically acknowledged the fictiveness of his own patternings of human experience, he romantically engages in the creative process of life by eagerly constructing new forms, new myths.'

16 Wallace Stevens, *The Necessary Angel: Essays on Reality and the Imagination* (New York: Alfred Knopf, 1951), pp. 174–5.

17 *The Collected Dialogues of Plato*, ed. Edith Hamilton and Huntington Cairns (Princeton: Princeton University Press, 1961), p. 1147; all subsequent references to Plato's dialogues are to this edition. J.G. Warry, in *Greek Aesthetic Theory* (London: Methuen, 1962), states (p. 46) that 'both Plato and ancient Greek thought in general closely associated Beauty, in its objective as in its subjective aspect, with a sense of harmony'; he notes (p. 35) that 'the apprehension of beauty described in the *Philebus* is quite obviously of an intellectual order.'

18 The parenthetical phrase is, of course, Derrida's, in *Positions*, p. 26. It seems to me that Wasserman was right only two times out of three when he wrote that 'the poem is Shelley's effort to locate life's worth exclusively in moments of extraordinary visitations of perfection, to come to terms with the intervening vacancies in life as a necessity imposed by

sublunary mutability, and to define a possible immortality' (*Shelley: A Critical Reading*, p. 190). The *Hymn* is devoted exclusively to mortal existence.

19 Ronald A. Sharp, in *Keats, Skepticism, and the Religion of Beauty* (Athens: University of Georgia Press, 1979), puts the matter succinctly when he writes that 'what Keats meant by beauty [is] that which is life-affirming' (p. 5).

20 J.F. Pollitt, in *Art and Experience in Classical Greece* (Cambridge: Cambridge University Press, 1972), writes that 'the recognition of order and measure in phenomena did more than simply satisfy their [the Greeks'] intellectual curiosity or gratify a desire for tidiness; it also served as the basis of a spiritual ideal. "Measure and commensurability are everywhere identified with beauty and excellence" was Plato's way of putting it in a dialogue in which measure is identified as a primary characteristic of the ultimate good' (p. 4). Neville Rogers, probably the most acute of the Platonic critics of Shelley, remarks in *Shelley at Work: A Critical Enquiry* (Oxford: Clarendon Press, 1967), that 'the identification of the Form of Beauty with the Form of Goodness was the basis of his [Shelley's] belief in the regenerative power of poets' (p. 153).

21 Bloom was the first to note this shift in *Shelley's Mythmaking*, p. 39. Wasserman observes that 'the hymn that begins with a prayer to a transcendent diety ends in reverence of the self' (*Shelley: A Critical Reading*, p. 195).

22 See Frank McConnell, who argues in *The Confessional Imagination: A Reading of Wordsworth's Prelude* (Baltimore: Johns Hopkins University Press, 1974), that Romanticism is a secularization of Protestant piety.

CHAPTER FIVE

1 See Norman Malcolm, *Ludwig Wittgenstein*, p. 93. Max Black proclaims his debt to Wittgenstein when he advances his 'functional theory of meaning' in *The Labyrinth of Language* (New York: Frederick A. Praeger, 1968), p. 166.

2 Kenneth Burke, *The Philosophy of Literary Form*, p. 61.

3 For a discussion of their symbolic significance, see Carlos Baker, *Shelley's Major Poetry*, pp. 72–7.

4 Notably by Harold Bloom in *Shelley's Mythmaking*, pp. 11–12; but see also Charles E. Robinson, *Shelley and Byron: The Snake and Eagle Wreathed in Fight* (Baltimore: Johns Hopkins University Press, 1976),

who remarks (p. 6) that Shelley's 'hopes were based on a Coleridgean conception of the imagination.'

5 Carlos Baker, *Shelley's Major Poetry*, p. 64.

6 Donald Reiman, in *Percy Bysshe Shelley*, says (p. 51) that 'the poem calls liberals from despair at the aftermath of the Congress of Vienna.' The possibility that Shelley may have thought of Byron as typifying this gloomy view of post-revolutionary prospects is examined by Robinson, in *Shelley and Byron*, p. 67.

7 'Dissemination *affirms* (I do not say produces or controls) endless substitution, it neither arrests nor controls play,' observes Derrida in *Positions* (p. 86). John Sturrock, in *Structuralism and Science: From Levi-Strauss to Derrida* (Oxford: Oxford University Press, 1979), p. 17, suggests the distinction between insemination and dissemination.

8 Northrop Frye, *Anatomy of Criticism* (Princeton: Princeton University Press, 1957), p. 34.

9 Thomas Paine, *The Rights of Man* (London: J.M. Dent, 1921), p. 94. Shelley was reading Paine's essay in 1817 while at work on *Prince Athanase*; see Mary Shelley's *Journal*, p. 87.

10 As Brian Wilkie, in *Romantic Poets and Epic Tradition* (Madison: University of Wisconsin Press, 1965), has observed (p. 139), 'moral persuasion is not only the goal of the poem but also an important subject. ... [Shelley's] epic not only preaches but is *about* preaching.'

11 Maintaining the thesis that Shelley 'did not regard poetry ... as an end in itself,' Timothy Webb, in *Shelley: A Voice Not Understood* (New York: Humanities Press, 1977), states (p. 65) that 'throughout his life Shelley regarded the writing of poetry as primarily a political function.'

12 Carlos Baker, in *Shelley's Major Poetry*, pp. 66–70, traces the 'Manichean scheme' of the poem to Peacock's influence; Earl Wasserman, in *Shelley: A Critical Reading*, p. 106, observes that 'Shelley's Manichean conviction [is] fully outlined in canto I of *The Revolt of Islam*.'

13 Donald Reiman, in *Percy Bysshe Shelley*, p. 51, eloquently writes that 'the noble example of love and forbearance exhibited by Laon and Cythna and other patriot-revolutionaries is more glorious, even in defeat, than is the cynical and brutal victory of the kings and their priestly allies'; Lloyd Abbey, in *Destroyer and Preserver*, p. 48, observes that 'their ministry brings them transcendence through martyrdom.'

14 Beginning from the premise that 'patriarchal order ... is a symbolic order into which we are born' (p. 4), Dale Spender, in *Man Made Language* (London: Routledge and Kegan Paul, 1980), argues that our language con-

structs a world of meanings encoded by men, that the rules of rhetoric
reflect masculine values of assertiveness and dominance, and that 'it is
no less an assault on someone's existence to make them change their
beliefs by oratory than it is by the sword' (p. 80). Mary Daly, in *Beyond
God the Father: Towards a Philosophy of Women's Liberation* (Boston:
Beacon Press, 1973), describes the voice of the prophet as hierarchical,
authoritarian, and 'phallic' (p. 165), and defines feminism as a move
away from the dichotomy of male and female 'toward psychic androgyny'
(p. 97).
15 Julia Kristeva, *Desire in Language: A Semiotic Approach to Literature and
Art*, trans. Thomas Gora, Alice Jardine, and Leon S. Roudiez (New York:
Columbia University Press, 1980), p. x.
16 G.M. Matthews, 'A Volcano's Voice in Shelley,' *ELH*, 24 (1957),
191–228.
17 See J.A. Wittreich's 'Opening the Seals: Blake's Epics and the Milton
Tradition,' in Blake's *Sublime Allegory*, ed. J.A. Wittreich and Stuart
Curran (Madison: University of Wisconsin Press, 1973), pp. 23–58. Wittreich comments (p. 33) that Milton 'recognized that literary forms carried ideologies.'
18 *Goethe's Literary Essays*, ed. J.E. Spingarn (New York: Harcourt, Brace,
1921), p. 100. Terry Eagleton, in *Marxism and Literary Criticism* (London: Methuen, 1976), states (p. 24) that 'the true bearers of ideology in
art are the very forms, rather than the abstractable content, of the work
itself.' Georg Lukács, in *Studies in European Realism*, trans. Edith Bone
(London: Hillway Publishing, 1950), observes that 'real changes in the
structure of society' must also be reflected in form, not just in content.

CHAPTER SIX

1 Michel Foucault, *The Archaeology of Knowledge*, trans. A.M. Sheridan
Smith (New York: Pantheon Books, 1972), pp. 41–2, and 219.
2 Stanley Fish, in *Self-Consuming Artifacts*, pp. 1–2, distinguishes between
the experience of a rhetorical form which confirms a reader's values and
the experience of a 'dialectical form' which challenges them. Anne
Mellor, in *English Romantic Irony*, p. 131, comments on Fish's distinction between 'a dialectical (as opposed to a rhetorical) presentation that
disturbs rather than satisfies the reader.'
3 G.W.F. Hegel, *Aesthetics*, II, 1079.
4 *The Works of Charles Lamb*, ed. William MacDonald (12 vols.; London:
Dent, 1903), II, 26. Sylvan Barnet shows how Lamb's theory of illusion

improves on Coleridge's in 'Charles Lamb's Contribution to the Theory of Dramatic Illusion,' *PMLA*, 69 (1954), 1150–9.

5 Mary Shelley's *Journal*, p. 93, shows that Shelley read Schlegel's book over a period of a week in March, 1818; he seems to have thought well enough of it to read it aloud to his companions on several occasions and later to pass it along to the Gisbornes (L, II, 17). Noting the influence of Schlegel on Shelley at this time, Stuart Curran, in *Shelley's Annus Mirabilis*, p. 32, comments that Shelley's 'recurring problem is formal. ... Abandoning the epic form on which he had invested his greatest labors, Shelley set to work in a variety of genres to create the vision that was its substance.'

6 Northrop Frye, *Anatomy of Criticism*, p. 250. Frye remarks (p. 107) that 'the drama in literature, like the ritual in religion is primarily social or ensemble performance.' Harold Bloom is of course right to stress Shelley's 'commitment to the mythopoeic mode,' but his exclusive attention in *Shelley's Mythmaking* to the traditional lyric Shelley obscures the political and social nature of the poet's achievement.

7 Thomas Love Peacock, *Memoirs of Shelley and Other Essays*, ed. Howard Mills (London: Hart-Davis, 1970), p. 45. Peacock reports on Shelley's experience of the theatre on pp. 45–6 and 70–1.

8 Stuart Curran, *Shelley's Cenci: Scorpions Ringed with Fire* (Princeton: Princeton University Press, 1970), pp. 39–40.

9 For a discussion of Shelley's use of and deviation from his manuscript source, see Curran, *Shelley's Cenci*, p. 43.

10 In *Shelley: A Critical Reading*, Earl Wasserman has argued convincingly that because Shelley 'can conceive of the poetic act indifferently as either a creation of ideal order ... or as a kind of discovery of the order created by the One. ... creation and discovery are only different ways of describing the same creative – not mimetic – act of the mind' (p. 217). He remarks in the course of this discussion that 'Shelley's poetics everywhere resolves itself into the problems and consequences of integral form' (p. 208). John S. Flagg, in 'Shelley and Aristotle: Elements of the *Poetics* in Shelley's Theory of Poetry,' *Studies in Romanticism*, 9 (1970), 44–67, discusses 'the general resemblance of Shelley's argument to Aristotle's' in the *Defence of Poetry*. Flagg remarks (p. 45) that Shelley's 'theory of drama certainly seems to owe more to Aristotle than to Plato.'

11 See Melvin R. Watson, 'Shelley and Tragedy: The Case of Beatrice Cenci,' *Keats-Shelley Journal*, 7 (1958), 13–21; Robert F. Whitman, 'Beatrice's "Pernicious Mistake" in *The Cenci*,' *PMLA*, 74 (1959), 249–53; James Reiger, *The Mutiny Within: The Heresies of Percy Bysshe*

Shelley (New York: George Braziller, 1967), p. 126; Stuart Curran, *Shelley's Cenci*, pp. 86–96; and Earl Wasserman, *Shelley: A Critical Reading*, p. 98.

12 See Michel Foucault, *The Archaeology of Knowledge*, pp. 219–20.

13 Curran, in *Shelley's Cenci*, pp. 100–1, notes that '*The Cenci* is remarkably rich in the kind of carefully structured image patterns associated with Shakespearean drama and generally absent from the work of Jacobean playwrights.'

14 The influence of Hazlitt on Keats's idea of 'negative capability' has been traced by C.L. Finney in *The Evolution of Keat's Poetry* (Cambridge: Harvard University Press. 1936), pp. 241–3, and by W.J. Bate, in his *John Keats* (Cambridge: Harvard University Press, 1963), pp. 244–59.

15 See Grabo, *The Magic Plant*, p. 303; Wasserman, *Shelley: A Critical Reading*, pp. 101, 127–8; James Reiger, in *The Mutiny Within*, p. 121, says the two dramas are 'halves of a single religious poem.'

16 Noting (p. 40) that at the beginning of the nineteenth century 'drama was still incapable of depicting the subtle subjective matter of *The Cenci*,' Terry Otten, in *The Deserted Stage: The Search for Dramatic Form in Nineteenth-Century England* (Athens: Ohio University Press, 1972), p. 14, argues that 'Shelley, perhaps unconsciously, was moving toward a new kind of drama, a drama which by the end of the century was to find full expression in Ibsen's late symbolic dramas and Strindberg's expressionistic dream plays.'

17 I.A. Richards, *Principles of Literary Criticism* (New York: Harcourt, Brace, 1930), p. 246.

CHAPTER SEVEN

1 Mikhail Bakhtin, *The Dialogic Imagination*, p. 270.

2 Northrop Frye, *Anatomy of Criticism*, p. 246.

3 Discussing mania and melancholia in *Madness and Civilization* (London: Tavistock Publications, 1967), Michel Foucault writes (p. 126) that 'the maniac [was] a sort of instrument whose strings, by the effect of an exaggerated traction, began to vibrate at the remotest, and faintest stimulus.' Foucault also discusses the historical use of music as therapy on pp. 160–1.

4 See Lamb's 'Sanity of True Genius' in *Works*, II, 73–7, and Lionel Trilling's meditations on 'Art and Neurosis' in *The Liberal Imagination* (New York: Viking Press, 1950), 152–71.

5 See Northrop Frye, *Anatomy of Criticism*, p. 74: 'Literary meaning may

best be described, perhaps, as hypothetical. ... In literature, questions of fact or truth are subordinated to the primary aim of producing a structure of words for its own sake. ... Where we have an autonomous verbal structure of this kind, we have literature.'

6 For a discussion of discourse as a practice of formation, see Foucault, *Archaeology of Knowledge*, pp. 49, 228. Shelley's ironic attitude toward signification must be what Bloom means by the 'prophetic irony' of *Prometheus Unbound*, which he feels was written in an 'awareness of the precariousness of mythmaking' (*Shelley's Mythmaking*, pp. 94–5).

7 John Dover Wilson, *Shakespeare's Happy Comedies* (Evanston: Northwestern University Press, 1962), pp. 21, 32.

8 Katherine Lever discusses the role of allegory and parabasis in Old Comedy in *The Art of Greek Comedy* (London: Methuen, 1956), pp. 123, 160–1. She concludes (p. 161) that the Old Comedy 'was a satiric, political, literary, fantastic, allegorical, witty, farcical, ribald, and operatic comedy.'

9 *Literary Criticism of Dante Alighieri*, ed. Robert S. Haller (Lincoln: University of Nebraska Press, 1973), pp. 101–2.

10 Northrop Frye, *A Natural Perspective: The Development of Shakespearean Comedy and Romance* (New York: Columbia University Press, 1965), p. 118. Frye states (pp. 49–50) that, in his view, tragedy and comedy are each 'the name of a structure,' and concludes: 'Structure, then commands participation but not assent: it unites its audience as an audience, but allows for variety of response.'

11 According to Mary Shelley's *Journal* (p. 127), Shelley read *The Tempest* aloud to her over three successive nights at the beginning of 1820; she had read the play herself in October, 1818. Shelley's earliest mention of *The Tempest* occurs in his preface to *Frankenstein* (1817). N.I. White, in *Shelley*, II, 366, remarks that *The Tempest* was 'his favorite play.' So immersed was the Shelley circle in *The Tempest* that lines from Ariel's song ('Nothing of him that doth fade / But doth suffer a sea-change / Into something rich and strange') were incorporated into the epitaph on his tombstone.

12 Helen North, in *Sophrosyne: Self-Knowledge and Self-Restraint in Greek Literature* (Ithaca: Cornell University Press, 1969), comments (p. 185) that 'some form of *kosmios* [order]. ... is the most persistent synonym of *sophron* [restrained, temperate, moderate] in all its varied connotations throughout the dialogues.' More specifically, she says (p. 167) that 'both Beauty – the object of the soul's desire in the *Symposium* – and the Good – the goal of reason in the *Republic* – are characterized by the orderly

arrangement that *Gorgias* associates with sophrosyne.' She also remarks (p. 163) that for Plato 'the cosmic order and the virtuous condition of the soul ... are products of art: the orderly arrangement of parts according to a pattern by a craftsman.' Gregory Vlastos, writing of 'Justice and Happiness in the Republic,' in *Plato: A Collection of Critical Essays*, says (p. 69) that they both depend on 'psychic harmony,' which he defines as 'the condition of the human soul when it is healthy, beautiful, and in an ontologically correct, hierarchic, internal order'; he also notes that psychic harmony is often described in terms of musical concord throughout the dialogues.

13 Frye remarks, in *A Natural Perspective*, p. 118, that 'the normal action of a comedy moves from irrational law to festivity, which symbolizes a movement from one form of reality to another.'

14 Bodleian ms. Shelley d.1; published with the permission of the Curators of the Bodleian Library and Oxford University Press.

CHAPTER EIGHT

1 The conception of dissemination as a kind of verbal dissipation is suggested by Derrida in *Dissemination*, when he observes (p. 149) that Plato's preference for dialectic over poetry reflects a preference 'for a seed that engenders because it is planted inside over a seed scattered wastefully outside: at the risk of *dissemination.*' In *Positions*, p. 86, Derrida adds that 'dissemination affirms (I do not say produces or controls) endless substitution; it neither arrests nor controls play.'

2 In developing his thesis that Romantic critical thought is characterized by a shift from a mimetic to an expressive theory of art, M.H. Abrams, in *The Mirror and the Lamp*, mentions (p. 50) that 'in place of painting, music becomes the art frequently pointed to as having a profound affinity with poetry.' This development in the aesthetics of the later eighteenth century is also discussed by Jean H. Hagstrom, in *The Sister Arts: The Tradition of Literary Pictorialism and English Poetry from Dryden to Gray* (Chicago: University of Chicago Press, 1958), p. 151. For the Greek view, see Werner Jaeger, *Paideia: The Ideals of Greek Culture*, trans. Gilbert Highet (3 vols.; New York: Oxford University Press, 1943), II, 224ff.

3 Friedrich Schiller, *On the Aesthetic Education of Man*, trans. Reginald Snell (London: Routledge and Kegan Paul, 1954), p. 27.

4 Newman Ivey White, in *Shelley*, II, 134, was the first to observe that '*Prometheus Unbound* at times suggests the opera rather than the drama.' Stuart Curran, in *Shelley's Cenci*, p. 182, remarks that Shelley's tragedy

was 'conceived along operatic lines,' and applies a similar metaphor to *Prometheus Unbound* when he likens it to 'the libretto to a supramundane opera,' in *Shelley's Annus Mirabilis*, p. 112. Curran's preference for exclusively literary sources, however, leads him to claim that '*Prometheus Unbound* derives its ethos from the Miltonic epic' (*Shelley's Annus Mirabilis*, p. 113). There can be no dispute that, generically and formally, *Prometheus Unbound* is a drama, even though Curran, preoccupied with epic vision, has argued that its four-act structure derives from Milton's brief epic and that '*Paradise Regained* is clearly the prototype for the four-book epics of the Romantic period: Keats's *Endymion*, Blake's *Jerusalem*, and Shelley's *Prometheus Unbound*.' See 'The Mental Pinnacle: *Paradise Regained* and the Romantic Four-Book Epic,' in *Calm of Mind*, ed. J.A. Wittreich (Cleveland: Case Western Reserve University Press, 1971), p. 136.

5 Arthur Schopenhauer, *The World as Will and Idea*, trans. R.B. Haldane and J. Kemp (3 vols.; London: Kegan Paul, 1907), III, 177. Schopenhauer shares with Shelley an instrumental conception of art in which he says, 'aesthetic effect is the criterion' (I, 331).

6 *The Autobiography of Leigh Hunt* (London: Smith Elder, 1872), p. 295; *Medwin's Conversations of Lord Byron*, ed. Ernest J. Lovell, Jr (Princeton: Princeton University Press, 1966), p. 5.

7 Friedrich Schiller, quoted by Thomas Mann, in *Last Essays*, trans. Richard and Clara Winston (London: Secker and Warburg, 1959), p. 56.

8 *Correspondence of Thomas Gray*, ed. Paget Toynbee and Leonard Whibley (3 vols.; Oxford: Clarendon Press, 1935), II, 810. Edward J. Dent, in *The Rise of Romantic Opera*, ed. Winton Dean (Cambridge: Cambridge University Press, 1976), p. 28, writes that 'Wagner's ideas of a *Gesamtkunstwerk* had been completely and entirely anticipated by Algarotti.'

9 See, for example, Milton Wilson, *Shelley's Later Poetry: A Study of His Prophetic Imagination* (New York: Columbia University Press, 1959), p. 44. Wilson also suggests (p. 40), without elaborating, the operatic analogue.

10 See Dent, *The Rise of Romantic Opera*, p. 15, and Lincoln Kirstein, *Movement and Metaphor: Four Centuries of Ballet* (New York: Praeger, 1970), p. 130. Dent remarks (p. 3) that 'opera, at any rate for the Romantic period, is by far the most important of all musical forms.'

11 See Neville Rogers, 'Music at Marlowe,' *Keats-Shelley Memorial Bulletin*, 5 (1953), 20–5. Jean L. de Palacio, in 'Music and Musical Themes in Shelley's Poetry,' *Modern Language Review*, 59 (1954), 345–59, ex-

plores the influence of Hazlitt and Novello on Shelley's musical taste. Leigh Hunt's reviews in the *Examiner* helped to pioneer the appreciation of opera in England; Theodore Fenner, in *Leigh Hunt and Opera Criticism* (Lawrence: University Press of Kansas, 1972), remarks (p. 226) that 'Hunt brought to his readers a new awareness of an art that had traditionally been regarded as an aristocratic perogative.'

12 Judith Chernaik, *The Lyrics of Shelley*, p. 53; the text quoted from J has been corrected in accordance with Chernaik's edition of the poem, pp. 196–7. Newman Ivey White demonstrated the identity of Claire and Constantia in his discussion of the poem, in *Shelley*, I, 507–8.

13 Peter Conrad, *Romantic Opera and Literary Form* (Berkeley: University of California Press, 1977), p. 72. Newman Ivey White remarks that 'the poem contains cumulative effects of changing rhythms far commoner to music than to poetry,' in *Shelley*, II, 134.

14 'The text offers itself as an instrument by means of which the reader can make a number of discoveries for himself that will lead to a reliable sense of orientation': Wolfgang Iser, *The Implied Reader* (Baltimore: Johns Hopkins University Press, 1974), p. 45.

15 Derek Beales, *The Risorgimento and the Unification of Italy* (London: Allen and Unwin, 1971), p. 46; Dent, *The Rise of Romantic Opera*, p. 173, who comments, 'The Italian public was ready to interpret every opera in a political sense. ... They were heralds of the Risorgimento.'

16 Sigmund Freud, *The Interpretation of Dreams*, trans. A.A. Brill (London: Allen and Unwin, 1923), p. 175.

17 Joseph Kerman, *Opera as Drama* (New York: Alfred A. Knopf, 1956), p. 108. Kerman argues that 'the drama of *The Marriage of Figaro* is Mozart's, not Beaumarchais's or Da Ponte's. Music here does not merely decorate what playwright or librettist had designed; Mozart's music creates a drama that they never suspected.'

18 Mark Van Doren, *Shakespeare* (New York: Henry Holt, 1939), p. 161. C.L. Barber, in *Shakespeare's Festive Comedy: A Study of Dramatic Form and Its Relation to Social Custom* (Princeton: Princeton University Press, 1959), remarks (p. 260) that 'the festive comic form which Shakespeare had worked out was a way of selecting and organizing experience which had its own logic, its own autonomy.'

19 Erik Erikson, *Toys and Reasons; Stages in the Ritualization of Experience* (New York: W.W. Norton, 1977), p. 136. Gerald McNiece, in *Shelley and the Revolutionary Idea* (Cambridge: Harvard University Press, 1969), stresses the ritual element in *Prometheus Unbound*, remarking (p. 134) that Shelley's long poems 'may be regarded as ritual enactments of the successful revolution they forsee.'

20 See Marian Hannah Winter, *The Pre-Romantic Ballet* (London: Pitman, 1974), p. 111; and Frederika Derra de Moroda, *The Ballet Masters before, at the Time of, and after Noverre* (Florence: Leo S. Olschki, 1975), p. 473.

21 Earl Wasserman, in *Shelley: A Critical Reading*, pp. 363–4, traces the dance metaphor of Act IV to philosophic notions of planetary dance and the literary commonplace of the Dance of the Hours; however, he neglects the possible influence of Shelley's more immediate aesthetic experience on *Prometheus Unbound*.

22 Roland Barthes, in *The Pleasure of the Text*, trans. Richard Miller (New York: Hill and Wang, 1975), p. 64, eloquently describes the relation between the reader and the text which evades determinate meanings: '*Text* means *Tissue*; but whereas hitherto we have always taken this tissue as a product, a ready-made veil, behind which lies more or less hidden, meaning (truth), we are now emphasizing, in the tissue, the generative idea that the text is made, is worked out, in a perpetual interweaving; lost in this tissue – this texture – the subject unmakes himself, like a spider dissolving in the constructive secretions of its web.' For his observations on the text as 'a site of bliss,' see p. 4.

23 Tilottama Rajan, 'Deconstruction or Reconstruction: Reading Shelley's *Prometheus Unbound*,' *Studies in Romanticism*, 23 (1984), 323–4.

24 Jonathan Culler, *Structuralist Poetics*, p. 107.

25 Julia Kristeva, *Desire in Language*, p. 142.

26 Writing of the 'bliss' (jouissance) made possible by the text, Roland Barthes, in *The Pleasure of the Text*, pp. 4–6, admits that while the text cannot guarantee pleasure, much less enforce it, it nevertheless 'desires' the reader in an erotic way. 'Writing,' he says puckishly, 'is the science of the various blisses of language; its Kama Sutra.' John Sturrock, in *Structuralism and Since*, p. 72, observes that 'what Barthes seems to claim is that the relationship between writer, Text, and reader is an erotic one.' The argument of Morris Eaves, in 'Romantic Expressive Theory and Blake's Idea of the Audience,' *PMLA*, 95 (1980), 784–801, can thus be extended to other Romantic poets, especially when he says that their relationship to their audience is 'a relationship not of entertainer to public, performer to judge, thoughtful person to thoughtful person, or teacher to student, but something closer to the relationship of lover to the beloved' (p. 791).

CHAPTER NINE

1 Irene H. Chayes, 'Rhetoric as Drama: An Approach to the Romantic Ode' *PMLA*, 79 (1964), 67–79. Stuart Curran, in *Shelley's Annus Mirabilis*,

agrees (p. 179) that 'the romantic ode is an intrinsically dramatic form.'
Timothy Webb, in *Shelley: A Voice Not Understood*, extends this notion
to Shelley's other public lyrics when he remarks (p. 85) that 'right up to the
time of his death, Shelley could never conceive of a poem as autotelic. ...
For him the poetry which really mattered projected itself outwards.'

2 Angus Fletcher, in *The Transcendental Masque: An Essay on Milton's
Comus* (Ithaca: Cornell University Press, 1971), comments on 'the main
characteristic of the masque: it always *presents* a vision' (p. 8; italics
added).

3 K.N. Cameron, in *Shelley: The Golden Years*, p. 346, has clearly explained the ambiguity on 'mask' in the title, while definitely establishing
'Masque' as Shelley's final choice. Stuart Curran has conclusively shown
Shelley's debt to masque traditions, especially as it was revived by Leigh
Hunt's 'Descent of Liberty,' in *Shelley's Annus Mirabilis*, pp. 187–90,
where he remarks, significantly, that 'in *The Mask of Anarchy* Shelley's
prototype is dramatic and pictorial in its immediacy.'

4 Analysing the irony of this phase of the poem, P.M.S. Dawson, in *The
Unacknowledged Legislator: Shelley and Politics* (Oxford: Clarendon
Press, 1980), concludes (p. 206) that 'in this world "Anarchy" wears the
mask of social order.'

5 The structural conventions of the masque have been ably delineated by
Dolora Cunningham in 'Jonsonian Masque as Literary Form,' *ELH*, 22
(1955), 108–24. She comments that 'by these means, a masque accom-
plishes its purpose of honoring magnificence, in the ethical sense, and of
inciting in the beholders a conscious moral imitation of the virtues
embodied in kingship.'

6 Stephen Orgel, *The Illusion of Power: Political Theatre in the English
Renaissance* (Berkeley: University of California Press, 1975), p. 38; he
concludes: 'Masques were games and shows, triumphs and celebrations;
they were for the court and about the court, and their seriousness was
indistinguishable from their recreative quality.'

7 Stuart Curran, *Shelley's Annus Mirabilis*, pp. 190–1. He believes, however, that political regeneration is to be accomplished merely 'through
the stripping of the masks of power that conceal its abuse.'

8 The 'Shape' that speaks with the earth's voice is another instance of that
volcanic imagery in Shelley's poetry which G.M. Matthews says indicates the poet's perception of how revolutionary activity must result
when 'irrepressible collective energy [is] contained by repressive power';
see his 'A Volcano's Voice in Shelley,' *ELH*, 24 (1957), 222.

9 See M.H. Abrams, 'The Correspondent Breeze: A Romantic Metaphor,'
Kenyon Review, 19 (1957), 113–30.

10 Desmond King-Hele, *Shelley: The Man and The Poet* (London: Macmillan, 1960), pp. 148-9; Stuart Curran, *Shelley's Annus Mirabilis*, pp. 192-3; K.N. Cameron, *Shelley, The Golden Years*, pp. 348-50; Michael Henry Scrivener, *Radical Shelley: The Philosophical Anarchism and Utopian Thought of Percy Bysshe Shelley* (Princeton: Princeton University Press, 1982), pp. 198-210.

11 See Fletcher's *The Transcendental Masque*, p. 126, where he notes that this 'governing persona is close to the poet himself.' Fletcher also remarks (p. 9) that, given 'the strongly teleological bias of this genre ... regal presence is its final cause.'

12 See Noam Chomsky, *Cartesian Linguistics* (New York: Harper and Row, 1966), where he says (p. 18) that 'language is a system with unbounded innovative potentialities for the formation and expression of ideas.'

13 See J.L. Austin, *How to Do Things with Words* (Oxford: Clarendon Press, 1962), p. 6ff.

14 E.P. Thompson, *The Making of the English Working Class* (London: Victor Gollancz, 1963), p. 682.

15 Scrivener, in *Radical Shelley*, observes in the course of his commentary on *The Masque of Anarchy* (p. 210), that in this poem 'Shelley is much closer to the socialistic Chartists than to the political forces which finally succeeded in passing the 1832 Reform Bill.' Thompson, in *The Making of the English Working Class*, states (p. 659) that Shelley's poem contains 'judgments which the greater part of Shelley's countrymen came to share.' For Shaw's remarks, see his *Works* (London, 1931), XXIX, 257.

16 Ludwig Wittgenstein, *On Certainty*, p. 49. Wittgenstein adds (p. 74) that 'the concept of knowing is coupled with that of the language game.'

17 See Louis Althusser, *For Marx*, trans. Ben Brewster (London: Allen Lane, 1969), where he says (p. 232): 'Human societies secrete ideology as the very element and atmosphere indispensable to their historical respiration and life.'

18 Shelley's *Ode* conforms to what Northrop Frye calls 'the primitive idea of drama, which is to present a powerful sensational focus for a community' (*Anatomy of Criticism*, p. 282). Frye adds that in 'the more public type of religious lyric ... the "I" of the poem is one of a visible community of worshipers.' Irene Chayes, in 'Rhetoric as Drama' (p. 72), writes that the *Ode* 'takes the form of a dramatic recovery and reversal by way of a pattern of rhetoric.'

19 Jacques Lacan, *Ecrits*, trans. Alan Sheridan (New York: W.W. Norton, 1977), p. 47.

20 See James Reiger, *The Mutiny Within*, pp. 181-2, where he writes that

the *Ode* 'evokes memories of the birth of language itself, the "perpetual Orphic song", and of villages where music had the potency of magic and the lyrist and the shaman were a single person. Shelley's poem concerns the human voice, which sets stones dancing and echoes the spheres.'

21 See *Shelley's Poetry and Prose*, ed. Donald H. Reiman and Sharon B. Powers (New York: W.W. Norton, 1977), p. 223n. Admitting that the *Ode*'s 'analogy between the seasonal cycle and human affairs is not a perfect one' in *Percy Bysshe Shelley* (p. 97–8), Reiman concludes that 'the conscious efforts of men of vision are required to turn the wheel past Winter to Spring.'

22 Louis Althusser, *For Marx*, p. 234.

23 Paul de Man, *Allegories of Reading* (New Haven: Yale University Press, 1979), p. 10.

24 Earl Wasserman, *Shelley: A Critical Reading*, p. 502.

25 Wasserman, *Shelley: A Critical Reading*, pp. 464–6.

26 Northrop Frye, *Anatomy of Criticism*, p. 97. He argues (p. 96) that 'the study of genres has to be founded on the study of conventions.'

27 Bernard Beatty, 'The Transformation of Discourse: *Epipsychidion*, *Adonais*, and Some Lyrics,' in *Essays on Shelley*, ed. Miriam Allott (Liverpool: Liverpool University Press, 1982), pp. 222, 227.

28 Jonathan Culler points to this species of authorization in *Structuralist Poetics*, p. 50, when he writes: 'Texts have meaning for those who know how to read them – those who, in their encounters with literature, have assimilated the conventions that are constitutive of literature as an institution and a means of communication.'

29 James Reiger writes that when the novel depicts in Victor Frankenstein 'the self-destructive pride of an adventurous soul,' Mary Shelley has her husband in mind: *The Mutiny Within*, p. 82.

30 Judith Chernaik, *The Lyrics of Shelley*, pp. 10, 148–9.

CHAPTER TEN

1 Ludwig Wittgenstein, *Philosophical Investigations*, p. 212e.

2 See Frank Lentricchia, *After the New Criticism*, p. 168.

3 Timothy Webb, *Shelley: A Voice Not Understood*, p. 203.

4 Gaston Bachelard, *The Poetics of Reverie*, trans. Daniel Russell (Boston: Beacon Press, 1971), p. 158.

5 James Reiger, *The Mutiny Within*, p. 221; Harold Bloom in *Shelley's Mythmaking*, devotes his final chapter exclusively to *The Triumph of Life*, stating (p. 220n.) that 'the *Triumph* is a myth-*unmaking* poem, and

is properly Shelley's last work,' presumably because (p. 275) the poem illustrates 'myth's necessary defeat.'

6 Tilottama Rajan, *Dark Interpreter: The Discourse of Romanticism* (Ithaca: Cornell University Press, 1980), p. 83.

7 Paul de Man, 'Shelley Disfigured,' in *Deconstruction and Criticism* (London: Routledge and Kegan Paul, 1979), p. 61.

8 Donald Reiman, in *Shelley's 'The Triumph of Life': A Critical Study* (Urbana: University of Illinois Press, 1965), p. 210, accepts the emendation of 'gold' to 'fold' in the last lines so that they read as follows:

> 'Then what is Life?' I said. ... the cripple cast
> His eye upon the car which now had rolled
> Onward, as if that look must be the last,
>
> And answered. ... 'Happy those for whom the fold
> Of

Reiman interprets (p. 83) the word 'fold' in Christian terms 'as a symbol of human salvation.' However, as this putative Christian metaphor is spoken by the demoralized Rousseau figure in the poem, there is no reason to assume that it represents Shelley's view. It could as readily be said that the important event in these lines is the fact that the Car of Life 'rolled onward' immediately the question is asked that would arrest its motion and fix its meaning. No doubt de Man has this possibility in mind when he writes that 'the structure of the text is not one of question and answer, but of a question whose meaning, as question, is effaced from the moment it is asked' (*Deconstruction and Criticism*, p. 44).

9 Jacques Derrida, 'Living On,' in *Deconstruction and Criticism*, p. 103.

10 Derrida, 'Structure, Sign, and Play' in *The Languages of Criticism and the Sciences of Man*, pp. 248–9. Frank Lentricchia, in *After the New Criticism*, concludes his commentary (pp. 165–6) on this essay by drawing a moral: 'The effect of Derrida's critique of centred structure is to urge us to stay inside the labyrinth of discourse and to become comfortable with the idea that all outlets are illusions.'

Index